CW00330496

Edward III's Faithful Knight

Edward III's Faithful Knight

Walter Mauny and His Legacy

Stephen Porter

Half title page: Rodin's figure of one of the Burghers of Calais, holding the keys to the city. (© Stephen Porter)

First published 2022

Amberley Publishing
The Hill, Stroud
Gloucestershire, GL5 4EP

www.amberley-books.com

ISBN 978 1 3981 0376 4 (hardback)
ISBN 978 1 3981 0377 1 (ebook)

British Library Cataloguing in Publication Data.
A catalogue record for this book is available from the British Library.

1 2 3 4 5 6 7 8 9 10

Typesetting by SJmagic DESIGN SERVICES, India.
Printed in the UK.

CONTENTS

ACKNOWLEDGEMENTS

For many years I have been burrowing into the history of the London Charterhouse, a set of buildings erected between 1349 and 2000 and for the last 400 years functioning as a quite unique almshouse, with Charterhouse Square acting virtually as its forecourt. The whole site was acquired as a burial ground for the victims of the Black Death by Walter Mauny, one of Edward III's leading commanders in the Hundred Years War, who also served him as a diplomat and administrator. Much of the history seemed to have fallen into place. Then a few years ago, when on holiday in Cadzand, at the south-western tip of the Netherlands, I realised with a shock that the soldiers who had captured the island, as it then was, from a French and Flemish garrison in 1337 – allegedly having smoked the inhabitants out of the church – were commanded by the same Walter Mauny who had acquired the site of the Charterhouse for plague burials and later established a Carthusian priory there. He also fought with the king at the battle of Sluis in the waters off the island in 1340, when a French and Genoese fleet was comprehensively defeated by an English one.

Moreover, I found that changing sea levels, the effects of reclamation and silting have made it possible if not exactly to 'walk the ground' of those battlefields, then at least to appreciate their setting. Following the thread laid down by Mauny at the Charterhouse leads to another generous charitable endowment, by Thomas Sutton, and then the evolution of the buildings and their reconstruction after extensive damage during the Second World War with, quite unexpectedly, the discovery of Mauny's grave. Together the various elements form a story which I felt should be told.

I am grateful to the Survey of London for assigning me to the Charterhouse project and giving me time to research the buildings' intricate history, and to successive Masters and Governors of Sutton's Hospital for their unfailing support and co-operation over many years. My wife Carolyn has listened and responded as the project developed, walking the sites with me and, not least, has provided invaluable help, especially through her astonishing ability to discover relevant illustrations, some of them in the most unlikely sources. The completion of this book owes much to her understanding, encouragement and patience.

I

HAINAULT AND ENGLAND

During the winter of 1372, Edward III and his sons, with various prelates and barons, attended a funeral in a small chapel in north-west London, just outside the city wall. The ageing king provided cloth of gold for what clearly was a special ceremony: the interment of Lord Mauny 'in the centre of the choir of the church at the foot of the high altar steps'. A generation before, Mauny had acquired the land as a burial ground for victims of the Black Death, and he had paid for the chapel to be built there. In the year before his death he had established a Carthusian priory on part of the site, and the chapel had become its church. Rather than be buried in St Paul's, Westminster Abbey or a church on one of his estates, he had chosen to be interred in the chapel, which commemorated his charity and piety. Alongside his munificence, through a long and distinguished career as a soldier, admiral and diplomat he had been a prominent figure at Edward's court, the members of which had now assembled to pay their respects. Mauny had lived a long life for the period, and a very active one.

Walter Mauny was born around 1310, the fourth of five sons of Jean le Borgne, lord of Masny, in the County of Hainault. His lively career spanned the first phase of the Hundred Years War, in which he was a prominent participant. Starting as a young courtier in the households of Queen Philippa and Edward III, he then honed his fighting skills during campaigns in Scotland and France and was promoted by the king to important commands at sea and on land, and he participated in the negotiations which, it seemed, might end more than twenty years of almost continuous warfare. From the profits of war and the king's favour he accumulated a fortune, part of which he used to acquire the aforementioned burial ground, erect the chapel and endow the priory. Mauny was a typical figure of the nobility in the mid-fourteenth century, engaging in war in a confident and aggressive manner while observing the chivalric code of the time, tackling the problems caused by the most devastating epidemic yet experienced, and displaying his devotion in founding a monastery.

The village of Masny is five miles east of Douai and thirteen miles from Valenciennes. Walter's mother was Jeanne de Jenlain; the lordship of Jenlain was to the south-east of Valenciennes and within Hainault. In 1325 his father was murdered at La Réole on the River Garonne, thirty-eight miles south-east of Bordeaux. Jean had mortally wounded a man during a tournament and made a pilgrimage to Santiago de Compostela as a penance for his action. During his return journey he was accosted at La Réole by relatives of the man he had killed and, despite his remorse, they murdered him in revenge. Walter and his brothers were left to make their way in the world and Walter entered the service of William I 'the good', Count of Hainault. It may be that he was brought up in the household of the count's brother John of Hainault (also referred to as John de Beaumont), who had a reputation as a fine soldier.

In the fourteenth century there was little consistency in the spelling of names and so subsequent generations had a certain amount of leeway when referring to an individual. Walter's name initially was Gauthier de Masny, which was modified by his contemporary the chronicler Jean Froissart to Gautier de Mauni. Following Froissart, the eighteenth-century French playwright Pierre Laurent De Belloy assigned him a role as a character in his play *Le Siège de Calais* as 'Mauni, Chevalier Anglais'. The author of a history of Saint Omer published in 1843 referred to him as Gauthier de Mainy, while giving the alternative forms of de Masny, de Manny, Dumainy and de Mauny.[1] The surname that most commonly came to be used by French writers was de Mauny, while English historians preferred de Manny, with his forename translated as Walter. The entry by James Tait for the authoritative *Dictionary of National Biography* of 1893 is headed 'Manny or Mauny, Sir Walter de, afterwards Lord de Manny', while that by Jonathan Sumption for the successor volumes issued in 2004 as the *Oxford Dictionary of National Biography* carries the heading 'Mauny [Manny], Sir Walter'. On the other hand, in his edition of Froissart's *Chronicles* published in 1904 by Macmillan, the editor, G. C. Macaulay, explained that 'proper names have been given in their correct forms, so far as that can be ascertained, but those which appear in an English dress, such as Walter Manny or Bertram of Guesclin, have not necessarily been made French again' and that 'the form "Manny" for "Mauny" is retained throughout'. During the late twentieth century 'Walter Mauny' came to be preferred, while the use of 'Manny' continued and was maintained by the London Charterhouse.

Hainault was a compact territory, bounded on the south by France and on the west by Flanders. To the north-east it shared a frontier with Brabant and reached almost as far as Brussels. On the east it had a short boundary with Namur and to the south-west lay the bishopric of Cambrai. These were among the group of states described as the Low Countries, between France, the Holy Roman Empire and the North Sea. Low-lying yet quite densely populated and economically well developed, they had varying political arrangements, so far as their rulers' feudal loyalties and allegiances were concerned. Hainault's capital was Valenciennes while its largest city, and Valenciennes' greatest rival, was Mons (the town's Dutch name was Bergen).

The county had a population of roughly 420,000 before the onset of the Black Death and was prospering.[2] It had a thriving linen industry with strong commercial links with England, which provided the high-quality wool required, and it was an agriculturally productive region, supplying the industrial towns of Flanders with grain, marketed through Ghent, the largest city in the region, with a population of perhaps 60,000, and so not that much smaller than London. Valenciennes stood at the head of navigation on the Scheldt and was a meeting point for traders from around the coasts of north-west Europe and those from the Rhine valley. It was well developed in terms of commercial organisation, with a merchant's guild there by the late eleventh century.[3] In terms of language and culture Hainault was at that time predominantly French, more so than the other territories in the Low Countries, although during the late Middle Ages Dutch language and culture came to predominate.[4]

Hainault had been jointly ruled with Flanders during the twelfth century but had reverted to the status of a separate county when

Joan and Margaret succeeded their father, Baldwin IX of Flanders, who was also Baldwin VI of Hainault. Margaret first married Bouchard d'Avesnes and their son John d'Avesnes became Count of Hainault as John II following a ruling in 1246 by Louis IX of France, acting as arbitrator, who assigned Flanders to the children of Margaret's second marriage, to William of Dampierre, and Hainault to the d'Avesnes line. The decision was accepted only after two wars between the parties, with the Dampierres supported by King Louis's brother Charles of Anjou, before a settlement was reached in 1254 which secured Hainault's separate identity. John II d'Avesnes ruled Hainault from 1280 until his death in 1304; the d'Avesnes family had also inherited the County of Holland and Zeeland and by the Treaty of Paris in 1323 Hainault's claim to Zeeland was formally recognised, ending its intermittent conflicts with Flanders but doing little to reduce the complexities of Low Countries politics, in which the French kings were involved as overlords of Flanders. John II was succeeded by William I of Hainault, known as 'the good', who was also Count William III of Holland, Count William II of Zeeland and Lord of Friesland.

The bulk of the county lay within the Holy Roman Empire, but a section of the count's territory was on the west bank of the Scheldt and was held by the count as a fief of the French king. That was the County of Ostrevent, which included Masny, and in the early fourteenth century it was the subject of jurisdictional disputes between the Count of Hainault and the French crown. Masny was close to the frontier, for nearby Douai was in Flanders, and it was in the diocese of Cambrai.

The diplomatic abilities of the counts of Hainault achieved a degree of security for their county and considerable prestige for themselves as rulers, and their court had a reputation for its chivalric atmosphere, with a seemingly endless succession of tournaments, jousts and feasts. That characteristic was established by the early twelfth century, if not earlier, and what seems to be the earliest use of the term 'tournament' was recorded there in 1114, with a mention of 'javelin sports, tournaments or such like'. Trazenies, on the border between Hainault and Namur, became the setting for one of the largest international tournaments, where the knights of Picardy, Flanders and Hainault periodically encountered those of France. Tournaments were mock fights between groups of knights, where they could polish and show off their fighting skills. Rules were accepted and adhered to, for the sake of safety, although wounds were sustained and fatalities did sometimes occur, as in the case of Jean le Borgne's adversary, and William II, Count of Flanders, who was killed at a tournament at Trazenies in 1251. In 1170 what should have been a tournament between groups of knights from Hainault and Brabant turned into a full-scale battle.

A joust was much smaller in scale, as a combat between two knights, but the participants were more exposed to the gaze of the genteel spectators, who often watched from stands, whereas a tournament could range across a stretch of open country. A joust offered the opportunity to win a name for skill and courage, as well as to draw the admiration of the court ladies. A young nobleman was expected, indeed required, to engage in such combats as soon as he was able to bear arms and gain celebrity through fighting, not only in his own lands but by travelling to distant places such as the Holy Land, or the crusades in central and eastern Europe. Hainault's own knights gained a formidable reputation for their military prowess and the county came to be referred to as a place 'where knights were exceedingly accomplished'. Those accomplishments included dress, deportment and eloquence; a knight was required to be both elegant and respectful of the ladies, never offering them any offence and taking vows that they would attain specific achievements in honour of their ladies. Those courtly skills would also equip a knight for diplomatic service on his prince's behalf. The chivalric culture, in which knights fought for their ladies' favour and finely dressed women accompanied them to the events, was the world in which the young Walter Mauny was immersed as he came of age. He was undefeated in 'fourteen combats lawfully approved', and presumably other informal ones as well.[5]

The martial skills and enthusiasm for combat evinced by the courtly culture of Hainault had an outlet in actual military campaigning. The county's high population provided enough men of fighting age who could be trained as soldiers and, when not required by the counts, loaned to other rulers on contracts, generating an income for the counts as well as maintaining their position in the diplomatic chess game. From the twelfth century Flanders and Brabant also hired out mercenaries. Hainault's proficient soldiers were a considerable asset and made the county a sought-after ally. Count William I ruled for over thirty years, from 1304 until 1337, skilfully playing off the tensions between his neighbours and deploying the tactic of dynastic marriages to help maintain his position. William's wife was the daughter of Charles of Valois, brother of Philip the Fair (Philip IV), King of France; their daughter Margaret married Lewis IV, the Holy Roman Emperor; and their other daughter, Jeanne, married William, Duke of Juliers.

The d'Avesnes family also maintained its prestige through its patronage of literary figures. John of Hainault encouraged Jean le Bel (d. 1361), a wealthy and worldly cleric whose Chronicles were commissioned by John, probably around 1352. In turn, le Bel was to be the benefactor of Jean Froissart (*c.* 1337–*c.* 1410), who drew upon le Bel's work extensively when writing his chronicles, which came to surpass those of his patron in terms of popularity and influence. Froissart's work became the principal contemporary account for historians of the period because le Bel's chronicles were unavailable, surviving only as a single manuscript which was not rediscovered until it was recognised in a library in 1861. Even then, his chronicles were not published until 1904–5, in Paris, as a two-volume work edited by Jules Viard and Eugène Déprez, and they were not translated into English in full until 2011. Le Bel and Froissart gave considerable attention to their fellow Hainaulters and provided positive impressions of them, especially John of Hainault himself and Walter Mauny, and their reporting of Mauny's exploits helped to perpetuate his posthumous reputation.

There is little doubt that both le Bel and Froissart knew Mauny and spoke to him about his career and achievements and that he took the opportunity to present himself in a favourable light in terms of the chivalrous standards of the age; they were glad to have his slant on affairs narrated in that way, providing them with the kind of tales which they wanted to record. In some sections the narrative was presented by Froissart in the first person, and although that was no doubt embellished and adjusted with the benefit of hindsight, it is plausible that his text was not too far removed from what Mauny had told him. When planning one risky escapade in Brittany, to release two knights under sentence of death, Mauny was said to have told his comrades, 'It would be a great honour for us if we could rescue those two knights. And if we were to try but fail, we would earn the gratitude at least of good King Edward, and of all worthy men who heard we'd done everything we could.' That summarised his motivation: to follow the honourable course, gain the king's approval and enhance his standing among men of a similar rank to himself.[6]

Other chroniclers mention Mauny and generally give the same impression of his abilities and achievements as Le Bel and Froissart. During the twentieth century a history of the London Charterhouse became available to scholars, having been unknown previously. It was evidently compiled by a monk of the Charterhouse during the last quarter of the fifteenth century, as the latest date in the manuscript is 1481. It naturally provided an assessment of Mauny, as the founder of the Charterhouse, and because it was written from an ecclesiastical perspective, not a military or diplomatic one, it gives a different slant on the man and his achievements from that of the chroniclers.

Mauny arrived in England in 1327 and it provided him with a whole new set of experiences. He may already have faced the problems that confronted any outsider, for the County of Ostrevent could have been regarded by the Hainaulters, including Count William's courtiers, as a rather distant and not entirely integrated area. As a Hainaulter in England he faced similar challenges on a much larger scale. William Langland's visionary character Piers the Plowman, looking across the Midlands from the Malvern Hills, saw 'a fair field full of folk ... Of all manner of men the rich and the poor, Working and wandering as the world asketh.' Langland was writing after the devastating plague outbreaks of the mid-fourteenth century; before then his imagined field would have been even more full.[7] The population of England could have been as high as five million or more on the eve of the epidemic, but in terms of population density and wealth there was a divide, with the east and south having far more people, commercial activity and prosperity than the north and the west.

For much of the thirteenth century the agricultural economy had been generally buoyant, both in the production of crops to feed a growing population and in the numbers of sheep producing wool chiefly for export to the cloth-making regions of Europe, especially Flanders and Brabant in the Low Countries, and parts of Italy. While not rivalling those in the urban areas of the Low Countries in the production of cloth and other manufactured items, English towns could flourish and grow during the period, attracting peasants from the countryside who marketed produce from their hinterlands, as well as supplying goods which could not be produced locally. London was by far the largest and wealthiest city in the country and, with Westminster, was steadily increasing its grip as the centre of trade, government, the law and culture.

England had evolved from the tenth century as a centralised state with a single monarch. In the late thirteenth century, Edward I had set about integrating into the realm those parts of Wales which had not hitherto been assimilated. But his attempts and those of his son and successor Edward II to gain control over Scotland met with failure. Powerful magnates existed within England itself, too, and some cities were insistent on maintaining their privileges and even extending them where possible, although none of them were strong enough to effectively defy the crown and local government structures were robust enough to implement the government's policies. That had implications for the raising of armies and financing of a war abroad, although the monarch needed the assent of parliament for the levying of taxes.

Locally, new taxes could be met with squeals of objection because of poverty and hardship, but by Edward III's reign a system was in place by which the Exchequer received from the tax collectors sums which were the outcome of their local negotiations with the taxpayers. As well as the crown's administrative officers, government was carried out by some members of the clergy, who chose a career route through the Church to effectively serve as civil servants in government administration and diplomacy. With the framework for tax collection in place and with the approval of parliament, Edward III could expect that adequate sums would be raised within the realm to finance a major military effort against France. Yet good harvests in three successive years – 1336, 1337 and 1338 – lowered the prices of agricultural produce to such an extent that the rural population began to plead poverty, with the complaint that 'common people must sell their cows, their utensils and even clothing'.

The contemporary writer Adam Murimuth attributed the low prices to the lack of money, which he described as 'a desperate shortage of cash among the people', blaming that on excessive taxation. So while parliament may have been willing to grant the king taxes to enable him to wage war, those who were given the responsibility of collecting them faced a difficult task.[8]

Greater instability within the political system was likely to come from the relationship between the king and members of the nobility. The nobles were jealous of their status, titles and functions and resented those who threatened to usurp their position. When a climate of mistrust arose as a result, plots and rumours thereof could lead to punishment by the king, including confiscation of titles, appointments and estates – and sometimes even execution. That was the case during the reign of Edward II (1307–27), who promoted his favourites beyond what some nobles regarded as acceptable. In 1312 their resentment of the king's favourite, Piers Gaveston, rose to such a pitch that their entourages united to form an army and overthrow him. The struggle between the king and some of his nobles led to the unprecedented killings of senior noblemen.

The King of England was also suzerain of large territories in France. In the late twelfth century these had been even more extensive, covering Normandy, Aquitaine (which came to the English monarch with the marriage of Henry II and Eleanor of Aquitaine in 1152), Anjou, Maine, Touraine and Poitou, until the loss of Normandy in 1204 and the recovery by the French crown of various territories, leaving Aquitaine as the largest remaining region still under English control. In 1259 Henry III renounced his claims to Normandy, Maine, Anjou, Touraine and Poitou in return for recognition as lord of Aquitaine as a vassal of the French king, and creation as a peer of France. Thereafter, English monarchs would hold the region on those terms, paying homage to the French king for it, which simplified a complex situation but was not to the advantage of the English crown. Much of western France around the fringes of Aquitaine was held in a complex pattern of tenures, with the rulers of various territories owing allegiance to the French monarch but also taking oaths of loyalty to the English ruler. To complicate matters, the counties of Ponthieu and Montreuil, on the Channel coast and along the River Somme, passed to the English crown on the marriage of Edward I to Eleanor of Castile in 1254. Brittany was an independent duchy and French kings naturally cast envious eyes upon it, and they hoped to maintain their influence in the north, especially in Flanders.

To put it mildly, the diplomatic position in north-west Europe was a tangled one and the region's stability could easily be upset if the monarchs of either France or England chose to enforce what they could reasonably regard as their full legal rights. But English kings were in an inferior position when dealing with France, for despite its political fragmentation it was a far larger and more populous country, with a population of between 15 million to 20 million, roughly three times that of England and Wales. In military terms, it was much more powerful, with its heavy cavalry widely respected as the most efficient fighting force in western Europe.

2

A NEW REIGN

The availability of Count William's troops after the end of the wars with Flanders was the basis for an alliance between Hainault and Edward II's queen, Isabella, sister of Charles IV of France, and her favourite, Sir Roger Mortimer. The royal marriage had become increasingly acrimonious during the early 1320s and threatened to split asunder after the queen did not return from Paris, where she was sent to negotiate for the return of territories adjoining the Duchy of Gascony. These lands had been lost to France in the short war of Saint-Sardos in 1324, named for a village in the Agenais that adjoined Gascony. Edward and his advisors possibly believed that the lost territories were more likely to be recovered by Isabella, with her strong connections to the French court, than by a diplomatic mission. She went to Paris in March 1325 and did achieve a settlement, but it was an unsatisfactory one from the English point of view.

Remaining in France with a small group of aristocratic adherents, in the winter of 1325/6 Isabella met Mortimer and they may have begun a liaison. Mortimer had spent some time at the court in Hainault after escaping from the Tower of London, where he had been incarcerated at the demand of Edward II's current favourites, the Despencers (Hugh, Earl of Winchester, and his son, also Hugh). Edward, Prince of Wales, born in 1312, had also been sent to Paris, to take the oath of allegiance to his uncle Charles IV on his father's behalf for the Duchy of Aquitaine, including Gascony. It was an uncomfortable arrangement, that one monarch should pay homage to another, and Edward II was reluctant to do so. Nevertheless, in September 1325 the young Edward was despatched to observe the necessary formalities. Having done that, however, he did not return to England. He was clearly acting on the instructions of his mother, who, with Mortimer, began to consider the possibility of supplanting not just the Despencers but also the unpopular king; the Count of Hainault's soldiers offered a ready solution to the problem of raising troops to carry out the rebellion.

As early as September 1324 the English court was receiving rumours that Mortimer might invade with a force of Hainaulters. Those reports were premature, but relations between the English government and Count William were at a low ebb, exacerbated by the seizure of English ships and their cargoes by Zeeland merchants and retaliatory captures of vessels on Edward II's orders. A meeting to resolve the issues should have convened in London in January 1326, but the Count's representatives did not show up. Against that background, an arrangement was reached between the queen on the one hand and the court of Hainault on the other, a part of which was that Philippa, William's second daughter, would marry the Prince of Wales, within two years of their betrothal, which was confirmed in August 1326 after Edward and his mother had travelled to Hainault to complete the agreement. Isabella and Edward's stay at the court in

Valenciennes provided an opportunity for William's courtiers to become acquainted with them, and the marriage of his daughter to the heir to the English throne clearly presented possibilities for an ambitious young man 'about the court', such as Walter Mauny. But the betrothal was a matter of state policy, not court politics, and the dowry consisted of soldiers, ships and money to be put under Isabella's control, which she was going to use for an invasion of England.[1]

Froissart wrote that the queen and her supporters, having been refused military aid from France, went to a small town near Cambrai, where she lodged with a knight 'who received her with great pleasure, and entertained her in the best manner he could'. Hearing of her predicament, John of Hainault, who was 'at that time very young, and panting for glory like a knight-errant', went to her and 'paid the queen every respect and honour'. He was greatly moved by her tale and promised to escort her and Edward to England and restore them to their rightful places; she reacted so emotionally that he could barely restrain her from falling on her knees and she did promise him that 'I and my son shall be for ever bound unto you, and we will put the kingdom of England under your management, as in justice it ought to be'.

That was quite a promise. John then escorted her to his brother's court at Valenciennes and set about gathering military resources for the enterprise; some of those he approached did not respond and Count William and his advisors initially thought it a hazardous undertaking. But his scruples were dispelled and he ordered that all assistance should be given for the assembling of the fleet which carried the invasion force to England. John was able to recruit enough men and assembled them at Dordrecht, where a fleet of ninety-five ships was collected and the force was embarked.[2]

Froissart's account of the preparations for the invasion is cast in a typically chivalrous style, describing a damsel (queen) refused help by her brother (Charles IV of France) and in such distress that she had to cadge from a poor knight, before being pitied by a gallant well-wisher (a count's brother) who comes to her aid and has the means to help her achieve her aim. That was how the noble and knightly classes of the fourteenth century wished to be seen, rescuing and comforting a lady in distress. But despite Froissart's account, the involvement of the d'Avesnes brothers in the displacement of Edward II was not altruistic or chivalrous, for John was said to have been paid at least £32,722 for the hire of his troops.

The queen, Mortimer and Edward landed on the Suffolk coast in September 1326 with a small army of roughly 1,500 soldiers, which included a contingent of 700 Hainaulters under John of Hainault. The queen's force had sailed past Harwich into the River Orwell and from there moved inland to Bury St Edmund's. They began to attract recruits, including many senior figures, while the king's support quickly ebbed away, partly because the Despencers had been so rapacious that they were highly unpopular. His problems were compounded by rioting in London, during which Walter de Stapledon, Bishop of Exeter and the king's Treasurer, was summarily executed. The queen and Mortimer continued their pursuit of the king, occupying Bristol on 26 October, where the elder Despencer was captured. His son and the king were subsequently apprehended near Llantrisant. London was secured when the queen despatched John of Hainault with just eight of his men to occupy the Tower, which dominated the capital and contained the country's arsenal.

John received payments from the English crown for four months from early November 1326, for his services and to secure his loyalty. His men were exempt from the order against carrying weapons in the city, which was allowed only to the watchmen in the wards and to 'the Hainaulters of the Queen, who are accustomed to go armed in the manner of their country'.[3] That made them the only effective force in the capital and may reflect the queen's confidence in them, or perhaps an acknowledgment of their power and the impossibility of disarming them. Meanwhile, the king's backing, both military and political, fell away so completely that he abdicated; his son Edward was proclaimed king as Edward III on 27 January 1327 and subsequently Edward II's death at Berkeley Castle was announced.

Isabella and Mortimer eventually arrived in London in early January 1327 and the new king was crowned in Westminster Abbey on 1 February. At his coronation 'there were present as many foreigners as Englishmen, particularly the mercenaries of queen Isabella his mother, whom ... she herself had invited from Hainault and Germany'. That arrangement could not last and after an inglorious campaign against the Scots, which was marred – among other things – by deadly clashes in York between the Hainaulters and the citizens, Edward 'sent back home the men of Hainault and the other mercenaries, who took with them as presents large sums of money and many choice jewels'.[4] Nevertheless, the Hainaulters must have gained a great deal of confidence from 'crossing the sea with so few to conquer such a kingdom as England in the face of its very king and all his supporters'.[5] They had indeed played a decisive role in the affairs of a country which was so much larger and more powerful than their own.

The connection was strengthened by the marriage of Edward III and Philippa that Isabella had arranged and which was a considerable diplomatic achievement for Hainault. It had gone ahead by proxy in November 1326, with a wedding ceremony to follow. Philippa and her entourage began their journey on 16 December 1327, crossing from Wissant, south-west of Calais, to Dover, and arriving in London on 22 December. Walter Mauny was one of the squires among Philippa's entourage when she travelled to England and that was probably the first time that he had set foot in the country where he was to make his name and fortune. The count did not travel with his daughter and the Hainaulters were under the direction of John of Hainault. The entourage included the count's chamberlain and the Grand Bailiff and Chamberlain of the county. The party travelled on to York, where the marriage was celebrated in the minster in January 1328.[6] Almost twenty years later Edward III and his army stopped briefly at Wissant on their way from their victory at Crécy to begin the siege of Calais; whether or not he was aware that this was the port from which his wife had begun her journey to England, when his troops departed 'Wissant was entirely burnt and all the land for six leagues in each direction'.[6]

Following the dethronement of Edward II, the government and the new king were under the control of the queen and Mortimer, who were the effective rulers. But as the young Edward matured he became dissatisfied with his subordinate role. He secured enough support at court and among the country's leaders to stage a coup, which he did in a daring escapade with a few followers at Nottingham castle in October 1330. Mortimer was captured in the castle and later executed, and Isabella's influence came to an abrupt end. From that point Edward was the actual ruler and not a titular monarch.

When the Hainaulters returned home, Philippa, now the queen, remained in England with 'few of her fellow countrymen except a young gentleman named Walter Mauny, who stayed behind to serve her and to wait on her at table'. He held the lowly position of trencherman; a trencher was a wooden plate to cut meat on at table, or, in another usage, a dried slice of bread used instead of a plate. From that lowly status he rose to become an effective tutor to Philippa as she established herself in her new role and environment; he may have been four or more years older than her (there are doubts about the year of her birth). Mauny was not only a success in the queen's household, but he made the difficult transition to that of the king (the two households were not amalgamated until 1360), where he held increasingly significant positions. He followed a careful path through the shifting sands of court politics, always remaining loyal to Edward and the queen.

Mauny was helped because friendly contacts between the courts of England and Hainault were continued. The count sent Edward a suit of armour, elements of which were copied by his armourer, Thomas Copham, on to a new suit which he was making for the king. Saddles were decorated with 'various beasts and images in the style of Hainault' and tunics were decorated 'in the Hainault and other fashions'. It is possible that Mauny was the principal go-between for the two courts, which would help to explain his support from Edward and Philippa, when other favoured young men were also vying for the royal couple's special attention and patronage. He would also have been well regarded as a protégé of John of Hainault, who had made a very good impression among the English nobility and had acted so well for Queen Isabella during the invasion of 1326 and in the subsequent securing of the throne, when he advised her council.[7]

After a period of parsimony during their early married years, Edward and Philippa created a court with a very bright and lively atmosphere, no doubt owing much to the queen's upbringing at her father's court in Hainault. Feasts, jousts and tournaments were held around the country as great social events, as well as opportunities for martial displays in which Edward proclaimed his role as a warrior king and cultivated the nobility's support. Theirs was a lively and ostentatious court; both king and queen became noted for their extravagant dress and their example was inevitably copied by their courtiers. Their favoured entertainments included hunting and hawking, as well as jousts and tournaments, with indoor celebrations such as feasting and dancing. Both king and queen retained several musicians, and performers such as acrobats and conjurors were engaged to entertain the court. In 1334 the queen sent her violist and two bagpipers to 'minstrel schools' on the continent; music was an important aspect of life at the Hainault court and Philippa's father was once described as the 'father of minstrelsy'.

More privately, the king and queen and their closest confidants played chess and chequers, and games of chance for money. Both of them regularly incurred large debts through gaming and either were poor judges when it came to gambling, or they deliberately lost money to those they played with, as a way of rewarding them and encouraging their continue loyalty. That was the atmosphere in which young courtiers such as Mauny lived and participated; demanding in terms of conduct and personal presentation and requiring good financial judgement, in being seen to be fully engaged in events without losing all their money, while constantly remembering that the king was the source of their patronage. Mauny, it seems, was adept at presenting himself as required, so retaining his patrons' favour.[8]

The chivalric culture was admired by the noble and knightly classes, who saw themselves as the successors of King Arthur, his court at Camelot and the brotherhood known as the Knights of the Round Table; the cult of King Arthur was taken up with enthusiasm by Edward III. This was informed largely by Geoffrey of Monmouth's *The History of the Kings of Britain*, which he wrote in the 1130s, based, according to his account, on 'a very ancient book in the British tongue'. So this court paid tribute to another by imitating many of its features, even though the latter was fabricated and had no genuine historical basis. Edward III espoused the model of King Arthur and his court with some fervour, either from a genuine interest or because he saw it as a means to unite the English warrior class by practising a common style of behaviour, which would produce a unity of purpose as well as conduct, especially in warfare and the social-cum-military events which it also engaged in.[9] He greatly developed the royal castle at Windsor, which he saw as an appropriate setting for a new court of Camelot, where tournaments and feasting would be held.

Some of Edward's tournaments were themed. At the events held in London in 1331 the king and other participants wore tunics and mantles decorated with Cupid's arrows and their costumes and masks resembled those of 'Tartars'. At one such event the mounted knights were each led into the arena on a silver chain carried by a lady. More provocatively, at the tournament held in Cheapside in 1343, the king and twelve companions dressed as the pope and cardinals.[10] Churchmen were not supposed to participate in warfare or its substitutes (although some of them did) and so the theme was a pointedly critical one. The popes were not neutral observers of the Anglo-French wars. For the whole of Mauny's life they were French speakers, and the papacy was based in Avignon, not Rome. Avignon was not a part of France, but its language and culture were French and the popes permitted the French kings to tax church lands in the country to help finance their wars against England.[11]

Edward III's policy on tournaments contrasted with that of Henry III, who was afraid that they would encourage disorder, and his own father, Edward II, who suspected that they were opportunities for political plotting and his leading opponents among the aristocracy were attending them so that they could intrigue together, protected by their knights assembled for the event. Edward II periodically issued prohibitions on the holding of tournaments.[12] Edward III was no doubt aware of those dangers but treated such events as outlets for the nobles' pent-up energies and martial aspirations, rather than risk leaving them to conspire together or settle their private scores violently in defiance of the crown. It was the warrior-kings – Richard I, Edward I and Edward III – who actively promoted the holding of tournaments and encouraged the chivalric culture of which they were a part.

The new regime and the freer mood at court saw the introduction of fresh and, some said, daring fashions; closely cut gowns for women and tight hoses for men left little to the imagination and disgusted those moralists who would have preferred the court to set a frugal and sombre example. As is ever the case, the newcomers took more than their fair share of the responsibility for the deplorable laxity in fashions and behaviour. In 1344 the so-called Westminster chronicler wrote that:

> Ever since the arrival of the Hainaulters about eighteen years ago the English have madly followed outlandish ways, changing their grotesque fashions of clothing yearly. They have abandoned the old, decent style of long, full garments for clothes which are short, tight, impractical, slashed, every part laced, strapped, or buttoned

> up, with the sleeves of the gowns and the tippets of the hoods hanging down to absurd lengths, so that, if the truth be told, their clothes and footwear make them look more like torturers, or even demons, than men.

Even the clergy were guilty of adopting those fashions. The women's clothes were so tight that 'they wore a fox tail hanging down inside their skirts at the back, to hide their arses'. This the chronicler judged to be 'the sin of pride' which 'must surely bring down misfortune in the future'.[13]

The impression of self-admiring young courtiers in fine clothes comes not only from the disparaging comments of their dour critics, but from the remorseful admissions of one of those finely dressed aristocrats. In Henry of Grosmont's 'Livre de seyntz medicines' he admits to his failings and cites examples of his vanity, such as being proud of the fine rings on his fingers, the elegance of his foot in the stirrup, stretching out his legs for the ladies to admire when taking part in jousts, his shoes, his armour, his garters, his ability as a dancer. He enjoyed hearing himself being praised, he relished food and drink to the point of overindulgence, he delighted in the sweet smell of ladies and owned up to indulging in the 'lecherous kisses' of common wenches. Regretfully looking back on his youth, he wrote, 'When I was young and strong and agile, I prided myself on my good looks, my figure, my gentle blood and all the qualities and gifts that you, O Lord, had given me for the salvation of my soul.' Henry was created Earl of Derby in 1337, succeeded his father as Earl of Lancaster and in 1351 was created the first Duke of Lancaster; he was a contemporary of Walter Mauny and the two campaigned together in Scotland, Flanders, France and Aquitaine. While his depiction of himself cannot not be taken as a portrayal of Mauny also, they were members of the same group of courtiers who served Edward III as soldiers and diplomats, presumably sharing characteristics in outlook, behaviour, style and appearance.[14]

As Mauny entered his twenties there were clear signs of the king's favour: he was designated one of his esquires in 1328 and he was knighted in 1330. In 1332 he and two other young men were noted as having the status of king's esquire, which, among other things, granted them access to the monarch's private apartments. He remained a member of that elite group, which in the late 1340s consisted of just seven men.[15] He was made a banneret, or principal knight, in 1338; the distinction between the two grades of knighthood was displayed on a battlefield or at a tournament or joust by a knight having a triangular pennon carried before him, while a banneret was entitled to a rectangular banner. Mauny's arms were distinctive, described in armorial terms as *or, three chevrons sable*. There was also an economic difference, as the financial obligations for a banneret were more onerous than those of a knight. When on military service he was required to provide more soldiers than a knight, and a banneret's daily pay was double that of a knight.[16]

That Mauny was raised to the status of banneret indicates that he had the means, while still in his twenties, to provide the services due from a man of that rank. That was possible because from the early 1330s the king's approval was marked by grants of positions and properties, raising Mauny's status among his contemporaries and increasing his income. When the Earl of Atholl defected to the Scots in 1335, Edward confiscated his estates and granted Mauny a large part of those in Buckinghamshire and Norfolk, with a contribution of £100 from the Exchequer until 'the king or his heirs shall grant the equivalent in land and rent within the realm to him and his heirs'.[17] When Atholl's lands were restored to him Mauny was compensated by grants of 'replacement' property, including the manor of Overstone in Northamptonshire, which he was able to retain despite a prolonged legal challenge. His property acquisitions in the 1330s included manors in Norfolk, Buckinghamshire, Northamptonshire and in Wales and he gradually expanded the area of his landowning: for example, in 1347 he bought the parish of Tunstall in Kent.

Mauny's career and fortune were also greatly advanced by his success in military actions, through the acquisition of plunder and, more rewardingly, the ransoms of prisoners of high rank. He campaigned with the English forces in Scotland, then in the Low Countries, and of course frequently in France during the Hundred Years War, which began in 1337. The tactic favoured by the English in France was the *chevauchée*; an armed raid in force on a wide front through enemy territory during which the people were beaten and robbed, crops, stores and buildings were burned, livestock were driven away or killed, and valuables were looted. Villages and towns were mercilessly plundered and high-ranking figures taken prisoner to be exchanged for ransoms that could pay for the deployment of more forces, so that the English military effort was financed by the enemy. Many prisoners who would not be ransomed were executed. That way of making war not only deprived the enemy of resources and leadership but also showed that he was unable to protect those under his rule, as he was obliged to do.

When the raiding army was pursued by a French detachment which was not strong enough to challenge it militarily but aimed to reduce its strength by harassing it and picking off stragglers, then the civilian population had to provide for both armies, which 'lived off the land' by taking what they needed without payment or other compensation. It was a ruinous practice for those in the territories across which the armies rampaged, but it could provide rich gains for the commanders through the system by which they bought prisoners and valuables from the lower ranks, at agreed rates, and sold them on to their seniors, or negotiated ransoms for their release.

The commanders needed to take plunder and prisoners who could be exchanged for a ransom so that they could cover their costs. They agreed a contract with the crown by which they would supply a fixed number and type of soldiers, receiving a fee, wages, necessary reimbursements and sometimes a 'regard', or bonus. The outlay on raising, equipping and paying the soldiers was recovered during the military operations. As taxation was out of the question when the territory was not to be occupied, that was done by plunder and taking prisoners. The most adroit commanders were therefore effectively military entrepreneurs as well as soldiers, making money from their operations on top of their pay. Campaigning in a poor area or one which had previously been stripped of its wealth by other troops was an unattractive proposition and so the area assigned to them to be raided was an important consideration.

Only the largest armies taken to the continent by the king were not recruited by contracts but were raised and administered by officials of the royal household. Froissart described the system at the outset of the Hundred Years War in terms of a decree stating that 'every knight, squire and fighting man serving the King in his war should draw the King's pay but that each should maintain himself according to his standing for half a year out of his own funds, any prisoner or other war-gains which he might make remaining with him for his personal profit'. In fact, a proportion of their profits was due to the king.[18] Mauny and his fellow commanders operated within that system and through his extensive campaigning in France he became a prominent military leader and typical chivalrous knight of the period.

3

SIR WALTER MAUNY: SOLDIER AND ADMIRAL

Worthy performances in tournaments were all very well and caught the eye, but to prove his real value a knight needed to participate in actual combat. The opportunity for Sir Walter Mauny came when Edward Balliol raised an army with which to invade Scotland. Anglo-Scottish relations were complex and became even more uncertain after the death of Robert Bruce in 1329. He was succeeded as king by his son David, who came to the throne as David II when he was five years old.

Edward Balliol was the son of John Balliol, who had been ousted from the Scottish throne, and he became the leader and figurehead of those who had lost their lands and positions north of the border that should have been restored to them by the 1328 Treaty of Northampton, but were not. If Balliol became king of Scotland he would be allied with England, whereas the lords who governed during David II's minority would maintain the alliance with France, and so pose a threat should Edward III launch a campaign to recover those territories bordering Aquitaine lost in the war of Saint-Sardos. Balliol decided to force the issue and in

August 1332, with a small army organised by Henry Beaumont, one of the 'dispossessed', landed in Scotland. He acted with Edward III's consent but not his active support, although Mauny and the other English lords and knights who joined his forces would have obtained their king's agreement before doing so.

Mauny's first military experience under Beaumont and Balliol went well and during a skirmish at Roxburgh Bridge he captured John Crabbe, a Flemish seaman in Scottish service formerly regarded as a pirate, but now a respected military man. Crabbe had taken a small fleet to besiege Balliol but had been defeated and had fled on foot. Among his earlier exploits was the seizure in 1310 in the Straits of Dover of a vessel carrying cloth, jewels, gold, silver and other goods valued at £2,000 belonging to Alice of Hainault, Countess of Norfolk, an incident which had diplomatic and trading repercussions. His later career under Edward III was concentrated more on supplying ships and as a military engineer, overseeing the construction of siege engines and the maintenance of fortifications.

Edward III ruled that Mauny should be paid 4,000 marks (£2,880) by Crabbe for his release and anything more which Mauny could extort from him, with Crabbe closely guarded until he had paid what he owed. But Crabbe then obtained permission to visit the English court and was able to persuade the king that he could be of help to him, so Edward paid Mauny 1,000 marks (£666 13s 4d, payable in six instalments) for him and took Crabbe into his service. Potentially, that brought Mauny the sum of £3,550, which was a considerable windfall for a young soldier-cum-courtier, from a prisoner valued not for his social standing or high military rank but for his soldierly abilities and specialist knowledge. Crabbe was valued because he was 'thought by the English to have experience in naval matters and knowledge of

French harbours' and, as was to be shown, the Flemish coast.[1] His transfer from Mauny's custody to that of the king was the kind of transaction that was to bring Mauny considerable wealth during future campaigns.

Balliol and Beaumont won a significant victory with an English army against heavy odds at Dupplin Moor near Perth shortly after the invasion. Beaumont had fought in Scotland during Edward I's campaigns there and had been with the army of Edward II which defeated an uprising by the Earl of Lancaster at Boroughbridge in 1322. Despite the success at Dupplin Moor, Balliol's cause wavered and he was surprised and narrowly escaped from his would-be captors in a skirmish in which his brother Henry was killed. After Balliol had fled to England, Edward III intervened personally, taking an army into Scotland, besieging Berwick and heavily defeating a Scots army which had come to raise the siege at the battle of Halidon Hill, in 1333. At both Dupplin Moor and Halidon Hill the knights fought on foot as men-at-arms. The Anglo-Welsh archers were positioned on the flanks from where they inflicted heavy casualties on the enemy ranks before they could get close to the English line. Mauny campaigned in Scotland with the king until 1336 and probably was present at both battles. In 1335 the king granted him an annuity of £100 'for his long service'.[2]

Jean le Bel described the nature of the war in Scotland, where the English captured 'numerous castles and even the greatest cities defended by fine moats and fortifications', as far north as Aberdeen. The Scots did not offer to fight a battle after their experience at Halidon Hill, preferring guerrilla tactics; they 'would often come and skirmish with the English army', attacking the troops whenever possible and raiding their convoys of supplies. The Scottish lords 'who so often came to skirmish with the English kept lurking in the wilds among dense marsh and forest where it was impossible to follow them; but they tracked the English so closely that there was fighting almost every day'. Le Bel twice mentioned Mauny as distinguishing himself in that kind of fighting, for he 'won much praise and esteem from the king and everyone ... of all the army he was one of those who exerted himself and risked the most'. When there was almost daily fighting 'Sir Walter Mauny earned the most renown, along with Sir William Montagu'. Le Bel described Montagu, who was a few years older than Mauny, as 'a strong an imposing knight'. The king rewarded him with privileges and grants and in 1337 created him Earl of Salisbury.[3]

Edward campaigned again in Scotland in person on three further occasions, in 1334, 1335 and 1336. The focus of his reign at that stage was very much upon developments there, reflected in the fact that he based himself at York for long periods and four of the five Parliaments called between December 1332 and May 1335 were summoned to meet there. In 1334 Balliol's rival, David II, was sent into exile in France, where he was given refuge by Philip VI, which proved to be another source of contention between Edward and Philip. Despite his efforts, Edward was unable to completely subdue Scottish opposition, and the attention of the English councillors and their king gradually switched to France. In 1336 two grand councils were held. The first, at Northampton in June, was attended only by magnates and prelates, who agreed that a delegation should be sent to Philip. The second was at Nottingham in September, where knights and burgesses could also attend, and at that meeting the failure of the negotiations with France presumably was high on the agenda.

Philip was being cajoled by Pope Benedict XII into mounting a crusade to recover the holy places from Muslim rule; the plans had gone so far that he had raised a considerable army and assembled a fleet. The English campaigns in Scotland therefore irritated the pope, as they prevented Philip from concentrating on the matter in hand while his ally's towns and countryside were being ravaged by English armies. Not only did relations between Edward and Philip deteriorate because of the unresolved Scottish conflict, which continued to threaten the security of England's northern border, but there was the continuing issue of the allegiance which English monarchs owed to the French kings for the Duchy of Aquitaine.

Charles IV died in 1328, the last of the Capetian dynasty, rulers of France since 987. He was succeeded by Philip of Valois, grandson of Philip IV, although Edward III had a claim as the son of Philip IV's daughter Isabella, a claim which was dismissed by the French because it passed through the female line. If that objection were to be set aside, Edward could argue that he had a stronger right to the French crown than Philip. He did not put forward his claim until 1340. More immediately, in May 1337 Philip declared the duchy of Aquitaine to be forfeit. This was was partly a response to Edward giving refuge to Robert d'Artois who had fled from France in 1334 disguised as a merchant, having clashed with Philip over his failure to support his claim to the County of Artois. Robert and his father, Philip of Artois, had connections in the male line with the Capetian dynasty.

In not returning Robert to France, Edward was breaking his oaths to Philip IV, and Robert was also thought by contemporaries to have had a more direct influence by goading Edward into making good his claim to the French throne, which of course meant war. The author of the poem *The Vows of the Heron*, composed around 1340, encapsulated that pressure on the king in a scene in which Robert, accompanied by three minstrels and two ladies, 'daughters of two nobles', present a heron to the king during a meal in September 1338. The breeds of birds were associated with certain characteristics, and the personality of the heron was that of 'the most cowardly of birds'. Robert declares that it is being presented to 'the greatest coward at the table'. That was an extremely challenging gesture and a comment which directly impugned Edward's honour; he is so riled that he bursts out with the promise that he will invade France to confront and fight Philip. When the king had committed himself so far, Robert demanded from his guests, who were leading members of his entourage including the earls of Salisbury, Derby and Suffolk, John Beaumont and Walter Mauny, separate oaths that they would support the king.

Mauny swore that he would attack 'a good town', fortified with towers and enclosed by marshes, which had long been held by Sir Godemar de Fay, and that he would set it on fire one morning 'and this town shall be ruined by me, and the people slain and lie with their mouths gaping'. He and his force would leave the town the same day unharmed. Robert's reaction to Mauny's oath was to be 'greatly pleased', while commenting that it would be difficult to achieve and that 'many a good man shall die before it is accomplished'.

Whether that incident actually occurred as the poet presented it, or whether it was intended to summarise several occasions when Robert pressed the king to act, is uncertain. Nevertheless, that he should be one of those allegedly provoked into giving such an undertaking does reveal Mauny's seniority in the royal entourage at critical times, and his oath, with its assurance of killing and destruction, is typical of that expected of a military man of action, and fits with the later representations of him during that period.[4]

Other provocations during those years were simmering hostilities which saw French raids on the ports of the south coast and Suffolk, the Isle of Wight and the Channel Islands, and the capture of English ships. They were challenging rather than damaging actions, supporting the Scots and drawing attention to England's inability to defend her own coastal waters. A complication was that the Count of Flanders owed allegiance to the French king. Philip was insistent that the obligation should be upheld and the count, Louis of Nevers, complied, which effectively allied Flanders to France. But the populations of the cloth-making towns of Ghent, Ypres, Bruges and Mechelen and their subsidiary regions opposed the count. The cloth industry was heavily dependent on supplies of fine English wool, for which there was no substitute, and so the rebels favoured an English alliance, encouraged by Edward's imposition in 1336 of an embargo on wool exports to Flanders, to demonstrate their dependence. Edward could use English wool supplies as an element of his economic and diplomatic policies, restricting its export and supplying it selectively to those cities and towns which he needed as allies in the looming conflict with France. His restrictions were extended to include corn and foodstuffs, and Flemish property was confiscated.

Those measures were very effective, producing unrest in the cloth-making cities and with starving Flemish weavers begging for bread as far away as Tournai. But he could not completely prohibit wool exports for long as they were an important source of income for the merchants and hence for the crown, at a time when he needed as much revenue as he could obtain to finance his military operations. He invited clothmakers to settle in England so that the country would develop its own cloth industry, rather than be mainly a supplier of raw materials.

The political divisions in the Low Countries which followed provided Edward with the opportunity to create an alliance with those cities and counties in the region which would give him a military base on the continent should he choose to attack France. To head off Philip's attempts to secure the support of those territories, in the spring of 1337 Edward despatched Henry Burghersh, Bishop of Lincoln, with two newly created earls, Salisbury and Huntingdon, on a diplomatic mission for that purpose. They secured the support of Hainault and Brabant and, after some hard bargaining, that of Jacob van Artevelde, who had emerged as the leader of the rebels in the Flemish cloth towns. He had found a policy of neutrality between England and France to be impractical and agreed to support England in return for an annual subsidy of £140,000. The French attempted to intercept Burghersh and his party on their way back to England; that failed, but the threat of capture combined with difficult weather conditions delayed the return of the delegates. Edward remonstrated with his naval commanders at the failure to get them home sooner, to provide him with the important intelligence which he needed.

The French used the island of Cadzand off the Flemish coast at the mouth of the Zwin as the base from which they attempted to intercept the English diplomats. The Zwin was of vital importance as it was the waterway which carried Bruges' trade. Bruges was a wealthy city that was roughly half the size of London in terms of population. It had an international significance in European trade, with industries which processed imported goods and a developing financial system that made it the centre in northern Europe for several Italian merchant houses. As the waterway between the city and the North Sea had begun to silt up, the Zwin was created in 1134 as a navigable waterway through the Sincfal Marshes to provide a connection between the sea and Damme, and hence Bruges. The town of Damme had come to serve as the city's outport, where goods were transhipped from sea-going ships to vessels with a shallower draught.

As the Zwin, in turn, began to suffer from silting, Sluis had been founded in the 1260s further downstream, at a point where a bend in the Zwin sheltered it from the North Sea. It developed so quickly that in 1290 it was granted its city charter. A garrison on Cadzand could control trade entering and leaving the Zwin, isolating Sluis, Damme and thus Bruges. The island had one significant settlement, served by a wooden church. As its population grew, a stone structure, the church of Our Lady Kercke, replaced it in 1250 and that was greatly enlarged in 1325 when a second aisle was built alongside the existing one, almost doubling its size.

After Philip VI's confiscation of the Duchy of Gascony in May 1337 and an invasion led by the Comte d'Eu in July, Edward began to assemble an army in southern England for a campaign in France. That would be launched from the Low Countries and would consolidate the support of his putative allies as well as threatening France from the north-east. On 11 August 1337 Edward appointed Mauny as admiral of the fleet north of the Thames. The rank of admiral was a relatively new one; in 1295 it was conferred upon Sir William Leyburn and Sir John de Botetort, who had previously been described as Captain and Under-captain respectively. It became customary to appoint two admirals, one responsible for the coast north of the Thames and the other from the Thames along the south and south-western coasts. Their chief duties seem to have been to raise and man a fleet, when required, for the English kings kept very few ships of their own and commandeered vessels when they were needed.

That made it very difficult to respond to threats of invasion or raids, whereas the French monarchs hired armed vessels from other states, such as galleys from Genoa and Castile, which effectively served as mercenaries. Their effectiveness in northern waters was limited by the prevailing conditions because their low freeboard and relative flimsiness made them unseaworthy if the seas were running high. Nevertheless, those arrangements gave the French the initiative in the tit-for-tat warfare of coastal raids and capture of merchant vessels, which was demoralising and disruptive.

Mauny's appointment anticipated action that would require a dynamic commander in the position of admiral; even so, the preparations to deliver wool supplies and the English ambassadors to the Low Countries were very slow. The operation was put back until 30 September 1337 and then delayed further. That left a contingent of men cooling their heels at Sandwich, who could be more profitably employed in action than waiting around using up resources, and it was too late in the season to mount a full-scale expedition. A fleet was fitted out to transport that small army of 1,450 soldiers, which consisted of both archers and men-at-arms, plus a consignment of wool in the custody of some wool merchants, which was needed in lieu of money to pay subsidies and to revive the cloth industry. Bishop Burghersh and three other members of the king's Council were aboard, who were to conduct the diplomatic negotiations with the Low Countries rulers. They were carried across the southern North Sea in a fleet of seventy-six ships, manned by 2,200 sailors, some of whom could of course serve as fighting men should the need arise.

The force was placed under the command of Mauny and Henry Grosmont, who had been created Earl of Derby in March that year; the two men had campaigned together in Scotland in 1333. To open communications into Flanders, to Bruges and on to Dordrecht, a developing river port in south Holland between the great rivers to the north and the cities of Brabant and Flanders to the south, Mauny had to dislodge the French and their Flemish allies from the mouth of the Zwin. If that were done, then the merchants, their cargo of wool and the diplomats could be conveyed inland with safety, and so the first step was a military action to open that route into the Low Countries.

Sailing into the Zwin, apparently not intercepted or deterred by whatever enemy force was on Cadzand, the English approached Sluis, but were repulsed or chose to withdraw having assessed the situation, for French galleys were stationed there. Indeed, the approach to Sluis could have been a feint to draw out the garrison, which could not permit Cadzand to fall into English hands and so obstruct the shipping between Sluis, and ultimately Bruges, and the sea. Perhaps Mauny's intention was to entice the garrison from its fortified town and engage it where conditions were more favourable for his men, especially the archers, although any operation would be difficult, requiring as it did a landing on a foreshore occupied by the enemy.

The English then sailed towards Cadzand, on 9 November, where the garrison consisted of 5,000 men, including 'many ... knights and squires, expert men of arms' who had been chosen by the Count of Flanders for that service, according to Froissart. Cadzand was not large enough to have maintained so many soldiers for long and some of them probably were from the garrison at Sluis, the only force close enough. The senior commander was Guy of Flanders, the count's illegitimate half-brother. To boost morale, sixteen new knights had been created in anticipation of an encounter. The defenders were positioned 'upon the dykes and the sands, with their banners in their proper position before them'.[5] It seems that there were no fortifications; neither stone or wood was readily available on the wind-swept island and its sandy soil would not provide secure foundations for any elaborate works.

The English decided that as the wind and tide were in their favour 'they would run close up to it' and positioning archers on the ships' prows, they 'made full sail for the town'. The first discharge of arrows 'did much mischief, and many were maimed and hurt' and because the defenders were unable to face the continuous volleys of arrows discharged against them they were compelled to withdraw from the foreshore. That enabled the men-at-arms to land and engage in hand-to-hand fighting. The Earl of Derby was so reckless in the assault that he was knocked to the ground and was in some danger until he was rescued by Mauny: 'By feat of arms, he covered him and raised him up and placed him out of danger.'

The English eventually gained the upper hand and drove the Flemish back. Froissart gave due credit to the senior knights, as well as pointing out that 'more of the Flemings than of the English' were killed and wounded 'for the English archers made such continual discharges, from the time they landed, that they did them much damage'. The Flemish crossbowmen's rate of fire was much lower than that of the archers and did little to deter the English. The small town was taken, pillaged and burnt, and those locals who had taken refuge in the church were smoked out. It was said that smoke from the burning buildings could be seen at Bruges, thirteen miles away. Among the dead on the Flemish side were more than thirty knights and squires and those who were captured included Guy of Flanders, who was passed on to Mauny, as the senior commander.[6]

Disembarking a force in the presence of an enemy has been a hazardous manoeuvre for armies throughout the ages and the victory was achieved at Cadzand largely through the archers clearing the way for the landing. The success of the operation was also a credit to the leadership of the commanders, as well as the skill and discipline of the troops and sailors. The success was a timely one for English morale and it also caused further dissension among the Flemish, rousing the rebels while dispiriting those loyal to the count and therefore French influence. Having neutralised the force at Sluis, much weakened after the battle at Cadzand, the English were free to move inland and at the end of the month Burghersh landed at Dordrecht, where the wool was unloaded. He then went on to Antwerp and from there to Mechelen to meet a gathering of rulers of the states in the Low Countries, who wanted to be updated. To placate them and secure their support he promised further subsidies. That, in turn, required contributions from the wool merchants, who were horrified at the scale of the levies that he imposed on them and which he required before the end of the following March, to secure Edward's position for the new campaigning season.

Mauny returned the fleet to England intact, with the bonus of some French ships carrying wine seized on the way back. He was then instructed to keep the fleet together, fill up the vacancies and re-provision it, in case it should be required; but within three weeks it was to be moved from the Orwell to Sandwich. The campaign both increased his reputation for military prowess and was also financially profitable for him, with the king paying £8,000 for Guy of Flanders. The arrangement was similar to that for John Crabbe, but the sum was very high compared to fees for other senior figures. The man who captured David II of Scotland at the battle of Neville's Cross in 1346 received an annuity of £500 for life, while in 1348 Edward paid £3,500 for the custody of Charles of Blois after his capture in Brittany.[7] Those were not ransoms as such but payments for the transfer of the rights to the captured person; the ransoms would have been higher. The sum which Mauny received partly reflects Guy's diplomatic value to Edward and partly his gratitude to Mauny for carrying out the operation so successfully.

The problem for Edward was that he could not recoup any of the money, for Guy's brother did not come to an agreement over a ransom before Guy changed sides, in 1340. In May 1338 the king ordered the collectors of customs and the subsidy granted to him in the City of London to pay Mauny 500 marks [£333 6s 8d] from the custom of the wool exported to Brabant. Edward made part of the payment to Mauny actually in wool, which was a not uncommon arrangement and was not necessarily to the creditor's loss, so long as its price remained stable.[8] It may not be quite true that the money received for Guy was the foundation of Mauny's fortune, for he was already accumulating land and other wealth from the king's largesse, but it surely gave it a considerable boost. To put Mauny's £8,000 in context, the average receipts of the English crown during the fourteenth century were roughly £30,000 per annum, without parliamentary taxation, and in a good year it received £100,000, including parliamentary taxes.[9]

The English success at Cadzand strengthened d'Arteveldt's position and he was emboldened to invite Edward 'to come thither ... certifying how the Flemings greatly desired to see him'. Edward would do so only with an army and a considerable fleet to transport his troops; in mid-March 1338 he again appointed Mauny admiral of the fleet north of the Thames, with Sir Thomas Drayton appointed as vice-admiral in July, when Mauny was 'attendant upon other business of the king' and so was unable to carry out his duties. Those included 'the power of punishing and chastising the mariners and others of the said fleet'. Lord Burghersh was appointed admiral of the western fleet at the same date, and he and Mauny were both replaced in February 1339, Edward having appointed them to organise the fleet for the planned invasion. That was not an easy task, for many owners and masters failed to respond to orders to make their vessels available for the royal service, to transport men, horses, supplies and wool. Indeed, some ships were 'alleged to have been removed by the masters and mariners to foreign parts and elsewhere' to avoid that duty and even to 'succour his enemies and their adherents'. Mauny and his deputy had the authority 'to arrest all ships now in port and those not now in port when they return, for the passage of him and his army to parts beyond the seas' and they pursued the defaulters. More than 300 ships were listed for refusing to go on that service during Mauny's time as admiral between 1337 and 1340, which is an indication of his efficiency as an administrator.

His men were rather too enthusiastic, if anything, and had to be instructed to release fishing boats from Blakeney, in Norfolk, and elsewhere which had been impounded, despite being exempt so that the fishermen could continue to ply their trade. In April 1338 the king sent Mauny a reminder that not enough vessels had yet been assembled, which was partly because of the high rate of evasions and desertions, for Mauny's operations had become very unpopular along the east coast.

Shortly afterwards he was ordered to prepare a fleet to transport wool from Ipswich for the merchants in Brabant, fulfilling part of Edward's treaty obligations. Mauny's problem was that although some orders requiring shipping specified the minimum tonnage of ships that could be ordered to join the fleet, others gave no such minimum and so those that were really too small, such as fishing vessels, were taken, leading to complaints. Yet by July preparations were completed and Edward and his army were able to cross the North Sea to Antwerp in a huge fleet of 346 ships crewed by 12,000 sailors. Mauny's efforts, however unpopular, had borne fruit and with his fellow admiral he had produced the largest fleet to leave English shores since the reign of Henry III, despite some evasion by the ports and shipowners. The unprecedented needs of the crown for shipping surely alienated some shipowners, which was a problem for the admirals. Between August 1337 and July 1338 Mauny gathered four major fleets, losing 152 ships from desertion, which represented 15 per cent of the vessels summoned. His successor, Morley, experienced a similar rate of attrition, losing 161 ships in 1339 and 1340.[10]

As the diplomatic negotiations progressed, Edward was appointed Imperial Vicar in September 1338. He continued to encourage his allies to maintain their support, despite France's war preparations. Those talks, and Edward's financial problems, occupied the remainder of 1338 and much of 1339 and despite French provocations, which included the capture of two of the king's finest ships and the execution of their crews, Edward's planned invasion of France did not begin until September 1339.

Mauny now relinquished his role of admiral and resumed that of a soldier. According to Froissart, before he left England he had 'promised before ladies and damosels' that he would be the first to enter France after a declaration of hostilities, capture a castle or town 'and to do some deeds of arms'. Now was the time to fulfil that promise and so with a force of forty men he rode through Brabant and Hainault and after some uncertainty as to what to do next, decided to capture the town of Mortagne, ten miles south of Tournai. Arriving before dawn, Mauny and his men found an unguarded wicket gate in the walls and so dismounted and entered the town, parading along the high street with his pennon, but the guard in the 'great tower' sounded the alarm.

Mauny's force was too small to challenge its garrison and so he contented himself with setting fire to houses in the high street, fifty of which were said to have been burned, and making the people 'much frightened, as they concluded they must all have been taken prisoners'. He and his men then withdrew and rode in a sweep to Denain and Bouchain. The raid was avowedly carried out to fulfil Mauny's quixotic promise supposedly given to Robert of Artois described in *The Vows of the Heron*, for de Foy was governor of Tournai and Mortgane probably came under his command. He was a senior commander who during the Crécy campaign in 1346 was entrusted with holding the fords across the River Somme to prevent the English from crossing the river, without being given the resources to do so.

Mauny's raid was a typical small action of the wars described by le Bel and Froissart; his precipitate approach and ruthless execution of a plan formed on the spot were well suited to such incursions. In a similar operation the Bishop of Cambrai's stronghold of Thun l'Evêque was surrendered to Mauny's men by its disaffected commander, on the payment of a bribe. It was then garrisoned under the command of Mauny's brother Gilles and its garrison subsequently 'gave such disturbance to the Cambrensians, as this castle was but a short league from the city of Cambray'. Gilles was killed outside Cambrai during a skirmish in 1340, part of the ongoing subsidiary war between his garrison at Thun and that at Cambrai. His brothers John and Thierry took his place at Thun and continued to harass the defenders of Cambrai 'in counteravenging the death of their brother'; all three of Walter's brothers clearly pursued the same warlike and chivalric vocation as did Walter.[11]

In campaigning in the Cambrésis Walter Mauny and his brothers were fighting in territory adjoining their home ground, the County of Hainault, and they had launched their raids from there. The count was so fearful of Philip's vengeance for permitting that to happen that he tried not to get involved in the fighting, although Philip held it against him that he had permitted Edward's forces to pass through his territory and that his brother, John, and some of his troops were campaigning with them. The count's position was complicated by the fact that he was a vassal of the French crown for the County of Ostrevent, and that was where the Mauny brothers hailed from, and so they, too, were defying their lord.

Philip's response to Edward's invasion of France was to confront the English with a large army and after some manoeuvring an agreement between the two sides for a set-piece battle seemed to have been reached. By that time Mauny had left his raiding operations and had re-joined, or had been recalled to, the army. He and a Flemish officer were sent forward to reconnoitre, killing some of Philip's troops and discovering the whereabouts of his army. Having received their intelligence Edward deployed the English army at La Flamengrie near La Capelle on 21-22 October. He adopted the arrangement which had proved so successful at Dupplin Moor and Halidon Hill, with the archers on the flanks protected by pits and ditches and the dismounted knights serving as men-at-arms in the centre at the crest of rising ground, which would tempt the French cavalry to charge and then slow them down before they reached the English front.

Edward rode along the line of his army to encourage the soldiers, accompanied by three of his senior commanders, including Mauny. But the French did not respond and eventually both sides drew off. According to Froissart the French 'were of contrary opinions among themselves, and each spoke out his thoughts'.[12] That had proved to be a disappointing campaign, with the French unwilling to offer the battle that Edward so looked forward to, and in truth quite badly needed, for a long period of diplomatic and military preparation had produced no positive results.

4

THE BATTLE OF SLUIS AND AFTER

Edward claimed the throne of France at Ghent in January 1340 and returned to England in the following month to raise funds and assemble a new army. That also required the assembling of a naval force, both to transport the king and his army to the continent and to clear the Channel of French and other raiders who were preying on English merchant vessels. French raiding parties occasionally attacked English ports, either with a quick raid or a more determined attack in which buildings were set alight or demolished. That was especially dispiriting for the citizens and disruptive of their trade. Portsmouth was plundered and burnt by a French force in March 1338 and Southampton suffered a similar fate in the following October, provoking an angry reaction from the king that more had not been done to defend the town.

England had not attempted to maintain the communications across the North Sea to the Zwin and from there into the Low Countries after Mauny's victory in 1337 and the subsequent diplomatic business. French naval activity and superiority along the coasts of the Channel and the southern North Sea alarmed the Flemish, fearful for their safety and property, and afraid of the disruption of their trade, should the French become aggressive. Flanders had entered an alliance with Edward despite the loyalties of many of its nobility, and the citizens continued to feel vulnerable, even though the English fleet had some successes in the tit-for-tat coastal raiding.

When it became apparent in the summer of 1340 that Edward was planning to return to the continent with an army, the French collected a fleet to deter him, or better still to defeat him in a naval encounter. That would open up the possibility of an invasion of England. The French fleet left Honfleur in Normandy on 27 May under its two commanders, Hugh Quireret and Jean Béhuetet, and sailed for the Flemish coast. It consisted of many 'great vessels ... so great a number of ships that their masts seemed to be like a great wood'. They included a few exceptionally large ships which, with their wooden castles at prow and stern, provided high platforms from which to attack the enemy in their more conventional vessels, with lower decks. The French fleet incorporated Genoese galleys, under Pietro Barbavera, in the absence of Carlo Grimaldi and Antoine Doria, who commanded the two largest galley squadrons contracted to Philip VI. Twelve of Grimaldi's galleys and three of Barbavera's were in the French fleet in June 1340.

Despite the size of the force opposing him, Edward set sail on 22 June 1340 from the Orwell estuary, intending to land at Sluis. He was intent on relieving the French military pressure on his allies, especially Hainault, and releasing the queen, who was pregnant, from being virtually held as a hostage in Ghent by his Flemish allies who were demanding payments due to them. The fleet was under the direction of Robert Lord Morley, Admiral of

North since the spring of 1339, a Norfolk man who was familiar at court and a shipowner with experience of seamanship, having been master of ships at sea. His recently appointed deputy was the irrepressible John Crabbe, whose familiarity with Flemish waters made him invaluable. Mauny was in the king's entourage and of course he knew the Zwin and nearby coast from his exploits in October 1337; in that expedition every English ship had a pilot aboard but there were none in Morley's fleet in 1340. That fleet consisted of more than 140 ships, perhaps as many as 200, carrying roughly 650 bannerets and knights, 7,000 archers and 12,000 sailors.[1]

On the afternoon of 23 June Henry Burghersh, Bishop of Lincoln, and Reginald de Cobham went ashore with a small party at Heist, a village on the coast to the west of the Zwin, to reconnoitre. Riding towards Sluis they could see, and count, the French ships in the Zwin, which had taken up a defensive position in the restricted waterway. The French admirals had arranged their ships in three lines, with the admirals commanding the first two lines and Barbavera the third. The ships were tied together; Barbavera took strong objection to those tactics, especially the practice of tying the vessels together, because it was restrictive and it nullified his vessels' advantage of manoeuvrability. The French heavily outnumbered the English in terms of ships and men, and their vessels were generally larger than the English ones, but the English ships were free to change their positions. The intelligence from Burghersh and de Cobham was sent to the fleet, where the king and his advisors decided to wait until the next day, 24 June, before attacking.

On the island of Cadzand the village had been burned, so that the inhabitants would have to move away for the time being and not be able to harass the French from the shore, if there was an action. Evidently its population had rebuilt the place within a couple of years after Mauny's earlier action there. They would not have been able to build during the first winter and so during the building seasons of 1338 and 1339 they had replaced the structures destroyed and damaged, only to see the new ones destroyed.

Early in the morning of the 24th the English fleet stirred and sailed east towards the Zwin, having waited for the tide and wind to be in their favour; when they reached the French fleet the sun would be directly behind them, in the faces of the enemy crews. The weather conditions favoured the English, for 'the wind had then been in the East for the whole fortnight before the King put to sea, but by the grace of Him who is Almighty, the wind shifted immediately to the West; so that, by the grace of God, the King and his fleet had both wind and weather to their mind'. They formed two, perhaps three, battle lines and Crabbe commanded a reserve force behind the main fleet. Like the French admirals, Morley placed his largest ships in the first line, which included his own ship, the king's vessel and that of Mauny, which was positioned close to Morley's. The tactics used at Cadzand were again employed, with the archers placed in the prows of the vessels; they were stationed in the larger ships, giving them the advantage of height, while the men-at-arms were in the smaller, lower, vessels. It may be that Mauny had a significant influence on the battle tactics adopted by Morley and Edward, drawing on his experience of three years earlier.

The English paused off the coast close to the Zwin, waiting for the tide to turn, and feigned a movement to turn their ships around and sail away. At least, that seems to be how the French interpreted the action and it prompted them to break their prepared line and move their ships forward, which required the uncoupling of the chains holding them. But that was not done soon enough for the vessels to gain sea-room before the action began, given the proximity of the English fleet and the rising tide, which turned at about midday. It did have the effect of breaking up the defensive formation into separate groups of ships which were likely to drift apart, which was to the English advantage. On the French side, the Genoese galleys were manned by crossbowmen, who, according to the requirements of the contracts issued by Philip to Grimaldi and Doria in 1337 and 1338, numbered just 1.35 per galley; as there were fifteen galleys in the fleet at Sluis, that figure suggests that they would have had roughly twenty crossbowmen among their crews, although more would have been provided by other commanders. They were vastly outnumbered by the quicker firing English longbowmen.

Ballistas and other projectile-firing weapons were mounted on the largest ships, firing arrows, big stones and flaming pitch. Sling-shot was another projectile deployed; Geoffrey le Baker wrote that many engaged in the fight 'had their brains knocked out by stones thrown down from the tops of masts'. The *Christopher* was one of the large ships captured from the English earlier and it was placed in the front rank of the French fleet, its height providing vantage points from which missiles could be directed at the English crews, until they captured it and turned it around, putting it to the same use against the French. The archers' rate of fire and accuracy subdued the crossbowmen and drove most of the French soldiers and crewmen to take shelter below decks, which prevented them from adequately defending their ships when the English men-at-arms came charging aboard to engage in hand-to-hand fighting. They moved from ship to ship and as they were better armed and more experienced in such close combat than were the French sailors and soldiers, they steadily captured almost the whole fleet. When the first line was taken they moved to the second one, and the action continued until after darkness fell. Mauny's ship was said to have been the fourth to crash into the French line and he attracted attention for his fighting prowess in the battle; according to Jean le Bel he 'fought magnificently ... and principally by the grace of God, the French, Normans, Gascons, Bretons and Genoese were finally killed, drowned and utterly defeated: very few escaped'.[2]

The French losses were estimated at 20,000 men at least, for the English took no prisoners, and modern estimates put the figure at 16,000 to 18,000. The death-toll was so high that, it was said, Philip's jester had the task of breaking the news to the king, which he did by saying that 'Our knights are far braver than the English' and when the king asked him why that was he responded with the comment, 'Because the English don't dare to jump into the sea in full armour.' It is unclear whether the king was amused. Both French commanders died, one during the action and the other was hanged from the mast of his ship after he had been captured. Edward decided that he had insufficient ransom value, and his death was also a punishment for the raids which he had conducted on English coastal towns.

Many of the French sailors and soldiers who were able to struggle ashore were set upon and killed by the locals, probably stirred up by the bishop and de Cobham on the previous day, but also taking revenge for the conduct of the French before the battle. According to Giovanni Villani, at Cadzand they had 'pillaged and burned and killed over 300 Flemings'. The English captured 166 ships, recovering those of the king which had been seized earlier, and destroyed twenty-four more, for the total loss was 190 ships. Only twenty-four vessels from the third line escaped, including the Genoese galleys and vessels under the command of a Flemish pirate. As daylight faded they were pursued by ships from Crabbe's flotilla, which may have captured some of them.

The action in the Zwin was the major victory Edward needed. It opened the way into Flanders for the English troops and supplies. His success also reduced for the time being the problem of the French capturing and plundering English shipping and raiding the coast, for so many ships had been taken or destroyed and so many sailors killed that the French Channel ports were left with very few seaworthy ships and able crews to man them for several years to come. That was doubtless one reason for the extent of the killing during the battle, for by eliminating experienced sailors, French naval power was greatly reduced, regardless of how quickly new ships could be built or hired. But the battle was not financially profitable for the English, for no prisoners were taken who could be ransomed and although many of the ships normally sailed as merchantmen, they were prepared in advance for military action and so were not carrying cargoes which could have been sold to offset the costs. That did not deter the king, who was wounded in the action, from acclaiming a great victory. He had five model ships made of gold, two of which he gave to Canterbury cathedral and the others to St Paul's, Walsingham priory and Gloucester abbey.

Edward's army then moved south to besiege Tournai, where he was joined by William II, Count of Hainault with a force of around 8,500 soldiers, making a total of 26,000 men. Mauny was among the commanders and was an active one. On one occasion, on 12 August, he and the Count led 'a *chevauchée* up to a town which is called Marchiennes, which was strengthened with walls and ditches, and took the town, and caused it to be burned; and they pillaged and burned the countryside all around and returned safe and sound the same day to the army with their company'.

On 27 August, during skirmishing with the defenders outside the city, the English pursued a party of Frenchmen to the Valenciennes Gate and during the fighting, 'Walter Mauny was stuck [sic] down off his horse, and his banner knocked down beneath the bridge of the gate, and because of this there was a marvelous assault, the greatest which occurred during the entire siege.' The sharpness of the fighting which followed Mauny's mishap suggests that his men were galvanised by the need to protect their commander while he recovered and was able to remount, and they were anxious to revenge the indignity he had suffered. Such incidents and other operations punctuated the siege. According to one chronicle, during the siege of Tournai, at St Omer:

> Sir Robert the Count of Artoys, Sir Walter de Manny, Jacob de Artefelde, and many other great men, assembled a great host of good people, horse and foot, well armed ... and began to throw great stones with their engines, to destroy the city. And when those within the city saw the compassing of our people without, they took counsel among them to open the gates and give battle to our people. And when our people perceived this, they withdrew, and with a good will allowed a great multitude of people to come out of the city.

The assailants then returned to the attack

> ...and boldly gave battle to the French; and all those who had taken the field met their death by evil mishap, for of the French there were slain 5210; among which dead were found ninety-five with gilt spurs. So that our people pursued the French as far as the gate of Saint Thomer, and there, right at the portcullis, were the Frenchmen all slain. And as for those who had escaped within

> the gate, they did not dare come any more out of the city, until our people had taken their departure for the siege of Torneye.

While that siege continued detachments of the army 'from day to day made incursions in the parts of France, and burnt, and took prey and prisoners, knights and esquires of great renown; and beasts, and corn, and other provisions had they, belonging to the King of France, so that the country, all round about the siege, was ravaged, burnt, and brought to destruction'. But in truth Edward's army had little chance of capturing the city itself; it was regularly supplied with provisions, he was short of money and as the siege dragged on he was unable to pay all of his men promptly. A truce was an appealing outcome for both sides and one was agreed at Esplechin on 25 September.[3]

The costs of the war and maintaining the support of his allies were proving very high for the king and his financial needs were acute, as he was not receiving an adequate return through captures and ransoms. The subsidies payable to his allies in the Low Countries came to £124,000 by the end of 1337. His credit was worsening and the two Italian merchant-banking houses of the Bardi and Peruzzi, which he had hitherto drawn upon for loans, were unwilling to lend him more. By September 1338 they had already advanced him about £70,000 and in 1340 he defaulted on the delivery of a consignment of wool, security for repayment of a loan in lieu of money or valuables. Their affairs elsewhere were increasingly shaky, which contributed to their reluctance to lend Edward further funds; the Peruzzi bank failed in 1343 and that of the Bardi in 1346, although in neither case was that largely attributable to the bank's over-exposure to the English monarchy.

An increasingly desperate Edward then raised money from merchants in Brussels and Mechelen, being forced to offer the earls of Derby, Warwick and Northampton as security. When he defaulted, Derby and Warwick were actually surrendered into custody, which was a personal humiliation for the king, as was the Archbishop of Trier having possession of the Great Crown of England as collateral for a loan and threatening to break it up to sell its gold and jewels. Pawning the crown had raised £2,250. Many items of large and small value were used as collateral for loans, including a war-horse of the king's which Mauny pledged at Mechelen and which was redeemed for £45. In November 1339 the king acknowledged debts of £349 10s to Mauny for his wages and those of his soldiers who had campaigned in France and Brabant.[4]

The queen's presence in Ghent was also effectively a pledge for payment of the subsidies due to the king's allies. Edward and Philippa's fourth son, John of Gaunt (Ghent), was born in St Bavo's abbey there in March 1340 and the queen did not return to England until the following November. By 1340 the crown owed roughly £300,000, was not receiving enough income to service the debt, could not supply the money demanded by the king's creditors (who would no longer accept wool in lieu) and so effectively it was bankrupt.

The king became exasperated with his financial officials for not providing him with adequate funds to pursue the war. He returned to London unexpectedly at the end of November 1340, arriving at the Tower's Watergate during the night with just seven companions, one of whom was Mauny. Edward dismissed the Chancellor, Robert de Stratford, brother of John de Stratford, Archbishop of Canterbury, and the Treasurer, four judges and other officials, imprisoning some of them. The archbishop was so fearful of the king's wrath that he claimed sanctuary at Canterbury Cathedral. The king's actions provoked a constitutional crisis in the following year and a political confrontation between the king and the archbishop. Whether Mauny's travelling in the king's small party when he returned to London was because he sought to influence Edward's actions cannot be known, but the army commanders had almost as much reason as the king himself to be annoyed with the failure to maintain supplies of arms, armour, other equipment and money for wages so that they could continue their campaigns. The outcome of the siege of Tournai certainly was a dispiriting contrast to the spectacular victory at Sluis.

Meanwhile the war had to be maintained and the king took loans from whoever could provide them, including Mauny, who advanced him £4,000. The acknowledgment of that debt stated that Mauny was someone 'to whom the king is bound, by letters patent and bills of his wardrobe, in large sums of money by reason of the war with France for defence of the realm and recovery of the rights of his crown'. The £4,000 was to be repaid in two yearly parts out of the sums collected in Essex as part of the subsidy granted by the previous parliament. Lending to a monarch whose normal expenditure was high and who was engaged in a major war was not a secure investment, but the loan surely boosted Mauny's status. By 1355 he was also a creditor of the king's eldest son, Edward the Black Prince, as were the earls of Huntingdon, Stafford and Arundel, the Bishop of Durham, five knights and at least five other men, as well as the king himself.[5]

Edward also owed Mauny £2,000 'for wages for the time in which ... [he has] stood with him in his war' in Flanders, which was to be paid as wool from Essex, also due to the crown by parliamentary grant. But that could not be advanced as the sum was also allocated elsewhere, and so £1,000 was to be paid from the Essex wool and the other £1,000 from fines received by the Justices in Kent. Mauny had been appointed Sheriff of Merioneth in December 1332, with the custody of Harlech Castle, the income from which was to cover £2,640 (4,000 marks) of a debt of £8,000 owed to him by the crown. Mauny also received income as Keeper of the Marshalsea Prison of the Court of King's Bench and various dues, such as those from the fairs held at Baldock in Hertfordshire. Those devices to pay the sums which the king owed to him further highlight the fragility of financial dealings with the king; on the other hand, Mauny's income from receipts for ransomed prisoners during 1337-40, in Flanders and northern France, was £3,000, in addition to the £8,000 he had received for Guy of Flanders. In 1345 the king granted him an annuity of £500, for life, a considerable sum; and in that year Edmund de Perrers quitclaimed him the manor and advowson of Knebworth in Hertfordshire. Mauny had become a wealthy man. He also obtained from the crown standard pardons for events during his time as admiral and for any escapes of prisoners from the Marshalsea while he held the post of Keeper, including 'all excesses' in the conduct of his officers and lieutenants at the prison.[6]

Mauny's administrative tasks for the crown included the management of the finances of Netley abbey, a Cistercian house on Southampton Water and near to Southampton, which was in the king's patronage, and needed help because 'in these days [it is] so depressed by the frequent coming thither as well of alien enemies as of other mariners calling there and passing over to foreign parts and other causes, that it cannot pay its debts'. Clearly, damage to its tenants' properties during French raids – and maintaining the tradition of hospitality to travellers at a time when more people were passing along Southampton Water because of the war – were seriously eroding its finances. Mauny and his officers were entrusted with rectifying the situation.[7] Similarly, lands held by one John de Brumpton from the priory of Ware which were in the king's hands 'by reason of the war with France' in 1359 were described as 'in the custody of Walter de Mauny'.[8]

An insight into Mauny's approach to administration comes from the case of a ship's captain from Zeeland in 1341 who had been imprisoned and his vessel seized because he had loaded wool on to it at London without declaring the cargo to the customs. On Mauny's request the case was brought to the king's attention and he pardoned the man and restored his ship to him, although the wool was retained by the crown. The man lost the cargo, but he could have been more severely punished for his offence and had his ship confiscated, which would have been ruinous. In a different context, in 1344 Sir Richard Stapelton and John Spring were both pardoned of any homicides, felonies and robberies with which they may be charged, provided that they agreed to stand trial if indicted and also that they 'go on the king's service when and so often' as they were required to do. Exercising clemency in that way was a standard procedure for grandees, using their influence to establish a body of people who owed them loyalty; Mauny was engaging in that practice. Similarly, he granted in 1346 a protection to Henry de Trafford which excused him from the expensive obligation of receiving knighthood.[9]

After the political crisis which followed Edward's abrupt return to England in 1340, the Stratford brothers were not re-appointed and the subsequent administration under William Edington, Bishop of Winchester, proved to be more efficient in raising revenue than theirs had been. Financing military campaigns became more certain and the king was increasingly able to employ English soldiers, reducing his dependence on his allies in the Low Countries for mercenaries. Some of those allies were, in any case, doubtful about the legality of campaigning in France themselves with their own troops, further reducing their value to Edward. Moreover, continuing instability in the internal politics of Flanders saw the count regain much of his authority and in 1345 Jacob van Artevelde was killed by a mob in Ghent. According to the chronicler Jean le Bel he had 'acquired such prestige and popular support that throughout all Flanders whatever he proposed or commanded was well and truly done' and no-one dare oppose his orders.[10] But that applied to the 1330s rather than the mid-1340s, when his personal ambitions and failure to account for the public funds expended lost him most of his earlier support. Under the count, Flanders became an ally of France once more.

In another major reversal, Hainault changed its adherence after being England's ally for twenty years and more; William II made peace with Philip in 1343 and subsequently he supported the French monarchy. That change would not have caused a problem for Mauny, for by the outlook of the fourteenth century an individual was loyal to his lord, to whom he had sworn allegiance, in his case to Edward and Philippa, and not to a state, be it Hainault or England. As the alliances with the states of the Low Countries diminished in significance, so the payment of subsidies to them could be reduced. That was not to say that the war with France could not be conducted through surrogate conflicts, and an opportunity to engage in such a proxy war soon arose in Brittany.

An experienced man-of-war such as Sir Walter Mauny was sure to be called upon when war erupted again. The impetuous style of warfare practised by some of Edward's commanders inevitably led to an erosion of their numbers, by death or captivity, creating openings for others. The king instilled a confidence and *esprit de corps* into his armies, which engendered a positive, self-confident approach, with swift movements and bold and decisive actions when the enemy was encountered, even when their own forces were dangerously outnumbered. That could lead to serious misjudgements. William Montagu, Earl of Salisbury, and his fellow-commander Robert Ufford, Earl of Suffolk, were captured in 1340 while carrying out a reconnaissance of the defences of Lille prior to a planned attack; they had apparently ridden forward with a protecting force of no more than forty men and were seized by members of the French garrison. Montagu was released on parole, on condition that he did not fight in France again; that restriction was subsequently removed as part of an agreement for the release of two French prisoners in English custody. One of those two men had been captured by Mauny in a raid, perhaps specifically targeted for his value in such a negotiation. In other words, holding a man for ransom could provoke the enemy into capturing someone judged to be of equal worth from one's own side for an exchange, to avoid paying the ransom. Montagu was able to resume his military career, but only after more than two years when he had been unable to fight. Ufford, too, was released, after the payment of a ransom, which included a contribution of £500 from the king, and he, too, was able to participate in the war again. But both men had effectively been taken out of action for more than two years by their ill-judged encounter before Lille, which made men such as Mauny, bold but perhaps not as rash as them and with sounder military judgement, all the more valuable, for Edward could ill afford the loss of such senior and experienced figures for so long.[11]

5

SIR WALTER MAUNY: THE FIGHTING YEARS

Edward involved himself in the disputed succession to the Duchy of Brittany following the death of Duke John III in May 1341. The rival claimants were John de Montfort, John III's half-brother, and Jeanne de Penthièvre, John III's niece and wife of Charles de Blois, the French king's nephew, who was supported by Philip. Edward was reluctant to see the duchy come under French control, not only because territory meant resources, but because of its strategic importance: the ports around its coasts could provide bases for privateers raiding English shipping sailing to and from Bordeaux and the other Gascon ports. He also regarded it as a possible territory from which to invade France.

A local war ensued between Charles de Blois and John de Montfort's forces, which brought quick successes for de Blois, assisted by some senior French nobles, whose troops overran most of the duchy and captured Nantes, surrendered by de Montfort, who was then sent to Paris as a prisoner. That was so alarming for the English that de Montfort's determined and influential wife, Jeanne of Flanders, was able to secure an agreement with Edward for his support. Mauny was sent there in April 1342 with a small force consisting of no more than thirty-four men-at-arms and 200 mounted archers. He complained that their departure from Portsmouth was delayed by the non-arrival there of three ships, the masters of which had been instructed 'to come to Portesmuth on a certain day now long past, where the king ordered the ships to be assembled for such passage'. Because of their failure to comply with this order 'the passage was delayed' and a warrant was issued for the arrest of the three offenders, who were protesting at not receiving their pay. Another example of the problem of supporting campaigns on the continent when the king had so few ships and his officers were obliged to hire merchant vessels for transport; their owners would prefer to continue with their existing trade than engage in the more hazardous service for the king, for erratic payments.

Rennes was surrendered to Charles de Blois in early May and those loyal to de Montfort retreated to the coastal town of Hennebont, where the defence was directed by Jeanne herself, adopting a martial pose and garb to encourage the citizens. In what Jean de Bel described as 'the boldest and most remarkable feat ever performed by a woman', during a French assault on the defences she led a foray which captured their camp and set it alight, before riding off to another castle for refuge. When she returned a few days later she again broke through the besiegers' lines to regain the town. Frustrated, they decided to split their forces, sending a part to besiege Auray while the remainder would break down Hennebont's resistance through the fire of 'twelve great engines', which had been used at Rennes, and not by assaults.[1]

Mauny and his soldiers managed to break the blockade and get into Hennebont, stiffening the defenders' resolve by providing professional guidance and carrying out morale-boosting exploits. Among Mauny's successes was a sally to destroy a siege engine which was regularly firing projectiles into the town; the archers drove off the guard and then his men-at-arms 'toppled the great engine and smashed it to pieces before charging into the enemy camp and setting it ablaze, killing plenty before the besiegers were awake and could respond'. But Mauny's force was so closely pursued as it withdrew that he and some of his men were obliged to turn and attack their pursuers to keep them at bay. That was a sound tactic of covering the withdrawal of the force which had sallied from the defences, but the action escalated. According to le Bel: 'Then a mighty fight began as the besieging army kept coming, and in the end the English and Bretons had to retreat to their fortress. There were many fine charges and captures and rescues made by both sides; and praise and honour were won above all by Sir Walter Mauny, and by his companions such as Sir Yves de Trésiguidi and the lord of Landreman'. The episode ended, in le Bel's narrative, with a characteristically chivalric flourish; after they had returned 'the valiant countess then come down from the castle and kiss Sir Walter Mauny and his companions two or three times in turn'.[2]

The archers within Hennebont were having such a deadly effect that Lord Louis of Spain, the commander of the besieging force, decided to abandon the siege for a while and take his troops to assist Blois at the siege of Auray. On the way they came to 'an old castle'. Meanwhile, discovering that the enemy were no longer blockading Hennebont, Mauny decided to pursue them and drive them away from the old castle, only to discover when his men arrived that it had been captured and the bulk of the enemy force had then left. Undaunted, Mauny's men assaulted the castle, forced their way in and 'killed all but ten' of its defenders before abandoning it and returning to Hennebont. Jean le bel thought that the episode was worth mentioning as it was an example of a castle 'which had been taken on one day and retaken the next, a feat of great prowess indeed'. In another incident during the siege of Hennebont, Mauny freed two English knights held prisoner and facing execution, using the stratagem of starting a skirmish and then entering the French camp when their soldiers were engaged in repelling his raiding party. Mauny and his men had taken two horses with them for the knights' escape, which was successfully achieved.[3]

Hennebont's garrison also engaged in a more substantial expedition under Mauny's direction, pursuing Lord Louis's troops, who were engaged in a plundering raid through the Breton countryside around Quimper. The force from Hennebont sailed around the coast until they found Lord Louis's ships, which they captured, killing the guards. They were amazed at the amount of plundered booty which they found aboard the vessels. Dividing their force into three they set off to locate Lord Louis's men and one of their divisions encountered and defeated them, with the help of the people who were themselves pursuing the enemy to try to recover their stolen possessions. Lord Louis got away but with his ships held by Mauny's men he had to do so in a small boat. Aware of the danger of being cut off by the enemy, Mauny took his force back to Hennebont, skirmishing along the way and attacking a castle 'which was very strong'. Their assault was at first beaten back, but 'Sir Walter urged his men on with a passion, and he himself was always at the forefront, in the greatest peril'. Eventually they captured the castle 'and put everyone they found there to the sword'.[4]

Jean le Bel's descriptions of those encounters presumably came from Mauny and so his courage and ability are emphasised; the actual events must have been confusing enough at the time and Mauny and le Bel may have distorted them, from Mauny's uneven memory and his wish to present a favourable impression of his role in the campaign, as well as the need to make sense of the operation to the reader. But le Bel's account does provide a sense of the nature of warfare during the fighting in Brittany; its small scale, the improvised tactics, often adopted in response to local intelligence, and its brutality, with death and destruction inflicted on combatants and non-combatants alike.

Those successes were minor operations in the wider scheme of things and Mauny's force was intended only as an advance guard to provide some support for Countess Jeanne until the main English army could be assembled and shipped to Brittany. When that failed to arrive, Mauny was clear-sighted enough to realise that the war had reached a stalemate and he proposed coming to terms with Charles de Blois for a truce. He returned to England to secure his prisoners and to report on the problems facing the Montfortian cause. But he was premature, for another English army, commanded by the Earl of Northampton, landed at Brest and had some initial successes before settling down to besiege Morlaix. There it found itself in danger of being trapped by a French relief force under de Blois, which arrived at the end of September. Northampton prepared his positions well and his army won a significant victory, despite being outnumbered. That encouraged Edward to persist with the war and not act upon Mauny's proposal for a truce.

Later in 1342 the king himself led an army of 5,000 men to the region; his primary objective was the capture of Vannes, and Mauny was instructed to make a reconnaissance of the city's defences with two other knights. They reported that it had weaknesses and could be taken by assault, but when the army arrived and launched an attack on the city, the assault failed. In January 1343 the Truce of Malestroit brought hostilities to an end under terms very favourable for the English. Montfort was released from imprisonment in the Louvre, while Jeanne accompanied Edward III to England, where she soon developed ill-health of some kind and was confined for much of the rest of her life in Tickhill Castle in Yorkshire, with payments for her care from October 1343. She died in 1374. There is debate as to her mental health, though some have suggested that she was confined on the orders of Edward III to increase his power in Britanny.

Campaigning in Brittany gave Mauny the opportunity to experience the practicalities of defending a fortified town during a siege, which required a different set of skills from those deployed by a commander in the aggressive role of directing and participating in raids. He was also able to take ransoms for seven noblemen captured during the fighting. But not all of the English commanders approved of that system and after taking noble prisoners at Auray they would neither accept offers of ransoms for them or allow the prisoners themselves to go away to raise the money, because once redeemed they would again be free to raise troops and resume the campaign. Instead, they sent them to regions under English control as prisoners-of-war. In that respect Mauny's way of making war was at odds with that of some of his fellow senior commanders.

While the position in Brittany had been stabilised for the time being, the problem of Aquitaine remained. Edward had declared his claim to the French throne in January 1340, partly because if the English monarch was also king of France, then no homage would be due for Aquitaine. Edward decided to re-start the war, renouncing the truce in June 1345 and launching a campaign in the region under the command of Ralph Stafford, the senior English figure in Aquitaine. That was in response to requests for assistance from the nobles there, who were faced with French successes, although the French strategy at this point was to act defensively and hold what they had, rather than launch further offensives in the region.

Stafford's forces were supported by an English expedition led by Henry Grosmont, who had now inherited the earldom of Lancaster from his father. He was clear about Edward's objectives and arrived with an aggressive intent, making the greatest possible impact with the forces under his command. His army reached Bordeaux on 9 August 1345; according to le Bel it consisted of 600 men-at-arms and 6,000 archers, and the king had allowed Lancaster 'as much gold and silver and as many supplies and troops as he required'.[5] Lancaster's army was merged with the local forces and was deployed in three divisions, with Mauny and Ralph Stafford commanding two of them. Mauny's retinue consisted of roughly eighteen men-at-arms and eighty mounted archers. He, Lancaster and Sir James Audley, whose retinue consisted of forty men-at-arms, were paid a *regard* by the crown, on top of the sums paid for wages. This was a relatively new element in financing war and was in effect a bonus paid to commanders to help them defray the costs of financing their contribution; a commander needed to draw on his own funds to maintain his soldiers, for payments were generally made in arrears and not always promptly paid even then. On 3 January 1346 Mauny claimed compensation for horses lost by his men, but he did not receive it until 1351. The standard rate for a *regard* was 100 marks for thirty men for a quarter of a year; the three commanders of this expedition were paid at one-and-a-half times that rate.

Of the £11,200 taken from the Exchequer to Aquitaine, Mauny received £1,795 10s.

Only 15 per cent of payments to Mauny were in cash; the remainder, two out of three payments to him, were in the form of assignments of money to be levied locally, which could take some time to administer and collect. The figures give an idea of the scale of the financial operation which Mauny was engaged in, but not an indication of profit, if indeed he made any money from the Exchequer for his commitment.[6]

Stafford had been tentative and had allowed himself to get bogged down besieging places of minor strategic significance. Lancaster quickly agreed a local truce to free up the besiegers of the castle at Blaye on the Garonne estuary and marched his army to join Stafford's men. He then launched an aggressive and effective campaign; less than two weeks after landing at Bordeaux the army captured and plundered the rich town of Bergerac on the Dordogne, known as 'the strong room of France' because of its fortifications. The English had sent scouts on a reconnaissance and on their return they told Sir Walter that the town's defences did not seem all that strong. Froissart cast the ensuing operation in a typical Mauny-like way. Lancaster and his senior officers dined early and during the meal Mauny said to him: 'My lord, if we were good knights, and well-armed, we might, this evening, partake of the wines of these French lords who are in garrison in Bergerac.' Lancaster's response was that it should not be his fault if they did not, and the others reacted by saying, 'Let us hasten to arm ourselves.'

The French sallied out to meet their assailants outside the town and during the ensuing fighting Mauny 'was the first to enter the suburbs' and he then pressed on 'so far among his enemies, that he was in great danger'. The English disengaged and spent the night in the suburbs and then, with the aid of the fleet, which had been sent for, they renewed the attack and eventually broke though the French perimeter. They then withdrew and left Bergerac to the English. The ensuing operations by the English army against crumbling opposition from the French were very successful and did what they were intended to do, restoring the English position in the region and distracting the French court from the two other campaigns mounted that year. But those campaigns did not go well for the English.

The Earl of Northampton's expedition to Brittany achieved only limited success and, although John de Montfort did homage to Edward III for the duchy in 1345, he died in September that year. That inevitably hindered the cause, although his son, the future Duke John IV, was to be brought up at the English court. Meanwhile the king's own plans for taking an army to Flanders were negated by the changing political situation there. But Lancaster's army in south-west France pressed on and was busy 'burning and wasting the country far and wide', capturing castles and walled towns to secure their position, including Aiguillon 'one of the strongest castles in the world and one of the best situated', which was surrendered. He then besieged the provincial capital at Périgeux. A French force raised that siege and forced the Anglo-Gascon army to withdraw, but during the campaign which followed, the French were heavily defeated while besieging the castle at Auberoche.

The fighting continued into the winter and included the capture of La Réole, a fortified town on the Garonne, in early January 1346. That was where Mauny's father had been killed and, according to Froissart, he offered a reward of 100 crowns to anyone who could show him where his father was buried. Mauny was shown the site by an elderly man; it was marked by 'a little tomb of marble' in a small chapel which had then been outside the town but had since been brought within it when a new circuit of town walls was built. He arranged for the bones to be disinterred and taken to Valenciennes and reburied in a friary there.[7]

The campaign was both a strategic success and a profitable one for the members of the army, which numbered fewer than 10,000 men, as the captured towns and castles yielded up much booty and some valuable prisoners. Le Bel wrote, 'No greater or finer campaign [*chevauchée*] was ever heard of, truly, than that conducted by the worthy earl of Derby [Lancaster], capturing so many well-fortified towns and impregnable castles. It involved some great and notable feats of prowess and remarkable adventures.' The English chronicler Geoffrey le Baker put the number of 'towns, cities, castles and forts' captured at 250, some of which were 'large, strong, well-fortified places'.[8] Ten prominent French noblemen were captured at Bergerac and those taken at Auberoche included one count, seven viscounts, three barons, two seneschals from the region, twelve bannerets, many knights and, to crown it all, a nephew of the pope. Froissart wrote that during the campaign the Count d'Lisle, nine other counts and viscounts and more than 200 knights were taken prisoner.

The ransoms which were demanded were put by one chronicler at £50,000, provoking a complaint that the sums were too high. But they may have been realistic, given the capture during the campaign of those regional and local leaders who were required to organise the resistance to Lancaster's incursions. In the circumstances they would be prepared to pay relatively high sums for their release and subsequent freedom of action. Lancaster was entitled to the major portion of plundered goods and ransoms, from which the army's costs had to be paid, but his senior officers were permitted their share and the campaign surely contributed significantly to Mauny's growing wealth. He was well enough off to invest in other financial transactions and property. For example, he was a creditor of the London merchant and vintner Sir John Stodeye, who traded with Gascony, and he lent £2,000 to Henry de Causton, a London citizen, on the security of a half-share of a tenement in the parish of St Thomas the Apostle.[9]

Mauny and his retinue probably left for England after the capture of La Réole, returning to Gascony in the spring for the new campaign. That saw the early English successes reversed by a large French army, under the command of Prince John, which set about recapturing the places taken by Lancaster in the previous year. This put the English under pressure but served Edward's purpose because it took men and commanders away from northern France, where he launched his invasion with a landing at Saint-Vaast-la-Hogue on 12 July. After the capture of Angoulême the French advanced along the valley of the Garonne until their progress was blocked by the English garrison of Aiguillon, a walled town at the confluence of the rivers Garonne and Lot. The garrison consisted of just 300 men-at-arms and 600 archers, yet for more than four months they resisted the French army, which was so large that Froissart said that it consisted of 100,000 men; an exaggeration which he later changed to 60,000 and was intended to convey the magnitude of the force rather than the precise numbers which it contained. The defenders were commanded by Ralph Stafford and included Mauny, who had remained there when Lancaster had withdrawn his field army. According to Jean le Bel, the leading role in implementing the defenders' tactics was played by Mauny, who

> ...should be remembered before all others; and certainly, he should wear the laurels here, for he bore the burden and responsibility, giving heart and spirit to all the defenders, and was always the first to arm, the first to go, the first into battle and the last to return, and nothing he saw or heard discouraged him.

The English commanders knew that a beleaguered garrison needed to maintain some initiative and not passively accept that it was hemmed in and could do no more than await the arrival of a relieving force. They carried out sorties to gather supplies and drive in cattle, harass the besiegers, destroy their works and their stone-throwing artillery. Mauny was to the fore in such operations. Froissart wrote that he 'made frequent excursions beyond the river, with about six score companions, to forage, and often returned with his booty in sight of the army'. In one incident he described a French foraging party numbering as many as 500 men were driving off cattle when it was intercepted by a force under Mauny:

> They immediately began an engagement, which was very sharp; and many were killed and wounded on both sides. The French were at least five to one. News was brought of this into Aiguillon, when every one sallied out for the fastest, and the earl of Pembroke with the foremost: they dashed into the midst of them, and found sir Walter Manny unhorsed, and surrounded by his enemies, but fighting most valiantly. He was directly rescued and remounted.[10]

The French were then driven off. Such skirmishes were hazardous in the extreme and sometimes involved the garrison in hand-to-hand fighting against heavy odds. Yet the dangerous sallies were undertaken not to flaunt the senior officers' fighting abilities or display their chivalric credentials, but for the sound military reason of unsettling the enemy and at the same time bringing in supplies and maintaining the garrison's morale.

On 26 August 1346 Edward's army won a complete victory at Crécy over the French under Philip VI in person; the tactics adopted at Dupplin Moor and Halidon Hill were successfully applied and the archers again played a major role. Edward then took the English army to Calais 'destroying all the country as he rode'. An itinerary of the king's movements included the comment that on 4 September he arrived at Calais 'and he will remain there until that town has been taken, with the aid of God, or the siege lifted by Philippe de Valois'. John of Tynemouth summarised the siege with the comment that 'the king of England began a long and expensive siege to the city of Calais'; the length of the operation, which lasted for eleven months, was understandable, for, as Froissart observed, it was 'one of the most fortified cities in the world'.[11]

In the aftermath of Crécy, Philip sent to Duke John ordering him to withdraw his force from the siege of Aiguillon, where the garrison not only still held out but continued to give the besiegers a bad time. As the French began to pack up their camp, the defenders, ignorant of the battle and mystified at the French preparations to withdraw, saw the opportunity to raid the camp, where they 'found great riches left behind', and followed that up with an attack on the rear-guard. A curious sidelight on that operation is that, according to le Baker, 'The townsmen were also considerably enriched by the tents they saved from the fire.'[12] Among the prisoners was a cousin of the Duke of Normandy who was also a member of his council. When the spoils of the operation were divided, he was assigned to Mauny, who questioned him and 'pressed him so efficiently that he revealed to him the whole business, and the journey that the king of England had made through Normandy, defeating the king of France and his forces at Crécy in Ponthieu and finally besieging the town of Calais. On hearing this, Sir Gauthier de Mauny and his companions were joyful and treated their prisoners better as a result of these tidings.'

Mauny then asked his prisoner: 'What sum of money he would be in a position to pay for his ransom. The knight replied that he would willingly pay up to three thousand crowns [£750].' Mauny told him that he would let him go free if he would go to Prince John and arrange a safe-conduct for himself and twenty men of his company, which would allow him to cross France unhindered and join Edward's army. The knight travelled to Paris, where the prince then was, and the prince granted the request, which he duly delivered to Mauny at Aiguillon. Mauny then cancelled the ransom, as he had promised to do, and left with his twenty men and he 'did not slink around but made himself known everywhere he went, and whenever he was stopped, he would show his letter and be released at once'. But one party of French soldiers who accosted the group did not respect the safe conduct and Mauny and his men were arrested and imprisoned in the garrison town of Saint-Jean-de-Angély. He escaped with two of his companions, but the others did not get away; they were subsequently released by Lancaster, who had been with his army about 40 miles away. Having heard of Mauny's predicament he led a raid to free them, which he then turned into a short and violent campaign.

Meanwhile, Mauny had resumed his journey to Calais, until he reached Orléans, where he was again detained before being taken to Paris and incarcerated in the Châtelet prison there. Prince John protested to his father that if Mauny was not released he would be dishonoured, and indeed it would be assumed that he had betrayed him, after granting the safe conduct. The king's initial response was that he would have him executed 'for he looked upon him as one of his greatest enemies'. The prince in his turn was pressed by a knight from Hainault, Sir Mansart d'Aisnes, to secure Mauny's release. Eventually the king relented and Mauny was not only released but all his costs were paid, and he was free to continue his journey. Perhaps as a recompense for his treatment, Philip invited Mauny to dine with him and presented him 'with gifts and jewels to the amount of a thousand florins'. Mauny responded that he would keep them only if Edward III approved. Edward did not approve because Mauny had served him loyally and the king hoped that he would continue to do so, commenting that 'we have enough, thank God, for you and for ourselves' and so Mauny did not need the gifts. He then returned them to Philip.

That was the kind of anecdote which Froissart included in his chronicle, as it showed the chivalrous conduct which the commanders on both sides displayed in their dealings with each other, and it emphasised that Mauny's loyalties lay with Edward and he would not take rewards without his approval. In returning the jewels he avoided any subsequent suspicion of conflicting allegiance.[13] Mauny's action in crossing France at such a time may have been unconventional and even mischievous but it was not irresponsible, for he had the guarantee of his safe conduct. Yet his actions inadvertently widened a split within the French royal family, with John resenting his father's actions in imprisoning and threatening someone whose security he had pledged.

By the time Mauny had completed his journey, Edward's army had begun the siege of Calais. After his arrival there, Mauny took a leading role in directing the operation and the retinue which he assembled consisted of 326 men, including nineteen knights and ninety-one squires; that was the fifth largest in the army, after those of the king, the Prince of Wales and the earls of Lancaster and Warwick. Because of the terrain and the town's fortifications the siege was a long and difficult process, requiring all the skills of Edward and his senior commanders to maintain the organisation of the large force assembled around the city. It also proved to be a very expensive operation and the king raised extra loans to help cover the costs. In July 1347 he called 187 urban delegates to a meeting to arrange the sums which their communities were to lend to the crown. The loans advanced included £1,333 6s 8d from London, £450 from York, £320 from Bristol and £100 from Norwich. Some £66 13s 4d was contributed by Robert Gyen, three times mayor of Bristol and the leading merchant of the city, which was the most important port in the West Country. Those figures provide a context for the scale of Mauny's financial involvement with the king, when London and three major provincial centres could lend only £2,203 6s 8d, despite being under pressure to support a major military effort. In 1351 the crown borrowed around £6,500 from its subjects to finance the war, when, among the towns of the second rank, Colchester, Grimsby and Hereford between them contributed £200.[14]

The prospects of success at Calais were much improved towards the end of June when a French fleet carrying provisions for the garrison was defeated at the mouth of the River Somme, with the English archers again playing a significant role. Despite the scale of the defeat at Crécy, the number of French casualties and the loss of leadership among the military classes, Philip had managed to raise a sizeable army by the summer of 1347 and he advanced towards Calais to attempt to break the siege. He did manage to bring his army on to the relatively high ground of Sangatte within a few miles of the city but declined to engage the English forces at a disadvantage and had to withdraw. That virtually settled the fate of the garrison and in July 1347 the defenders realised that they could expect no further aid from Philip; within the city things had become quite desperate and 'for defaute of vitailles & of refresshyng they eten hors, houndes, cattes & mys'.[15]

On 1 August the governor, Jean de Vienne, requested a parley; Mauny and Lord Basset were sent to negotiate the terms of surrender. One account says that the defenders had asked that Mauny should be one of the commissioners with whom they were to negotiate. His reputation and perhaps, too, his origins as an Hainaulter and so a fellow Low Countryman, may have prompted their request. Negotiations for the surrender of a town were a delicate matter. The garrison would wish for guarantees of their own safety when they had laid down their weapons and that they could march out without being molested, so that it was clear that they had yielded on terms without having been defeated and their honour would not seem to have been besmirched. The citizens required undertakings that the garrison would not try to settle old scores before they left or that the besiegers would not take reprisals, and their leaders would wish to settle on a reasonable fine for the town's payment towards the besiegers' costs and to buy off the besieging soldiers, to prevent it from being sacked and its inhabitants harassed. Those soldiers, though victorious, were likely to harbour resentments and, out of sheer boredom and the discomforts of life in the camp, take out their pent-up frustrations on the citizenry by wrecking the place and destroying its resources. That would be the last thing which their commanders wanted, especially after such a large-scale and prolonged operation. Those arranging the terms of surrender had to be skilled in negotiation and trusted by all sides; Mauny met those requirements.

Edward's original demands were that all those within the town should be at his mercy, to be ransomed or put to death, which Vienne regarded as far too harsh. Mauny made the point to the king that if he put any of those in the town to death after the surrender his own soldiers would be reluctant to serve in a garrison, for that could be used as an example to justify the execution of his garrisons if they surrendered and so 'we would suffer the same fate in a similar position, even though we were doing our duty'. His point was supported by 'divers other lords that were there present'. According to le Bel that reasoning 'greatly softened the king's heart' and he may have been aware that those circumstances had applied to English garrisons which had been left without support as Edward marched across northern France; after they had been captured the defenders had been killed.

Eventually, Edward relented and agreed that if six of the principal citizens should come out of the town 'in their shifts, pure and simple, with nooses round their necks and the keys of the city in their hands', then the remainder of the citizens would be spared. Vienne put the proposal to an emotional meeting of the citizens in the marketplace and they agreed to it, under the leadership of Eustace de Saint-Pierre, the wealthiest citizen, who volunteered to be one of those who submitted to the English. Five others did the same, describing themselves as 'citizens of Calais, great merchants and members of its longest established families'.

The governor handed them over to Mauny with the keys to the town and declared that 'they be and were to-day most honourable, rich and most notable burgesses of all the town of Calais'. Edward ordered that they should be beheaded at once, despite pleas from his own entourage for mercy. Mauny pleaded with the king that he was 'renowned and famed for all noble qualities' but that reputation would be lost if he now committed such a cruel act. The queen had arrived during the siege and now intervened; she 'weeping bitterly, fell on her knees before her husband and said: "Ah, my worthy lord! Since I crossed the sea – in great peril, as you know – I've asked for nothing. But now I beg and implore you with clasped hands, for love of Our Lady's son, have mercy on them."' The king eventually gave in to her entreaties and presented the prisoners to her. She had them taken to her chamber, where their halters were removed and they were newly clothed and then set free. The other citizens of Calais were also spared. There is no proof of the story, but whether or not the queen's intercession actually happened, Mauny's arguments as a military commander on the burghers' behalf surely carried some weight with the king.

They were not original. Savary de Mauléon had made a similar point to King John after his capture of Rochester castle in 1215 when he threatened to have the members of the garrison hanged; if the fortunes of war were reversed the same fate might be meted out to his soldiers, and who would serve him if they were put at such a needless risk?[16] That argument was undeniable, indeed was self-evident, but Mauny's repeating it at such a moment gave it the extra cogency needed. And it surely took some courage to argue with a wrathful Edward for the lives of the six burghers when he seemed to be implacable. Yet perhaps the episode could have been a case of stage-management on the king's part, intending all along to spare their lives but making the maximum impact by delaying their reprieve until literally the last minute, thereby emphasising his clemency. Only those present who knew the king so well that they could gauge his true intentions were able to make such a judgement.

Edward threatened to massacre prisoners on other occasions during his campaigns in northern France but never carried out those threats. A similar negotiated surrender of a town under threat of being sacked by Lancaster's army had occurred during the campaign in the south-west, when the citizens had deputed two knights to negotiate on their behalf for a surrender and they made contact with the English through a herald. Lancaster himself, with Stafford and Mauny, went to negotiate the surrender and at first he was implacable, demanding that the town be surrendered unconditionally, which would have exposed the citizens to reprisals and allowed the troops to plunder the place. But after negotiations an agreement was reached that the town should surrender and place itself under Edward III's suzerainty, with twelve of its leading citizens sent to Bordeaux as hostages for the completion of the terms. That suggests that Mauny's approach was more conciliatory than Lancaster's and that he prevailed.[17]

Another parallel – albeit in a totally different context – had occurred at a major series of jousts in Cheapside in 1331. The queen and her ladies were watching from a temporary grandstand, which collapsed under the weight and several of the spectators were injured. The angry king immediately swore that he would have revenge on the carpenters who had erected the staging, but the queen forestalled his vengeance by pleading on their behalf, and he relented. The royal couple were much younger then and the accident was a sudden one that could not have been foreseen, whereas the surrender of the burghers had been anticipated.

It is possible that at Calais the king's pardon was agreed in advance, that the burghers were enacting a version of a traditional ritual symbolising the town's submission to the king while knowing that they would be reprieved. The episode was characteristic of incidents included by le Bel and Froissart, from which the reader could develop a wider impression of the period than from just the prominent and better-known events. The attention subsequently given to the burghers' fate was partly because of the successful pleading by the compassionate queen for their lives, as well as the sensible professional objections raised by Mauny. Both were Hainaulters, as were le Bel and Froissart, so the telling of that tale may have owed much to their common background. Only le Bel and then Froissart included this affair in their descriptions of the surrender, and their principal source had probably been Mauny. Geoffrey le Baker described how John de Vienne had gone to Edward III 'sitting on a little nag as he could not go on foot because of the gout, and with a halter tied round his neck'. He was followed by 'other knights and townspeople on foot, bare-headed and without shoes, and also with ropes around their necks'. Vienne offered the king a sword, as a sign that he was 'the prime prince of battles among all Christians and one who had mightily taken that town with all knightly chivalry from the greatest king in Christendom'. He handed over the keys of the city and pleaded for mercy. Edward accepted the surrender and sent Vienne, with fifteen knights and fifteen townspeople, to England 'enriching them with generous gifts and allowing them to go where they wished'. Le Baker did not mention the queen's intervention or Mauny's pleas on the burghers' behalf, nor the role of Eustace de Saint-Pierre. Nor were they mentioned in the Brut chronicle, in which the capitulation was but briefly dealt with.[18]

After the surrender Mauny and the earls of Warwick and Stafford were ordered to take possession of the town, securing all knights and mercenary soldiers.[19] Other undesirables were to be expelled, for Edward intended that Calais should become an

English town and provide a base on the continent for trade and military operations in the Low Countries and northern France, regardless of the political situation in Flanders and the adjoining states.[20] He declared that 'I wolle repeople agayne the towne with pure Englysshemen' and offered inducements to those who were willing to settle there; almost 200 people received grants of tenements and lands, both artisans and men who had financed the king, so it may be that the Calais grants included some made to repay debts owed by the crown. Mauny was among the recipients, being granted several properties as part of the process of replacing the former owners, including 'all the tenements and void plots which before the conquest of Calais belonged to John Morel'.[21]

Mauny's military career had developed enormously during the 1340s and he was given increasing responsibilities, culminating in his role at the siege of Calais, an operation to which the king attached great importance because the capture of the town was a major aspect of his strategy. He displayed great courage and was a more than able fighter in hand-to-hand encounters, was prominent in action and distinguished himself during armed raids and skirmishes; he had also proved himself to be a capable officer in besieged garrisons. He possessed qualities which the king admired and through his loyalty and competence he retained Edward's support. According to le Bel, Mauny was 'a knight he dearly loved for his outstanding service in a number of perilous missions'.[22] He was not reticent in displaying the fruits of his success, which helped to attract capable men to join his entourage. During the Brittany campaign his force rode horses that were worth much more than the average value, and his own warhorse was worth £100, the highest figure for any of the horses recorded.[23] As well as his military commitments, Mauny's family obligations also increased, especially after the killing of his brother Gilles by the French at Cambrai.[24]

Mauny had returned to England by November 1347 and was ennobled in time to answer the summons to attend the parliament called by the king to meet on his thirty-fifth birthday, 13 November 1347. He would have strengthened the court's spokesmen who could describe in an authoritative manner the progress of the wars in France. In 1348 the Commons admitted that they were too 'ignorant and simple' to express views on the wars and would defer to the 'magnates and wise men' of the king's council.[25] Mauny was summoned to all the subsequent parliaments during his lifetime, when the average number of lords, constituting the English nobility, was roughly sixty. He had become a member of that elite group, the most senior in the country.

6

THE BLACK DEATH

Two months before the sitting of the first parliament which Mauny attended, a shipload of Genoese escaping from the siege of Kaffa on the Black Sea had landed at Messina in Sicily; the Black Death epidemic followed, spreading inexorably across Europe and the Middle East. In the mid-1340s alarming news had reached Europe of a great mortality which was causing havoc in the Black Sea region. Unbelievably high numbers were said to be dying, with scarcely anyone left alive after the pestilence had struck. That was not just a ghastly rumour and the disease followed quickly after the news. By the spring of 1346 it had reached the region between the Caspian Sea and southern Russia and from there spread to Constantinople in 1346 and to Sicily in 1347, spreading across the island and then reaching the mainland. It then moved remorselessly across the continent, through the Mediterranean basin and across North Africa, even infecting Iceland and remote valleys in Scandinavia. The full horror of the catastrophe quickly became obvious and the consequences inescapable.

Not since the eighth century had the continent been afflicted by plague. It struck everyone, the rich in their castles, the poor at their gates, clergy, monks and nuns, lawyers and physicians, townsmen and countrymen, soldiers and sailors, all succumbed to the onslaught. The early signs displayed by victims were no more than a cough, headaches and nausea, but they were quickly followed by spitting blood, excruciatingly painful blotches beneath the skin and swellings of the lymph nodes in the groin, under the armpits and on the neck. Some victims lost their self-control completely with the pain and ran wildly around the streets, shunned by those who could have helped them, because the visible symptoms and effects of this unknown affliction caused widespread terror. They were also fearful that they might catch the disease through any contact, or even by going close to sufferers, as well as being repelled by the foul smells emanating from the sick, caused by anal seepage, bad breath and the oozing of matter from the swellings, or buboes, after they had burst. Although the bursting of the bubo when it was ripe could save the victim, that required the subsequent cleansing and regular changing of the dressing of the wound, and without nursing care that was unlikely.

The discovery of bacteria and the specific cause of the plague bacterium *Yersinia pestis*, with the understanding of the nature and spread of disease, were still centuries away and physicians could offer no solutions or explanations. During the onset of the plague in the 1340s, which in the nineteenth century came to be described as the Black Death, not only was bubonic plague present, but so too were the pneumonic and septicaemic forms of the disease. Bubonic plague is transmitted by fleas infected with the bacterium, which is transferred to the victim's blood stream and lymphatic system by the flea's bite. If the bacteria break out of the buboes they reach the lungs and are spread in water droplets on the victim's breath, so that close contact would indeed produce direct transmission from person to person in the form of the disease known as pneumonic plague. Septicaemic plague is caused by a flea bite, but the bacilli enter the bloodstream directly, not through the lymphatic system, also resulting in a more rapid death than with the victims of bubonic plague, and before buboes have formed. Those who were infected with bubonic plague died within a week or so of displaying the symptoms, but those afflicted with pneumonic or septicaemic plague passed away within twenty-four hours, or at most forty-eight.

Innocent of such matters, contemporaries suspected that the disease was carried by venomous atoms which were conveyed in foul and polluted air, and could lodge in merchandise such as textiles, especially those with a thick texture, such as woollen cloth. But why was such a disease being inflicted on mankind at this time? The church's explanation was that plague was a punishment sent by God to chastise a sinful people, so that reform and repentance were urgently needed if God was to end the scourge; living purer lives in future might prevent the recurrence of the disease. An Italian chronicler explained that the divine purpose was first to threaten and then to strike the human race 'with enormous and unprecedented blows' so as to bring repentance and reform:

> His terrifying judgement began firstly in the furthest part of the world, in the countries of the East. After he had struck at the Tartars, Turks and all the other unbelievers ... the unprecedented plague crossed the sea and so came to the Veneto, Lombardy, the March, Tuscany, Germany, France and spread through virtually the whole world.[1]

Some explanations were based on the conjunction of the planets at a crucial time before the outbreak, and others attributed it to earthquakes and volcanic eruptions in the years immediately preceding the epidemic, which had ejected foul subterranean airs into the atmosphere. The influential medical faculty of the University of Paris was called upon by Philip VI in 1348 to provide an explanation, which was that at one o'clock in the afternoon of 20 March 1345 there had been a conjunction of Saturn, Jupiter and Mars. A conjunction of Saturn and Jupiter was held to bring death and depopulation, while Jupiter, as a warm and humid planet, drew up foul vapours from earth and water, and Mars was a very hot and dry planet and so set fire to the vapours. The great heat and dampness favoured pestilential fumes, which were a likely cause of the plague. The report came to be widely accepted, even though it was believed that no planetary conjunction's effects lasted more than two years and as the epidemic had continued beyond that time, perhaps it was not its true origin.

While physicians and theologians pondered the reason for the disaster, the early news of the awfulness of the disease and the numbers of dead were confirmed. The accounts of those chroniclers who produced descriptions of the epidemic conveyed their shock and horror, as they tried to absorb and make sense of the scale and impact of what was happening, or had happened. The indefatigable traveller Ibn Battutah was in the region of modern Syria in May and June 1348 and he noted that in Ghazzah the death rate was more than a thousand a day. In Homs about 300 died on the day of his arrival and when he returned to Damascus he found that the citizens had been fasting for three days and that the number of victims was about 2,400 a day. He and his party then travelled overland to Cairo, where the death-toll had risen to 21,000 a day.[2]

A Benedictine abbot reported that conditions in the south of France were terrible:

> The death rate was unbelievable at Marseilles, where the illness arrived by land and sea, at Montpellier, throughout Provence and in Avignon ... and throughout the whole country round about. Travellers, merchants, pilgrims and others who journeyed through the area reported that animals roamed freely through the fields, towns and waste land, that barns and wine cellars stood open, houses empty, and that few people were to be seen. In many towns, cities and settlements, where there had originally been 20,000 people, scarcely 2000 remained; in many towns and villages 1500 people were reduced to barely 100; and in many regions the vineyards and farms were left uncultivated.

The abbot later described the equally dreadful situation in his own city of Tournai, where he believed that more than 25,000 people had died:

> The strange thing is that most of the deaths were among the more influential and wealthy inhabitants. Few or none died among those who drank wine and who avoided bad air and visiting the sick. But others, who visited or lived among the sick, either became seriously ill or died; and they died especially in the streets in the market area, and more people died in narrow lanes than in broad streets and open squares. When one or two people had died in a house, the rest followed in a very short time, so that often ten or more died in a single house, and in many houses the dogs and cats died as well. Thus no one, rich, middling or poor, was safe, but each one of

> them spent every day awaiting God's will. And certainly there were many deaths among the parish priests and chaplains who heard confessions and administered the sacraments, and also among the parish clerks and those who visited the sick with them.[3]

Other chroniclers told similar tales of suffering, death and disruption. Geoffrey le Baker observed that 'very, very few, in fact hardly anybody at all bounced back to life and health, once infected'.[4] But throughout the crisis the numbers of dead reported were speculative and by no means accurate. The clergy were best placed to estimate the numbers, but they were among the most vulnerable groups and suffered disproportionately, both senior figures and parish priests. Leicester did provide some figures: in 'the little parish' of St Leonard more than 380 died; in Holy Cross parish more than 400; in St Margaret's parish 700, and then, lacking further numbers, the chronicler added 'and a great multitude in every parish'.[5] The numbers who died could not be established, or records were not kept, for no administrative arrangements could continue to function efficiently in such circumstances, if they had existed at all; that was a less pressing issue than the deaths themselves and attempts to avoid catching the pestilence.

Processions and services to assuage the divine wrath proved to be futile and the numbers of clergy were reduced as they fell victim to the plague. Nor could the physicians claim any success at all. Guy de Chauliac was the most senior member of the profession at the time. Trained at Toulouse and the medical faculty at Montpellier, he became a physician in ordinary to Pope Clement VI and has been described as 'the father of French surgery'. He contracted the plague yet survived and later wrote that the disease 'was most humiliating for the physicians, who were unable to render any assistance, all the more as, for fear of infection, they did not venture to visit the patients, and if they did could do no good and consequently earn no fees, for all infected died with the exception of some towards the end of the epidemic, who escaped, as the boils had been able to mature'. The Persian physician and polymath Muhammad ibn Zakariya, known as Rhais (854-925), had commented that anyone could escape from plague and sickness by following the advice to 'Start soon, flee far from town or land / On which the plague has laid its hand, / Return but late to such a place / Where pestilence has stayed its pace.'[6] Those aware of the progress of the plague scarcely needed such guidance. The Sorbonne's physicians advised Philip VI to leave soon and go far away, which was all very well if a safe refuge could be identified, but the speed with which the disease spread and its apparent ability to kill people anywhere made that difficult advice to follow. Crossing from the Mediterranean littoral to that of the Bay of Biscay, the plague had reached Bordeaux by the spring of 1348 and erupted in Paris during the summer.

In England, Edward III and his councillors were focused on the war with France, in the aftermath of the victory at Crécy and capture of Calais, a port which the king intended would be a launch pad for future military campaigns. The corresponding port in England was Sandwich and frequent voyages between the two towns became part of the English military effort. Trade with other ports along the coasts of France and the Low Countries was also common, so that it must have seemed impractical, if not impossible, to prohibit the ships engaged in it, or to stop fishing crews from carrying on their routine trade. Checks could be made but, of course, given the virulence of the disease and complete ignorance of its nature and means of transmission, no checks could have been effective. The authorities did not know what they were looking for and the parasites carrying the deadly bacillus could not have been excluded without a total ban on shipping.

The English court had been made directly aware of the progress of the plague when the king's fourteen-year-old daughter Joan died in Bordeaux of the disease on 1 July 1348, on her way to marry Peter, heir to the Castilian throne. It is unclear why she had been sent on the journey when the plague had probably reached the city by the end of March, and news of its presence there had been reported to the English court. Her death should have further alerted Edward III's council to the danger that the disease would soon reach England. Yet no restrictions were placed on shipping entering English ports at that stage; it is likely that the merchants would have been strongly opposed to any such measures and the government needed to keep open communications across the North Sea to the troops in Calais and the Low Countries.

Edward and Philippa were greatly affected by the death of their daughter. The king wrote to Alfonso XI of Castile, who would have been Joan's father-in-law, on 15 September saying that she had gone to Bordeaux, 'But see – with what intense bitterness of heart we have to tell you this – destructive Death, who seizes young and old alike, sparing no-one, and reducing rich and poor to the same level, has lamentably snatched from both of us our dearest daughter (who we loved best of all, as her virtues demanded).' Their grief must have affected everyone at court and brought home the dangers of the disease, which had spread to England by the time that the letter was written.[7]

A contemporary chronicler noted that the disease arrived in England on board a ship from Bordeaux that put in at the south coast port of Melcombe. As plague was reported there around midsummer 1348 and the symptoms would have taken some time before they became apparent, it is likely that its arrival occurred in the late spring. Coastal ships and fishing vessels carried commodities harbouring infected parasites and they helped to disseminate the plague around the coasts of southern England, moving it more quickly than overland communications would have done. Within weeks it was dispersed across the south of England and into the Midlands, eventually spreading to the north of England and Wales, and indeed across the British Isles, continuing to claim victims until late 1349.

Chroniclers in England described the impact of the plague in no less dramatic and heartrending terms than their continental counterparts; one of them described it as 'that great and universal pestilence' and another, viewing the world from Louth in Lincolnshire, adopted a wide perspective when summarising the disaster: 'This blow struck the whole world with immense terror. So great a pestilence had not been seen, or heard, or written about, before this time.'[8] According to Geoffrey le Baker, after the disease had reached the Dorset coast it 'almost stripped the countryside of its inhabitants' and more generally he commented that it 'completely emptied many rural towns of every individual of the human species'. Henry Knighton was an Augustinian canon at Leicester and the information which he received from Bristol was that 'virtually the whole town was wiped out'. He added that 'cruel death took just two days to burst out all over a town'. Burial of the dead quickly became an urgent problem because there were 'hardly enough people left alive to bury the dead, or enough burial grounds to hold them' and as the graveyards became full 'people chose places in the field to bury their dead' and the bearers may have decided to dump bodies almost anywhere rather than risk going into a graveyard.[9]

Using a range of evidence, modern historians think it likely that the overall mortality level was roughly one-third, but that covers a range of different communities. Whatever the numbers who died, or the proportion of the population which was carried off, such a heavy loss in a relatively short time was a dreadful collective experience, summarised by John of Reading, a monk at Westminster: 'There was in those days death without sorrow, marriage without affection, self-imposed penance, want without poverty, and flight without escape.' The chronicler of the cathedral priory of Rochester was appalled by the impact on society, for he believed that labourers and skilled workers became so rebellious that the judges were unable to enforce the law and punish them, 'and more or less the whole population turned to evil courses, became addicted to all forms of vice and stooped to more than usually base behaviour, thinking not at all of death or of the recently experienced plague, nor of how they were hazarding their own salvation by uniting in rebellion'.[10] His bald summary indicates that the epidemic was socially divisive and economically disruptive.

Londoners would have anticipated the plague's onset with trepidation and fear, aware that their large and populous trading city could hardly escape the general catastrophe. Its population was probably around 75,0000, most of whom were crammed into the area within the city walls, in narrow streets of tall houses, many of which incorporated workshops for the artisans, their apprentices, journeymen and families, who formed the largest group of citizens, while the merchants, although far fewer in number, were the wealthiest category. Since the reign of King John early in the previous century the city had enjoyed a considerable degree of self-government, while the economic muscle of its wealthier citizens gave it a measure of leverage over the government's policies on such matters as trade, in terms of taxation and loans.

Plague was causing deaths in London towards the end of October 1348 and thereafter the death-toll increased dramatically. If the number of wills made in the City's Court of Hustings reflected the number of deaths, then they rose almost fivefold between October and December. That put immediate and relentless pressure on the existing arrangements for services and interments; the number of priests available to administer the last rites and conduct funerals was reduced as some of them succumbed to the plague, and those who carried out the burials found that they had far more bodies to inter than they could ever have imagined.

Space for burials was a problem, for the churchyards of the more than a hundred parishes were small, especially those in the centre, and were quickly being filled. Geoffrey le Baker later wrote that 'a host of people beyond counting passed to the next world, and a multitude of monks and other clerics known only to God'. Whatever the arrangements for burials that were followed, in London 'so great a multitude eventually died there that all the cemeteries of the aforesaid city were insufficient for the burial of the dead. For which reason very many were compelled to bury their dead in places unseemly and not hallowed or blessed; for some, it was said, cast the corpses into the river.'[11]

Extra burial space was urgently required and three new cemeteries were opened, provided by the crown, the Bishop of London and Walter Mauny. To the north of the Tower an area of about four acres was made available by John Cory, a clerk in the royal service, who had been acquiring property there since 1346, probably for the king, possibly so that he would found a monastery there, perhaps a Carthusian priory. The Carthusians emerged from groups of hermits who, in the eleventh and twelfth centuries, chose to remain outside the Benedictine order, which they considered too wealthy and secular. The Carthusian order was established by Bruno Hartenfaust and in 1084 he founded the first charterhouse in the mountainous countryside near Grenoble, which met the Carthusians' desire for isolation. But in 1132 its buildings were destroyed by an avalanche and were replaced by another monastery, La Grande Chartreuse, on a new site on the fringe of the French Alps. Only one other Carthusian priory was founded in the eleventh century, but there was a steady increase in their number over the next 200 years and in the fourteenth century more than 100 charterhouses were established. From the French Alps, the order spread across much of Europe, with a concentration in the Low Countries and Picardy.

The Carthusian order had come to be respected for the strictness of its rules and the austerity of the monks' lives, shut away from the world in their priories. A Carthusian house would have been regarded as the appropriate endowment for a monarch. Holy Trinity priory was the owner of part of the ground acquired by Cory and the site was designated the New Churchyard of Holy Trinity. It was dedicated by the Bishop of London, Ralph Stratford, who had been bishop since 1340 and was a nephew of John Stratford, Archbishop of Canterbury, who died on 23 August 1348. Ralph was entrusted with diplomatic missions and acted as a member of the regency council in 1345, when Edward III was in Flanders. He also provided the second of the new cemeteries, acquiring a plot of three acres north of Smithfield, which was designated Nomanneslond and may have been in use for burials before the end of December 1348.

The third of the new burial areas was by far the largest, covering 13¼ acres to the north-east of St Bartholomew's priory and Smithfield and on the south side of Nomanneslond. The site was acquired by Mauny, who had asked his staff if they knew of a suitable place and one of them told him that 'the master of the hospital of St. Bartholomew in Smithfield and his brethren have a place enclosed outside Smithfield aforesaid which is called Spitell Crofte where you might very well be able to obtain the accomplishment of your devotion'.[12] As the Hainaulters' general conduct and particularly their mode of dress at court was suspected to have provoked God's wrath, and so unleashed the plague, it may have been thought appropriate that the most renowned of them should provide a resting place for the victims, as an act of penance as well as charity. Because of his prominence and wealth, Mauny would have been the obvious person to atone for their collective sinfulness in this way.

Mauny came to an agreement with the hospital and took a lease of the land for twenty-one years, initially for a yearly rent of £8 and later in exchange for the rents of one of his manors in Cambridgeshire. The arrangements were completed around the turn of the year and the cemetery was in use by 26 January 1349. The Bishop of London went in a procession with Mauny and 'a great multitude' to bless the site, which was dedicated to the Holy and Undivided Trinity and the Annunciation of Our Lady. Spitalcroft was suitable because it was available immediately and its owners were willing to come to an agreement quickly. Its size and position, just outside the city, were ideal, so was its configuration; a gently sloping plot which drained south-westwards to a brook at the side of Smithfield. A further advantage was that the plot was 'enclosed by walls on every side'. Until then the land had been ground where Londoners could take their recreation and play sports, reached from Smithfield by a passageway which was to become Charterhouse Lane.

On the Feast of the Annunciation, 25 March, the foundation stone of a new chapel was laid, roughly in the centre of the site. The Bishop of London, Mauny, the Mayor (John Lovekyn), the sheriffs, aldermen 'and many others, nearly all barefooted and with a most devout procession' went to the cemetery, where the bishop preached a sermon on the word 'Hail'. Then the bishop, Mauny and the Mayor laid the foundations of the chapel. The king was absent because the court was peripatetic during those perilous times and after Christmas he was at King's Langley in Hertfordshire and Woodstock in Oxfordshire; a visit to London and Westminster would have been regarded as unduly risky, even for such a solemn event as the dedication of Mauny's new chapel.

The chapel's construction had been anticipated, for when Gerard Larmurer drew up his will on 3 March he left his estate to his wife and two children and, if they predeceased him, it was to go to 'the new chapel of the Blessed Virgin Mary outside Aldersgate, to have and to hold in perpetuity, on condition that the ... chapel be required ... to maintain a priest who shall celebrate mass in perpetuity for the souls of my father and mother, my ancestors and all the faithful departed'. He probably lived in St Bride's and not in one of the adjoining parishes of St Botolph-without-Aldersgate and St Sepulchre, so his was not a local bequest but a more general charitable one.

The date of his will suggests that planning for the chapel was so far advanced that he had the certainty that it would be built, or that building had already begun and the ceremonies on Lady Day did not mark the beginning of the work but were formal services of dedication held on the appropriate day.[13] As constructed in 1349, the chapel was a simple rectangular building of five bays,

97 feet by 38 feet, and a lofty structure, with walls at least 33½ feet high: it was divided into presbytery, choir and nave, with a wooden screen carrying a rood loft separating the choir from the nave.[14]

Although the cemetery was certainly needed, the number of burials there was uncertain. Robert of Avesbury was a commissary clerk on the Archbishop of Canterbury's staff at Lambeth Palace and he left an account in which he stated that between 2 February and 12 April 'more than 200 corpses were buried almost every day in the new burial ground made next to Smithfield,' which suggests a total of almost 14,000 interments at Spitalcroft during the epidemic. But his phrase was that they occurred not daily but 'almost every day', and the pattern of interments revealed by recent excavations shows them to have been less dense than the numbers based on his comments would suggest. On the other hand, a petition to the papacy from Mauny in 1352 requesting a relaxation of a year and forty days for penitents who visited the chapel stated that in the burial ground were buried 'more than sixty thousand bodies of those who died of the epidemic'. At the end of the sixteenth century John Stow, the historian of London, remarked that he had seen and read an inscription on a stone cross in Spitalcroft which stated that more than 50,000 bodies were buried there. Those are implausibly high numbers in the context of the city's population before the epidemic. Perhaps Mauny set the number at that level to emphasise the significance of his role: the more burials, the greater his contribution. A Bull issued by Urban VI in 1384 refers to Spitalcroft as a place where 'twenty thousand and more dead are buried', a more modest but still striking figure.[15]

By the summer of 1349 the epidemic had come to an end in London; plague had killed at least a quarter and perhaps more than a third of the city's inhabitants since the previous autumn. The scale of the death-toll and the process of burials had been unavoidable and depressing features of the outbreak. Yet the Chronicle of London described this catastrophe with the laconic comment that in 1348 'was the grete pestilence at London', while Froissart also gave it only a glancing mention, observing merely that 'in that time of death there was an epidemic of plague'.[16]

Mauny was involved in two other new establishments during the mid-fourteenth century: Gonville Hall and the College of Corpus Christi and the Blessed Virgin Mary, both in Cambridge. He and his co-founders had the example of Queen's Hall, later Queen's College, founded at Oxford in 1341 by Queen Philippa's chaplain Robert de Eglesfield as a 'hall of scholars, chaplains and others'. In 1347-8 Mauny assisted Edmund Gonville in his efforts to establish a new college, which was dedicated to the Blessed Virgin Mary. The charter was granted in January 1348 and it stated that Mauny had been Gonville's agent in the royal court, presumably using his considerable influence with the king and his circle to ensure that the grant was approved.

The connection was surely through Henry Grosmont, Earl of Lancaster, who was alderman of the Corpus Christi gild at Cambridge, instituted in 1350; Mauny became a member shortly afterwards. Such gilds were founded in the wake of the pestilence, to ensure that the celebrations at the feast of Corpus Christi were carried out fully and with due reverence. The gild of St Mary was much older, dating from the late thirteenth century. Lancaster petitioned for the new college's charter, which was granted in 1352; the college was unusual in that it was formed by the united gilds of Corpus Christi and St Mary. Its chapel was the parish church of St Benet and, after the Reformation, when the formal title smacked too much of Catholicism, the college became popularly known as Benet College.

Mauny was not directly involved in the creation of the third college founded in Cambridge in the aftermath of the Black Death, which was Trinity Hall, established in 1350 by the efforts of William Bateman, Bishop of Norwich since 1344. Gonville died in 1351, with the hall which bore his name incompletely established and Bateman, his bishop and executor, then took over the project. He moved the college from what is now part of Corpus Christi College to a site close to the university schools and his own Trinity Hall. (The college would be refounded more than 200 years later as Gonville and Caius.)

Mauny's connection with the new colleges was presumably through his estates in Norfolk and Cambridgeshire and his long-standing links with Henry Grosmont and senior figures in those counties. In 1331 the Earl of Norfolk had assigned to Mauny 31 marks a year (£20 15s), out of the sum which he received from the county. Gonville was rector of Terrington St Clement and a member of an old Norfolk family, while Bateman was a significant figure as bishop of the diocese and had wide experience as a diplomat. In the early 1350s he was involved in negotiations for a truce with France. It is probable that he and Mauny would have been well acquainted.

Spitalcroft was brought into use again when the plague struck for a second time, in 1361. Further interments were made in later outbreaks in the early fifteenth century, perhaps during the epidemics in 1407 and 1433-4.[16] It was used as a burial ground into the fifteenth century, but not in the sixteenth. The cemetery was not kept exclusively for the burial of plague victims. Mauny noted that he had established it for 'poor strangers and others' and Stow confirmed that, commenting that it was for 'the burial of poor people, travellers, and other that were deceased'. An arrangement had been made to avoid contention between the deceased's parish and the clergy at Spitalcroft by which the funeral was held in the parish church and then the body was taken to Spitalcroft for burial.[17] Stow's figure for the total number of burials there was 100,000, again an implausibly high number but an indication that he judged that as many people had been buried after the Black Death as during the epidemic. Modern researchers accept that the various contemporary figures are too high and one estimate puts the number of burials as low as 2,500.[18]

The burial ground came to be known as New Church Haw and was used for playing games and filth was dumped there, until both were prohibited by Pope Gregory XI during the 1370s. The unused parts of the ground were large enough to allow for the possibility that they could be developed for other purposes. In 1351 Lord Mauny obtained papal approval for the establishment of a college with a warden and twelve secular priests, expressed as 'a college of twelve or more chaplains'. That proposal probably was another result of Mauny's connection with Henry Grosmont who, from 1355, established a similar college in Leicester. That was an enlargement of a foundation created there by his father containing a warden and four chaplains. Henry's college contained a dean, twelve canons, thirteen vicars, three clerks and a verger. Its income was also suitably increased, to a level nine times that of the former establishment. Henry's model was that of Edward III's foundation of St George's, Windsor. Only six such colleges were ever created in England, by the king, three dukes and one earl.

Mauny did not attempt to emulate the king's foundation at Windsor or that of Henry Grosmont in Leicester by proceeding with the plan. Although the expenses would have been high, he surely could have met them. Perhaps he deferred to Grosmont with his endeavours, or as seems most probable, he was already considering an even larger scheme. That took time to mature, however, and by 1354 a hermitage had been built close to the cemetery chapel for two anchorites, who were to offer continual prayers for those buried there. A pulpit house was also built on the south side of the chapel, so that sermons could be delivered to congregations in the cemetery. The chapel, hermitage and pulpit house do not explain the comment by Geoffrey le Baker, of Swinbrook in Oxfordshire, who completed his chronicle in the late 1350s, possibly in 1357. He wrote that 'The bishop of London bought that piece of land in London called 'Nomansland,' and Sir Walter Mauny bought that which is called 'the new Charterhouse,' where they founded religious houses for the burial of the dead'.[19]

No religious house was established at Nomansland, by the bishop or anyone else, although the cemetery chapel of 1349 known as Pardon Chapel remained in use. Nor had Mauny established his proposed college, and the reference to 'the new Charterhouse' indicates a Carthusian priory, which was not founded until 1371, many years after le Baker had completed his account. It suggests, however, that the intention to establish a monastery of that order was in Mauny's mind by the late 1350s, and furthermore that it was widely enough known for le Baker to refer to it, anticipating its completion.

A delay then followed, with the cemetery still used for burials but no further buildings erected there. The delay may have been because Mauny was aware of the king's intention to establish a Carthusian priory in London, perhaps on the site where he did in fact found a Cistercian house, St Mary Graces, in the aftermath of the Black Death. He had earlier, in March 1347, decided to found a Carthusian priory on Cadzand, an intention which was recorded on a Chancery patent roll for 1347-8.[20] That perhaps was intended as a recompense to the inhabitants for the treatment which they had received at English hands during the fighting in 1337 and, according to one chronicle, also after the battle of Sluis in 1340, when Edward's 'people passed on unto the isle of Cagent [Cadzand] and slew all who could be found therein; and there they obtained great riches, and then ravaged the whole of the said island with fire'.[21] But the Count of Flanders recovered control of the island before the scheme could be implemented, which made it more likely that Edward would establish a priory of the order in England. Mauny would not have acted in a way which seemed to pre-empt the king.

A second plague epidemic struck western Europe in 1360-1, causing a reported 17,000 deaths in Avignon between March and July 1361 when, according to Guy de Chauliac, it 'raged furiously ... so that in many places it did not leave behind more than half of the people'. The outbreak reached northern France by the following September and was identified in London in the spring of 1361; the Chronicle of London recorded that 'in this yere was the second gret pestilence'. Ranulf Higden's *Polychronicon* noted that in 1361 'a great pestilence of men began in London and then it steadily advanced from the south of England to the rest of the country killing many men but few women ... there was a great mortality'.[22] The return of the disease confounded those who believed that society had reformed to such an extent that it would not need to suffer more divine punishment of the kind endured in the late 1340s. On the contrary, it confirmed the views of those mournful observers and critics who were convinced that the people's continued sinfulness and lasciviousness invited such punishment. It showed that the plague was not a one-off experience and further epidemics in 1369, which was 'great beyond measure', and 1374-9, during which 'a large number of Londoners, from among the wealthier and more eminent citizens, died,' indicated that intermittent eruptions of the disease were probable.[23]

The first reactions to the disease had to be reconsidered in the light of the repeated outbreaks. Without any rational explanation for them, plague could be seen, with famine and war, as one of God's three mortal arrows, which he could unleash to punish sinners or send as warnings to repent. An epidemic did seem to resemble the effect of a cloud of arrows fired into a crowd, killing some at random and leaving others untouched. It provided an opportunity for the clergy and lay moralists to condemn the population for its woeful behaviour and plead for reform, so that God would relent and end the plague. Services and processions were held and the saints were beseeched to intercede so that the community would be spared before being completely wiped out. Some saints were especially venerated for their influence in times of plague, such as Saint Roch and, through the analogy with arrows, Saint Sebastian.

That was a potential source of conflict between the clergy and the civil authorities, who disapproved of people gathering together in case the disease was spread further. The clergy could claim that none of the measures taken by the civil governments were effective and that the plague could be halted only through the intercession of the saints, while the authorities could counter-claim that for all the prayers and processions the virulence of the disease was not the least diminished. They could not have known it, but in some outbreaks the proportion of the population that died was as great as during the Black Death.

The practical, rather than spiritual, measures taken to restrict the spread of plague were based upon the isolation of households where the infection was identified and, if possible, of communities. That had been tried during the first eruption of the disease and may have been successful at Milan, although it had failed at Gloucester. Closing the trade routes by restricting travel, especially of merchants and their goods, particularly textiles, or limiting access to vessels or vehicles which had been issued with a certificate stating that they were not from an infected area was a policy which came to be widely adopted. Some international co-operation was required for such policies to be effective, as was the freedom and ability to transmit news, warning of the presence of the plague and its spread.

Other steps could be taken, based upon observations of the disease. Corrupt air that had not emanated from beneath the ground was thought to be caused by putrid and decaying matter or stagnant water in pools, lakes or wells and came to be acknowledged as an important factor in the cause and spread of the disease. The efficacy of clean air was widely recognised, with cold northern air being good for health and warm southern air being detrimental. Houses should therefore be built with windows and doors facing north so far as possible, and any facing south ought to be kept closed during warm summer weather. Cleanliness in private houses and public places was both advocated and pursued, with cities and towns enforcing regulations preventing the accumulation of filth and the presence of standing water, which could stagnate and so harbour the foul air, or miasma, which harboured the plague.

Those measures evolved but were not adopted with any consistency and the disease continued to be a major scourge. For the warring governments in north-west Europe, the sharp decline of population and economic activity surely made recruitment of manpower and the financing of warfare more difficult, not only because of the deaths of so many people, but the checks to demographic recovery caused by the periodic epidemics. Social changes inevitably came in the wake of the disease, as those who owed labour services simply left their manors and sought work elsewhere and were welcomed without restraint or punishment, as labour was in short supply. If no questions were asked about where an individual had come from, no lies need be told. Marginal lands were slowly abandoned and branches of farming which required less manpower than cultivation came to be preferred, especially sheep farming.

Edward III's government anticipated that labour shortages would lead to demands for higher wages and tried to stem the process and maintain wage-rates at pre-plague levels, through the Ordinance of Labourers and then the Statute of Labourers. Despite assiduous attempts to enforce those measures, they were sure to have little effect in the long run; that proved to be the case and a period of wage inflation followed. The government was neither deterred from renewing its military operations nor hindered from doing so by the new circumstances. Perhaps some of those who were freed from their manorial obligations chose military service, preferring the chance of rewards from dangerous, profitable engagements to familiar drudgery.

7

LORD MAUNY: DIPLOMACY AND PHILANTHROPY

After the dedication of the chapel at Spitalcroft Mauny went with the earls of Northampton and Huntingdon on a diplomatic mission to renew the Truce of Calais. That had been agreed in September 1347 and in November 1348 was continued for one further year and, although its terms were by no means fully observed, further negotiations were held at Guînes in March 1349, where Mauny represented the king. The extent of the death-toll from the plague could not have been known then; the epidemic was still claiming victims across England and Wales and in France, and there was no means of collecting statistics. Yet from the scale of the disaster it must have been apparent that not only would economic activity be reduced, with crops unsown and livestock neglected, so that the wool clip would be reduced, but the numbers of men available to serve in the armies, garrisons and fleets would be much diminished. There was every reason, therefore, to continue the truce, which was renewed periodically until June 1355; Mauny was twice a representative at the negotiations.

Because of those commitments, Mauny was not present at the tournament held at Windsor and the establishment of the Order of the Garter there on 21 April 1349, and so was not one of the original twenty-four members. Edward III had for some time been fascinated by the Arthurian legend of the Knights of the Round Table and the Order was his version of that brotherhood of warriors under their king. The number of members was fixed and so admission could occur only on the death of one of the knights; six new members were admitted to the Order before Mauny was granted that honour in 1359, following the death of John, Lord Grey of Rotherfield. In truth, although he was among the foremost of Edward's commanders and distinguished himself with his bravery and decisiveness in action, as well as following the behaviour appropriate for a chivalric knight, he was by no means the only one of them to display such characteristics. The king had given the English nobility a collective self-confidence which had emboldened them to carry out the kind of operations which Mauny engaged in.

While soldiers needed not only physical courage but the character to display a fearlessness in action, they retained an underlying dread of sudden death, without having confessed their sins. To die unshriven would carry the risk of sending their soul to purgatory. That concern was increased by the added danger of death from plague, when the priesthood's normal practices came under severe stress because of the high numbers requiring a deathbed confession and the reduced numbers of priests able to carry out those duties, as they, too, were carried off by the pestilence. It therefore became the practice for the Pope to issue licences to individuals allowing them to choose a confessor 'who shall give them, being penitent, plenary remission at the hour of death'. On 4 March 1351 such a licence was granted by Pope Clement VI to 'Walter de Mauni, knight, of the diocese of Cambray'.[1] He was regarded as lord of Masny and not described by any of his English titles. Clement had granted similar permission to the queen and some of her household in 1344; Mauny was not among them and probably had left Philippa's household some years earlier.

Mauny had been involved in two hazardous military actions in the period before the licence was granted. One was to thwart a French attempt at the very end of December 1349 to capture Calais by subterfuge, by suborning the defenders to leave open a gate to the town. Hearing of the plan, Edward III went himself, with the Black Prince and Mauny, to organise an ambush of the attackers as they entered. As with all of Edward's military operations, large or small, careful preparations were made; false walls were built within the barbican to conceal troops and when the enemy had penetrated that far the portcullis was lowered at the perfect moment, trapping many of them within, where they were surprised and defeated by the soldiers emerging from behind the false walls. The exultant English forces then surged out through the gate.

The king fought incognito under Mauny's command but became too confident when pursuing those outside the town, who were placed there to exploit the opportunity presented by the capture of the gate, which had not occurred, and so they had not been engaged and were still fresh. With a few companions the king became separated from the main body of the English troops and was in danger of being cut off until he was joined by the Black Prince. They and their supporters fought so stoutly that other English troops were able to arrive and drive off their attackers. It may have been an exhilarating encounter, but the dangers of hand-to-hand combat for a man who was now well into middle age were made all too plain, let alone the folly of the monarch exposing himself to danger so directly and in what was a minor operation that would not influence the outcome of the war.

Nevertheless, Edward again placed himself in a potentially hazardous position during the naval battle off Winchelsea in the following summer. He commanded an English fleet which intercepted a Castilian flotilla of forty-seven ships returning down the Channel from Sluis; they had been allied with the French as mercenaries until the arrangement was nullified by the declaration of a truce and the consequent ending of the French subsidies. The sea was too rough for the English archers to be effective and the action consisted of boarding the enemy vessels and fighting by hand. The king and Mauny were prominent among those who boarded the enemy vessels and battled with the soldiers and sailors. A half of the Castilian fleet was captured or sunk and the English were victorious. But that was the last occasion that Edward took part in such a fight.

A week before the battle off Winchelsea, Philip VI had died, on 22 August 1350. That raised the possibility of a lasting peace, but Prince John now took the throne as John II and was determined to recover the French losses and so he continued the war. Negotiations proved to be difficult and in October 1355 Mauny addressed a joint sitting of both houses of Parliament, describing the diplomatic and military events of the past eighteen months, in many of which he had been involved. He conveyed the king's wish for 'a hasty battle (hastif batail)', in other words a decisive encounter in which he would again defeat the French and so be able to dictate the peace terms. Mauny was followed by William Shareshull, the Chief Justice, who added the news of the Scots' resumption of the war and their capture of Berwick. The king was requesting a renewal of the wool subsidy to help finance a new military campaign; that was granted for the six years which he had requested. Mauny's eloquence and reputation, with Shareshull's unwelcome news, evidently were enough to persuade the Commons that the king's entreaty should be met.

As well as being summoned to every Parliament after January 1348, Mauny became a regular attender of meetings of the king's council. He undertook political assignments, such as that in 1356 when he headed a deputation to negotiate with the clergy for an unprecedently high level of taxation. He was less successful than in his address to Parliament and the Convocation of Canterbury refused to meet the king's demands, conceding just one-sixth of the level of imposition which had been asked for. Such requirements were less pressing after the news of the crushing French defeat by the Black Prince's army at Poitiers in 1356, during which John II was captured and subsequently brought to England, pending an agreement for a ransom. That changed the crown's financial circumstances, for surely the ransom of the French king alone would provide a considerable treasure for the royal coffers once it was agreed, and if it was received.

Mauny had come to act regularly as a negotiator and conciliator. The Court of Chivalry came into being as a formal body during the siege of Calais in 1346, when knights from across England and Wales were assembled together in large numbers, really for the first time during Edward's reign. As they displayed their arms, a vital aspect of their chivalric identity, so the rights to bear them were called into question in some cases. The court therefore sat to adjudicate in such matters, acting as a safety valve by peacefully settling disputes. The long siege would have had periods of relative inactivity, providing the opportunity for violent solutions for the resentments and jealousies which arose from the vexed questions over coats-of-arms, had there not been another way of resolving them. Mauny was one of its six judges, the most senior being Henry Grosmont, now Duke of Lancaster, as Steward of England, and the others were the Earl of Huntingdon and four knights, including Mauny.[2]

Among Mauny's diplomatic duties were discussions in 1350-1 with Margaret of Hainault, widow of the Emperor Louis, on the affairs of the Low Countries; presumably he was chosen for that task because of his continuing connections with Hainault. Edward had agreed to act as arbitrator between Margaret and her son Count William in a jurisdictional and territorial dispute. Henry of Lancaster was put in charge of the English delegation, but resolution of the issues proved to be difficult to achieve. Mauny replaced Lancaster as the head of the English mission and was granted a safe conduct to go to Bruges. A settlement was eventually reached that owed at least as much to military victories by Count William as to arbitration. Mauny and Lancaster were assigned to the same diplomatic missions on other occasions, which were major undertakings, with the deputations arriving in an appropriate style. The English embassy for the negotiations which led to the Truce of Calais required 443 horses, of which 204 were for Northampton and 106 for Mauny, with forty-six for the Earl of Suffolk and thirty-three for the Bishop of Norwich.[3]

Pope Clement VI died in December 1352 and his successor, Innocent VI, made a concerted effort to conclude the war. Negotiations at Calais were so promising that ambassadors from England and France were summoned to meet at Avignon. The English delegation was led by Henry of Lancaster, who chalked up an impressive amount in expenses. Despite the high hopes, there was no agreement and the war continued.

Military activity had continued during the early 1350s, despite the truces, intermittent negotiations and the economic and demographic effects of the pestilence. Mauny continued to have a responsibility for Calais and in 1351 he and Robert Herle, the Captain of Calais, carried out a spectacular raid into France to provision the town. According to Geoffrey le Baker, they looted 'a great swathe' of French territory 'and brought back great numbers of cattle, oxen, sheep and pigs. With these they so restocked the larders at Calais that one fat cow was barely worth fifteen pence sterling.'[4] The English court remained anxious for the security of Calais and its vulnerability, as the garrison controlled a relatively small area around the city. In 1352 the king ordered Mauny to report on the condition of the city's fortifications and those of its subordinate forts. Presumably as a result of that review, two years later Edward ordered that new fortifications should be built there, with the principal gate reconstructed and the high ground at Sangatte, close to the town, fortified. Work continued until 1360, when Mauny, with Guy de Bayeux and Roger de Beauchamp, were sent to report on the outstanding wages for the workmen.[5]

Lord Mauny campaigned with the king in Artois and Picardy in 1355 and when the army returned to England to deal with the new threat from the Scots he was sent on ahead of Edward's forces to direct operations at Berwick. The castle was separated from the town by a moat crossed by a bridge, which the French and Scots had attacked soon after they had captured the town early in November 1355. Mauny's advance guard entered the castle and he took command, directing the efforts to recover possession of the town. His detachment included 120 miners, who began to undermine the town's walls; the French had withdrawn and the garrison had no prospect of being relieved, so when the king arrived with the main army on 13 January 1356, it quickly surrendered. The terms were generous and, according to Geoffrey le Baker, 'Life and liberty were given to all found within the town.'[6] Clearly, the king could be merciful when taking the surrender of a garrison.

Another truce with France was arranged following the battle at Poitiers. Mauny did not campaign with the Black Prince, remaining a member of the king's household, and he was attending the king's council when the news of the battle arrived at Westminster. Under John's eldest son and heir, the Dauphin Charles, the French nobility could barely retain control of the country in the following years and in some regions they lost their authority to bands of freebooters who terrorised the population. In January 1359 Mauny was sent to France to negotiate an extension of the truce, which was due to expire in April. A peace settlement seemed to be a possibility. Edward thought that his case at the negotiating table would be strengthened if he were to be crowned king of France in Reims cathedral, the traditional place for the sovereign's coronation. Should a French army challenge his expedition to the city Edward was confident of defeating it, emphasising English military superiority and moving the negotiations forward. In the summer of 1359, he began to raise an army and Mauny gathered recruits at Calais from his native Hainault, Brabant and some German states. Edward then used Calais as he had intended, as the launching pad for an incursion into France. His army of about 10,000 men arrived there in late October and Mauny, with his 1,000 recruits, joined it. Despite the lateness of the season, the army left Calais on 4 November with, in Froissart's words, 'the best supply train ever seen', which must have owed something to Mauny's organising abilities at Calais as well as the efficient administration of the English forces under Edward.

The army reached the vicinity of Reims without being challenged and may have hoped that with the support of the archbishop, the king would be allowed into the city. Such expectations were to be disappointed and as the army was not equipped to mount a close siege a loose blockade was formed around it. That was probably in the hope that Charles could not, in all honour, allow an enemy force to march so freely across a part of his realm unchallenged and so would have to bring an army to end the siege. But he did not rise to the bait and the city's defences were strong enough to deter Edward from mounting an assault. In the ensuing stalemate the English could not collect enough provisions to maintain their positions and so the army drew off.

During skirmishing about 20 miles from the city, probably by a foraging party, Geoffrey Chaucer was captured by the French and was released four months later after the payment of a ransom to which the king contributed £16. Chaucer was not from the knightly class; he came from a merchant family in London, where his father was a prosperous vintner. He had been placed as a page in the household of Elizabeth, wife of Edward III's son Lionel of Ulster, and from that beginning he may have had some aspirations to achieve knighthood. That was not pursued, but he was employed by the crown for diplomatic missions and as a negotiator of trade deals with the Spanish and Italian states. In 1374 he was appointed controller of the wool custom and wool subsidy, living until 1385 in rooms over the gate at Aldgate. Chaucer's career had begun in a similar way to Mauny's, but his path diverged from Mauny's as he did not pursue a military career. Both men were favoured by John of Gaunt.

After leaving Reims the army marched in a broad sweep to the east and south of Paris, eventually reaching the city from the south. Paris was an even harder nut to crack than Reims and was well prepared. The English army burned villages and estates around the capital and the suburbs were set on fire, according to some accounts by the besiegers under Mauny's direction, but more probably by the defenders to prevent the English from using them for shelter and as cover to approach the defences. An impasse had been reached and so it was logical for peace negotiations to be held, which they were on Good Friday, 3 April 1360, in a leper house. The Duke of Lancaster was the head of the English delegation of five members, who included Mauny. Nothing was achieved. The English army marched away and reached Chartres; a truce was then arranged and the peace negotiations were resumed at Brétigny, south of Paris, on 1 May. Mauny was one of Edward's seven representatives; the others included Lancaster and the earls of Northampton, Warwick and Suffolk. A peace treaty was agreed there, by which King John was to be permitted to return to France on payment of the first stage of a ransom, leaving several hostages as a pledge for the execution of its terms, including his son Louis, Duke of Anjou. Edward was to drop his claim to the French throne and would thereafter hold Aquitaine and its adjoining territories in full sovereignty.

The English army marched back to Calais, where John waited for several weeks in 1360 while the arrangements agreed in the treaty were put in place; Mauny was entrusted with his care while he was there. Lancaster and Mauny acted on Edward's behalf at the ratification of the treaty at Calais in October 1360.[7] John was then released, but Louis escaped in 1363 and the king felt that it was his duty to voluntarily surrender himself and return to England, where he died in 1364.

During the 1360s Mauny was less occupied with military campaigns and more with diplomatic duties, membership of the king's council and other services to the crown, as he grew older. Among his responsibilities was attending King Peter of Cyprus when he was in London in 1363 during a tour of Europe, trying to obtain support for a crusade against the Turks to reconquer Alexandria. According to Froissart, Edward told Peter that he was too old for such exploits. He would surely have been reluctant to engage in what could only be a diversion while peace with France had not been fully achieved, despite the Treaty of Brétigny, the terms of which had not been completely implemented and were certainly unacceptable to many of the French nobles as being too harsh. During Peter's stay, the mayor of London, Henry Pickard, hosted a feast for what the seventeenth-century antiquarian Thomas Fuller described as 'a mess of kings, Edward king of England, John king of France, David king of Scots, and the king of Cyprus, besides Edward prince of Wales, and many prime noblemen of the land'.[10]

Charles V succeeded his father as king of France in 1364 and patiently began to restore the country's position and subdue those armed bands which had terrorised, and in some cases taken control of, parts of the realm. He also set out to recover the areas of the south-west that had been assigned to England at Brétigny; coming to terms with the lords of territories around the fringes of Aquitaine, which had been annexed by England but yet owed their feudal loyalty to the French crown. Sporadic warfare continued and the French captured towns and castles, gradually regaining lost territory.

Edward III's response was to send a force of roughly 6,000 men, and possibly as many as 8,000, through France from Calais in 1369 under John of Gaunt, Duke of Lancaster, with Mauny as second-in-command. John was Edward III's fourth son and was to become the leading English military figure after his brother

Edward the Black Prince gradually succumbed to a debilitating illness from the late 1360s. Among the other leading figures on the campaign were the earls of Salisbury and Warwick, Sir Frank Hale and Sir Henry Percy. The raid was designed to take pressure off the English in Gascony and to protect Calais, which was threatened by a resurgence of French military activity that included the capture of the English garrisons in Ponthieu. In fact, the French were seriously engaged in planning an invasion of England, which Gaunt's expedition disrupted, although the English court may not have been fully aware of how far advanced those plans were.

To all intents and purposes the expedition by Gaunt's army was a grand *chevauchée*, destructive but ultimately inconclusive, with his force crossing Picardy into Normandy as far as Harfleur before returning. At Tournehem, near St Omer, it was confronted by the Duke of Burgundy's army, but no major action occurred, which was frustrating for 'many on both sides' who hoped for a battle. It was suggested that a formal set-piece encounter should be arranged and Mauny was one of the two English supervisors who selected the site; but once that was done the French nobles refused to allow a battle to happen. Then, according to Froissart, one night the English guards saw fires in the French camp and interpreted that as preparations for an attack and so put their troops into battle order, but nothing happened. Gaunt asked his senior officers what they advised and 'some replied one thing, and some another,' so the duke asked Mauny what he recommended. Mauny said that the English should draw up in battle formation and move slowly forward, for it would soon be daylight and they would be able to see what the situation was; others disagreed and only a small force rode forward on a reconnaissance. Mauny then told Gaunt that he expected that the French would have withdrawn and that he should make the army ready to pursue them 'and I will engage that you shall have a fine day of it'. Gaunt did not take that advice as he would not act against the recommendation of his council.

When the scouts returned soon afterwards, they confirmed that Mauny had been right, the French were gone and as they left had set fire to their quarters, which is what the English guards had seen; all that the scouting party had found were 'some poor victuallers, who followed the army'. An opportunity had been missed, although the incident did bring Mauny 'great credit', for his military judgement. Burgundy went to St Omer and the English army marched back to Calais, where the Earl of Warwick died, perhaps of plague.[11]

With fewer semi-independent commands and usually serving as a commander in the king's army rather than on detached duties, in his later career Mauny had less opportunity for raising money from ransoms than he had done previously, but the English tactics of devastating a region brought in booty and he should have profited from Gaunt's campaign. A French prior in the diocese of Sens described the process during a similar English incursion into his region in 1358:

> They captured the castle and that same night set fire to almost all the countryside; afterwards they brought the whole country under their rule, ordering all the owners of both great and small estates to pay ransom for themselves, that is to say, for their lives, their goods, and their chattels, or their houses would be burned – and this they did in many places. Roused and terrified by this, very many people came to the English and agreed to buy themselves back, promising to give florins and flour and oats and many other necessaries for food if they would cease for a while their persecutions, because they were killing many men in divers places.

1. Philippa, Queen of England, being greeted outside Paris by her brother Charles IV of France in 1325. (Author's collection)

Above left: 2. Philippa sailing to England with an invasion fleet, 1326. (Author's collection)

Above right: 3. Edward III's coronation, 1327. (Author's collection)

Above left: 4. A tournament on London Bridge in the reign of Edward III. (Author's collection)

Left: 5. Knights jousting in front of an audience of ladies. (Author's collection)

Below: 6. Walter Mauny's seal. (Author's collection)

Above: 7. The shoes of the princes, the sons of Edward III. (Author's collection)

Right: 8. A depiction of Edward III, on the wall of St Stephen's chapel, Westminster, *c.* 1355; copied before the fire of 1834. (Author's collection)

9. A royal feast, accompanied by a harpist. (Author's collection)

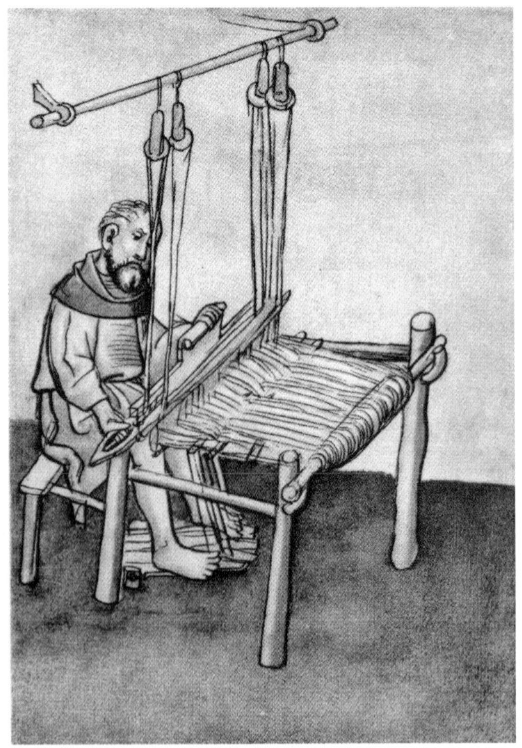

Above left: 10. Jean Froissart shown writing his Chronicles. (Author's collection)

Above right: 11. Weavers in the Low Countries relied on English wool for their raw material. (Author's collection)

Above left: 12. A scribe, perhaps writing a chronicle of contemporary affairs. (Author's collection)

Above right: 13. The capture of Berwick by Edward III's army in 1333. (Author's collection)

Right: 14. Cadzand Church. (Author's collection)

15. The English ships at the battle of Sluis in 1340. (Author's collection)

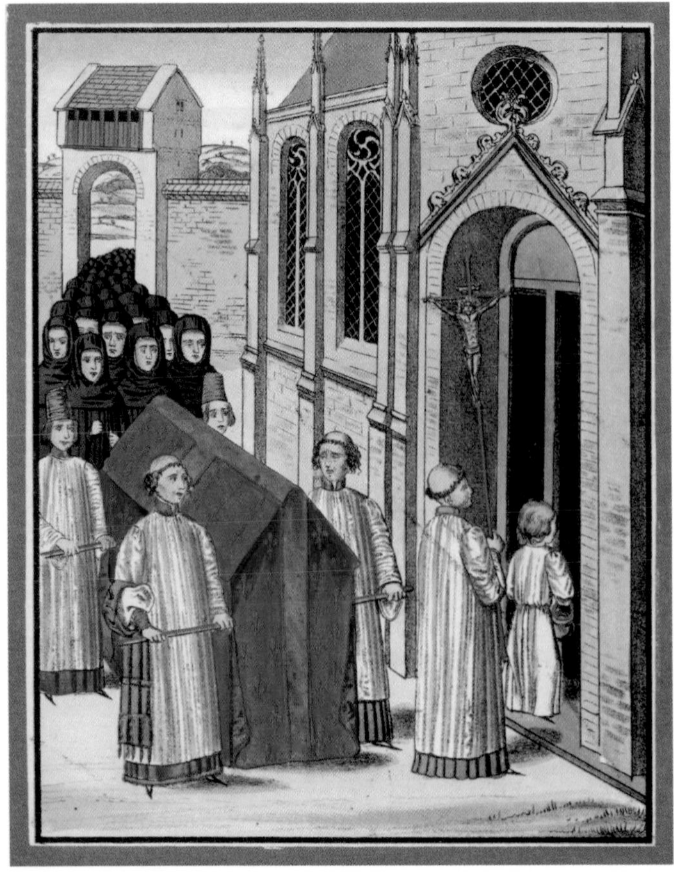

16. The funeral of the French king Philip VI in 1350. (Author's collection)

17. The siege of Hennebont, 1342. (Author's collection)

18. Killing, burning and plundering at Aalst in Flanders after its capture. (Author's collection)

Above: 19. The French attack on Calais in 1350, repelled by Mauny and Edward III. (Author's collection)

Left: 20. Charles V's coronation in Reims Cathedral in 1364. (Author's collection)

Above left: 22. The English siege of Reims, 1359–60. (Author's collection)

Above right: 21. Edward the Black Prince, copied from a painting on the wall of St Stephen's Chapel, Westminster. (Author's collection)

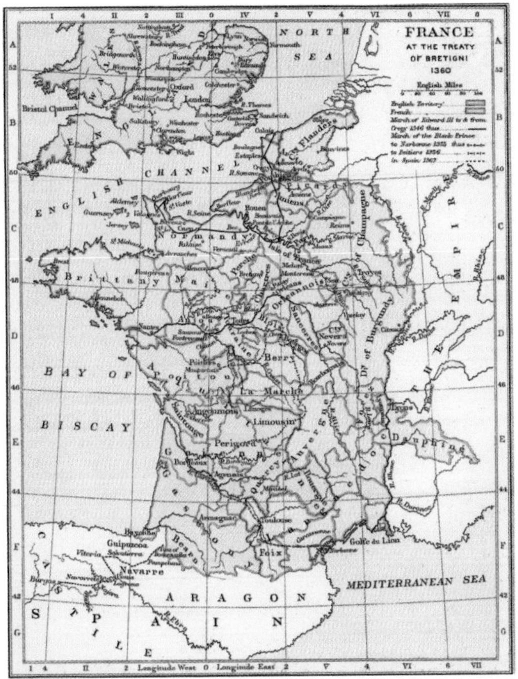

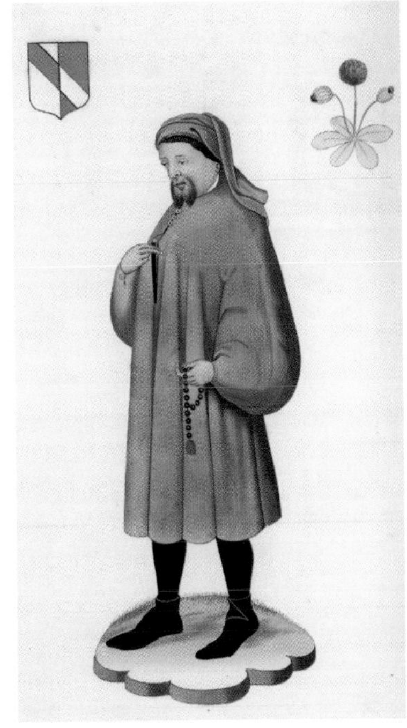

Above left: 23. Map of France in the mid-fourteenth century. (Author's collection)

Above right: 24. Geoffrey Chaucer, who served with the English army which besieged Reims in 1359–60. (Author's collection)

Above left: 25. Edward III in later life, by Edward Lutterell (*c.* 1650–1737). (Author's collection)

Above right: 26. The doorway of Cell B at the London Charterhouse, as restored by Seely & Paget. (Author's collection)

27. The London Charterhouse in the mid-fifteenth century depicted on a plan of its water supply. (© Historic England Archive)

28. A maid serves wine to a groom. (Author's collection)

29. John Ball preaching to the rebels during the Great Revolt. (Author's collection)

30. The killing of Wat Tyler in Smithfield, by William Walworth, Mayor of London. (Author's collection)

Left: 31. The Charterhouse and Charterhouse Square in the mid-seventeenth century; the site of the Black Death burial ground. (© The Charterhouse)

Below: 32. Auguste Rodin's *The Burghers of Calais*. (Author's collection)

33. The medieval revival in Mons in Hainault: the slaying of a dragon *c.* 1910. (Author's collection)

34. The effigy of Thomas Sutton on his tomb in Charterhouse Chapel. (© Stanley Underhill)

35. Lord Mauny's grave at the Charterhouse uncovered in 1947. (© The Charterhouse)

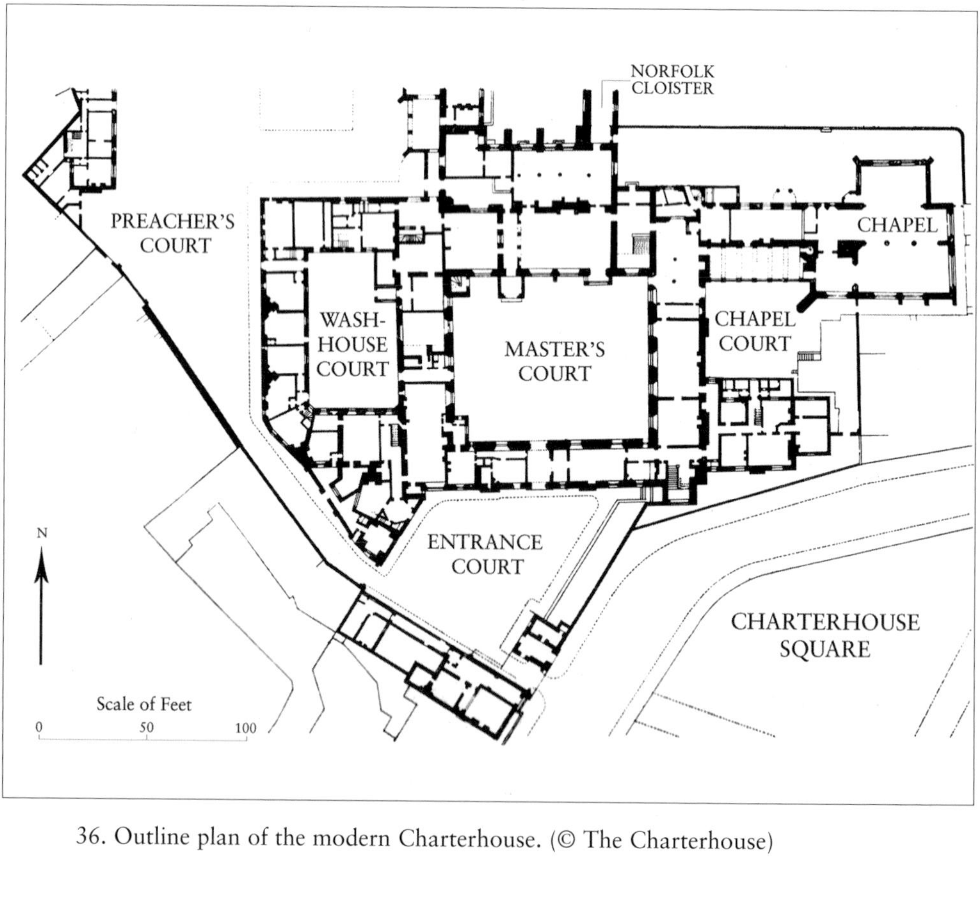

36. Outline plan of the modern Charterhouse. (© The Charterhouse)

37. Chapel Court, the site of the Black Death chapel and Mauny's grave, *c.* 1920. (© The Charterhouse)

38. The seal of the bulla granted to Mauny by Pope Clement VI in 1351. (© The Charterhouse)

Left: 39. David Acton as the Earl of Salisbury, whose escapades resemble those of Walter Mauny, in the Royal Shakespeare Company's production of *Edward III* in 2002. (Photo by Jonathan Dockar-Drysdale; © RSC)

Below: 40. A section of the Charterhouse priory buildings in Wash-house Court. (Author's collection)

The sums would have been divided among the raiding party according to rank. Diplomatic duties also supplemented Mauny's income. When the Bishop of London visited Bruges in 1365 'to treat of the King's business with the Council of Flanders' he was reimbursed for all his expenses and was paid a daily rate of £3 6s 8d for his services, producing a claim of £113 6s 8d for the 34-day embassy. It is unlikely that Mauny would have been paid less than the bishop for similar duties.[12]

The campaign of 1369 was Mauny's last, for he was now quite elderly for undertaking the rigours of military operations. And the world which he had inhabited for so long was changing. Henry of Lancaster had died in 1361 and Sir John Chandos, whose career had paralleled that of Mauny in many ways, died on 1 January 1370 from wounds inflicted in a skirmish. Queen Philippa, Mauny's first patron, died on 14 August 1369. That would not have diminished Mauny's influence with the king, but the companionship of a group at court, of Hainaulters and others, which had lasted for more than forty years, was disintegrating.

Jean Froissart was at the English court from 1361, making a journey to Scotland in 1365 and on another occasion touring the Welsh Marches and the Severn valley; he also went to the Black Prince's court at Bordeaux in 1365-6. The queen appointed him her secretary and while in England he took the opportunity of adding to his knowledge of the wars. With her support he travelled around and, as he later wrote, 'Wherever I went, I made enquiry of the ancient knights and squires, who had taken part in feats of arms, and could speak of them rightly; and also of ancient heralds, to verify and justify all these matters.' The help which he received from 'lords, kings, dukes, counts, ladies and knights of whatever nation they might be' he attributed to their 'love of the noble lady to whom I belonged'. He also had access to senior Frenchmen who were prisoners in England, pending the agreement for their ransoms; at least sixty such 'great personages' were being held as prisoners or hostages, with little to do and no doubt eager to put their memories of events and points of view to a reputable chronicler. Other Hainaulters were drawn to the English court by Philippa's patronage.

Froissart wrote that the queen favoured Hainault and that 'above all things she loved, valued, and praised its people'. They included Andre Bieuneveu from Valenciennes, sculptor and painter, whose patrons included Charles V of France, Louis de Male, Count of Flanders, and Jean, Duc de Berry, the sculptor Jean de Liège and perhaps Geoffrey Chaucer's father-in-law, the herald Sir Payn Roelt. All of them left after the queen's death brought that source of patronage to an end.[13]

Some senior members of the court who were wealthy enough chose to endow religious institutions. Edward, the Black Prince, re-founded a house of canons, the Brothers of Penitence, or Friars of the Sack, at Ashridge in Hertfordshire, which had originally been founded in 1283. He was also instrumental in converting a college at Edington in Wiltshire founded by William Edington, Bishop of Winchester, in 1351, to a house of a small order known as the Bonhommes. The Bonhommes followed St Augustine's rule and were one of the austere orders which were then in favour because of their disdain for wealth and power. The Carthusians were the largest of such ascetic orders, whose self-discipline was likely to make their prayers more effective; certainly those of the Benedictines and Cistercians had failed to save humanity from God's wrath in the form of the successive outbreaks of the pestilence.[14] The Duke of Lancaster, in addition to his involvement with the institutions at Cambridge, was patron of the college of the Annunciation of St Mary in the Newarke at Leicester.

Ralph Stafford created a house for Augustinian friars at Stafford in 1344, where prayers were to be said for the king and for Stafford's first wife and her relatives; he also endowed a perpetual chantry at Cold Norton Priory, Oxfordshire, for the salvation of his soul and that of Margaret Audley, his second wife.[15] That was the context in which Lord Mauny contemplated founding a Carthusian priory on Spitalcroft.

In 1354 Mauny married Margaret Brotherton, and in doing so became a member of the royal family, because she was a granddaughter of Edward I. Margaret was the eldest daughter of Thomas of Brotherton, Earl of Norfolk, the eldest son of Edward I from his marriage to Margaret of France, his second wife. Margaret Brotherton had married around 1335 John, Lord Seagrave, and after her father's death in 1338 she became co-heir with her sister Alice of most of the Brotherton estates, their brother, Edward of Norfolk, having died as a child and predeceased his father. In 1351 Alice was beaten to death by her husband Edward Montacute, the Earl of Salisbury's brother, and some of his retainers, making Margaret Thomas's sole heir. But her marriage with Seagrave was in trouble and she was arrested for defying a royal prohibition on travel to go to obtain papal approval for a divorce. In fact, Seagrave died in 1353 and Margaret then received a large jointure from the Seagrave estates. She offended the king by marrying Mauny because they had not obtained a marriage licence from the king; after their marriage the Brotherton estates were confiscated and for a time she was imprisoned in Somerton Castle, Lincolnshire, although that was surely a case of comfortable house-arrest rather than harsh incarceration. In 1354 those estates were restored.

Both husband and wife were capable administrators of their estates and at the time of Walter's death in 1372 they owned land in eighteen English counties, as well as his property in Calais. Mauny's brothers had all predeceased him and so he came into possession of the family estates in Hainault, at Masny, Jenlain, Roucourt and Wasnes. He continued to lend money, acknowledging in 1362 the receipt of 19,000 gold florins from Margaret of Hainault, just part of a debt which she owed him. Her son, Duke Albert, was also indebted to Mauny at the time of his death. It has been estimated that when he died in 1372 Lord Mauny was worth £15,000, or the equivalent of more than a half of one per cent of the net national income at the time. That qualifies him as being among the 250 wealthiest people in Britain since the Norman Conquest in 1066.[16]

Mauny's wealth should be seen against the changing demographic context and the finances of his contemporaries. Edward the Black Prince's landed estates were generating an average annual income of £10,000 during the mid-1370s. He was the king's eldest son and heir to the throne, and his holdings were greater than Mauny's, despite the latter's assiduous accumulation of property. Both held estates in Wales and Mauny's lands were also widely spread across England, yet he must have experienced the declining income faced by the prince and indeed all landlords, as rents and dues fell in the wake of the plague outbreaks in the late 1340s and in 1361-2. The changed demographic altered relations between them and a much-reduced workforce, as well as a fall in demand for produce and declining economic activity, for example in the market towns, which generated tolls for the owners of the market rights.[17] While efficient administrative policies could mitigate the effects of the epidemics, they could not remove them and it is likely that by the early 1370s Mauny's landed income was less than it had been, say, ten years earlier.

Margaret Brotherton not only pursued wealth but was tireless in maintaining her status. She claimed to have inherited the Norfolk title and styled herself Countess of Norfolk, because she was Brotherton's sole heir. This was duly acknowledged on 29 September 1397 when her grandson Thomas Mowbray was created Duke of Norfolk and she was elevated from the rank of countess to that of Duchess of Norfolk, thus becoming the first Englishwoman to be made a duchess in her own right. That was a part of Richard II's overhaul of the peerage; on that same day four men who were already members of the aristocracy were given ducal titles, three new earls were created and the Earl of Somerset, John of Gaunt's eldest son, became Marquess of Dorset. Margaret also styled herself Countess Marshal, on the basis that her father had held the hereditary office of Marshal of England. But that post was granted to others and she was not allowed to perform the duties of the role at Richard II's coronation in 1377, yet in the 1370s the crown did address her as Margaret Marshal. Part of her success can be attributed to her longevity. She died in 1399 aged about 80, having outlived her two husbands, her siblings, her niece, her four children and one of her grandchildren.

It was customary for a testator to make a will only when he or she was so ill or infirm that death seemed to be inevitable. Lord Mauny's will was dated 30 November 1371, suggesting an illness or a steady decline in his health before his death at his wife's manor at Great Chesterford in Essex on 15 January 1372. That was 'to the great grief of all the barons and knights of England, on account of the loyalty and prudence they had always found in him'. He was buried in the chapel which he had built at Spitalcroft, having instructed his executors to bury him there in a custom appropriate to his rank but without 'worldly show, and without too much expense, but in a reasonable style, according to current fashion'.[18] His choice of place was significant, for he could have been interred at Westminster, in St Paul's or a parish church, or at Masny in Hainault or Cambrai cathedral. Writing in the 1380s, Sir John Clanvow, a knight of the royal household, held the opinion that 'a thing that worldly men desire greatly is that their fame might last long after them upon earth'; in Mauny's case that can be interpreted as wishing to be remembered for acquiring the burial ground and founding the priory. Remembrance was also achieved by the form of the monument raised over their grave. Mauny specified that his tomb was to be of alabaster with 'a knightly effigy with my arms, like that made for John Beauchamp [who died in 1360] at St Paul's in London, in remembrance of me and so that men may pray for me'.[19] As he had decided on the place of his burial and the form of his tomb by the end of November, it is possible that work on the monument was under way before his death; it was customary for the family of the deceased to have completed the monument within a year after the interment. For Mauny, 'family' meant his wife, and she was brisk and purposeful in most matters, so that the monument, with his effigy, may have been in place by the end of 1372.[20]

Mauny's grave was in the centre of the choir in front of the step of the high altar, with a suitably laudatory inscription. His funeral was attended by the king, those of his sons who were in England at the time, lords and prelates, and poor people. The inscription on his tomb described him as the priory's founder and its anonymous chronicler wrote that he was 'an approved man, and in all things laudable, both in matters relating to religion and those of human knowledge, and particularly accomplished'. Mauny left a penny to each of the poor people who attended his funeral 'to pray for me and for the remission of my sins'.

The payments from that clause in his will could have been considerable, as there was no restriction on the numbers. He was well regarded for his acquisition of Spitalcroft as a burial ground at a time of dire need and had continued it in use, and he had founded the large priory of the prestigious Carthusian order there. John of Gaunt paid for 500 masses to be said for Mauny's soul as 'our most dear companion, one of the knights of the garter'.[21]

Mauny was outlived by his wife Margaret and daughter Anne, who was seventeen years old when he died; she had married John Hastings, Earl of Pembroke, in 1368 and was a founder of one of the monks' cells at the Charterhouse. Mauny's only son, Thomas, pre-deceased him and his two illegitimate daughters, Mailosel and Malplesant, had entered convents; he bequeathed £10 to one of them. Mauny was not unusual in his century not to establish a dynasty; a quarter of noble families died out in the male line every twenty-five years.[22]

Jean le Bel placed Mauny very favourably in terms of military renown and in the 'true deeds' carried out by Edward III and his captains:

> [They] fully deserve to be held and reputed as worthy, despite the fact that there is much debate as to which of them should be regarded as most worthy – whether it be the noble person of the king himself, his son the prince of Wales in his youth, the duke of Lancaster, Lord Reginald de Cobham, Lord Walter de Manny, Lord Frank de Hale, or various others… [They all] showed themselves to be so valiant that they must be held to be worthy and doubly worthy.

He was especially fulsome in his praise of Mauny, who 'gained such favour with the king and all his barons that he was welcomed into the most privy and august council of the land; and in time he achieved countless feats of prowess in many places, and so many bold missions ... that he was deemed the worthiest knight known. And he should indeed be considered the most valiant of all, after the noble King Edward and the worthy Duke of Lancaster, who surpass all others in deeds and renown.' He depicted him as 'that worthy knight Sir Walter Mauny, always more mindful of honour than money', and as one among the king's entourage 'in whom he placed great faith'. Le Bel also stressed Mauny's popularity: his 'many feats of arms and prowess in Scotland and elsewhere had earned him such favour with the king and all the English, great and small' that the king had taken him into his 'innermost council' and granted him great estates.[23]

Mauny's reputation was enhanced by the embellished descriptions of his escapades provided by chroniclers, especially his fellow Hainaulters Jean le Bel and Jean Froissart, but his achievements were substantial even without their advocacy. And he came well out of Froissart's shorter and more considered version of his Chronicles, written in 1395. Froissart concluded that Edward III and Philippa did deserve the fine reputation as monarchs which he had given them, and that their reign had been successful partly because they had taken the wise advice of men such as Mauny.[24]

As well as his sagacity, Mauny was outstandingly brave, a talented fighter and a skilled commander whose tactics at Cadzand surely contributed to the style of warfare developed by Edward III. His role in both domestic and foreign talks suggest that he was also a capable mediator with a conciliatory manner; those aspects of his character which had helped him to become well-liked by the king and queen in his early years in England would have stood him in good stead when negotiating. Mauny's employment by the king in such matters as preparing a fleet suggest that he recognised him to be a proficient organiser. He undoubtedly followed contemporary practices of warfare and benefited from royal favour in amassing a fortune, which allowed him to invest in philanthropic projects at the time of the Black Death and later in the foundation of the Charterhouse. Through his abilities and by taking the opportunities which came his way, the orphan boy from the village of Masny became one of the most prominent figures in Edward III's England.

8

THE PRIORY

Before his death Mauny returned to his project of founding a Carthusian priory at Spitalcroft. The delay before he did so may have been due to his many other commitments and perhaps waiting to see what the king's intentions were, in case he wished to make such an endowment. Mauny would have been aware of several precedents and surely, too, of the scale of funding needed to make a Carthusian house viable. It was partly for their piety and otherworldliness that the Carthusians attracted patronage from senior figures, but their monasteries were expensive to endow and maintain.

The d'Avesnes family, Counts of Hainault, were benevolent in supporting institutions for the poor and the church, as was expected of members of a royal house. In 1288 the Bishop of Cambrai, the count's brother, founded a Charterhouse, which was moved to the outskirts of Valenciennes in 1297 by Count William. But not until 1325 was it put on a sound financial footing by the count and his family, with the addition of property, rents, money and jewellery to the endowment; their example was followed by the gentry and citizens of Valenciennes as well as the clergy. The priory was also granted some exemptions from taxation. It was a single house, consisting of a prior and twelve monks, accommodated in fifteen cells, one each for the professed monks and the converts, with the full set of buildings commonly provided in a charterhouse. The monks came together daily for matins, mass and vespers, on Sundays and some feast days they dined together in the refectory, or frater, and they also met in the chapter-house on Sundays.

At other times they led austere and contemplative lives in those individual cells; the order's statutes of 1259 directed that each monk should have a writing desk, pens, chalk, two pumices, two inkhorns, a penknife, two razors or scrapers for scraping parchment, a pointer, an awl, a weight, a rule, a ruler for ruling, tables and a writing style; in other words the implements required for writing or copying documents. When Thomas Golwyne transferred from the London Charterhouse to Mount Grace in 1520 his belongings consisted of clothing, bedding, some kitchen utensils, a number of books, writing implements and a loom. Clearly, when not at worship or prayer he spent his time writing manuscripts or weaving. The re-endowment of the priory at Valenciennes occurred before Mauny left for England; it offered an exemplar and a cautionary guide to the establishment of a Carthusian priory.[1]

Before the plague epidemic in 1361 Mauny had been encouraged by Michael Northburgh, Bishop of London since 1355, to establish a Carthusian priory at Spitalcroft. Northburgh was pursuing a typical career for a senior churchman of the period, holding several benefices, canonries and prebends, and taking positions in the royal service. In 1349 and intermittently thereafter he was described as the king's 'secretary' and was entrusted with diplomatic missions. He was with the army on the Crécy campaign in 1346 as the royal clerk and held the office of Lord Privy Seal from 1350 until 1354. During his journeys he visited and was impressed by the Carthusian priory in Paris, founded in 1257. In the early years of the order the Carthusians had chosen remote sites for their priories but increasingly they were founded in or near cities and towns, perhaps encouraged to do so by lay patrons, who wished the fruit of their munificence to be more widely seen than would be the case among mountains. The extensive site of the priory in Paris was donated by the king, Louis IX (known as Saint Louis), and Northburgh also cited the charterhouses at Avignon, Bruges, St Omer and Cologne as precedents for a similar foundation in London, 'where the concourse of the whole kingdom is'.[2]

Northburgh was especially keen to see a Carthusian house in London and was aware that Spitalcroft offered a suitable site. He approached Mauny, who could assign the land and was wealthy enough to provide the funds that would be required. In May 1361 the two men came to an arrangement by which Mauny was designated the principal founder of the priory, yet gave Northburgh leave to act as he thought fit. At that stage the priory was to be a single house, of twelve monks and a prior. Mauny's widow and heirs were not to have a claim on the patronage of the priory, but were to be the first after Mauny and the bishop in all 'masses, memorials, prayers, orisons, and hours' within the priory church.[3] But the scheme was not proceeded with: Mauny was active on campaigns and engaged in diplomatic negotiations at that time, and Northburgh died four months after the agreement was made, bequeathing £2,000 and a dozen properties in London to the projected priory. A considerable delay followed before the proposal was taken up, with Mauny's encouragement, by

John Luscote, prior of the charterhouse at Hinton in Somerset. Mauny made him aware of Northburgh's legacy and asked him to approach the bishop's executors 'and entreat them towards the same plan'. Luscote enlisted the support of Simon Sudbury, Northburgh's successor as Bishop of London, but they met with opposition from the Master of St Bartholomew's Hospital, the Bishop of Ely and the Dean and Chapter of St Paul's, among others, chiefly on the grounds that the new foundation would be to the detriment of the other houses in England. Even a hermit living close to the chapel was obstructive.

Luscote was probably unable to make much headway against such figures, but progress quickened after Mauny's final military campaign in 1369, suggesting that he could then give more of his attention to the project and used his authority and influence to reconcile, or overcome, the objectors. Mauny had given Luscote encouragement in his dealings with the 'devils' who were obstructing his progress. An anecdote reported him telling Luscote after overcoming an obstacle: 'Lo, we have conquered the devil of such a place: now pray earnestly instantly for victory over such a devil, for he is very strong.' He also applied to the Carthusian's General Chapter for Luscote's appointment as rector of the new house, implying that he would not support the scheme further if that was not done. Luscote was duly appointed, having to resign as prior of Hinton, and when the London house was formally established he was made its prior, a post which he held until his death in 1398.[4]

As the land was held on lease, an important step was to acquire the freehold and Mauny obtained the title from St Bartholomew's in November 1370, in exchange for two of his manors. Edward III granted a royal licence for the foundation of the Charterhouse in February 1371, and Mauny's foundation charter followed in March. The house was the largest of the four Carthusian houses hitherto established in England, for unlike Northburgh's proposed priory it was a double house of twenty-four monks and a prior. There was insufficient space for the larger house now established and a further four acres of land on its east side were acquired from the priory of the Hospital of St John in 1377, specifically for making gardens for the monks' cells. There must have been an assurance from the outset that this plot would be transferred, and the delay before it was granted to the Charterhouse may simply indicate that it was not formally conveyed until required.[5] Other acquisitions brought the area available to the priory up to about 30 acres.

Somewhere around mid-May 1371 Mauny appointed Henry Yevele as mason, effectively architect, to set out the site and begin building the monks' cells and the great cloister. Yevele first worked for a member of the royal family when finishing the hall at Edward, Prince of Wales's manor of Kennington in Surrey, in the late 1350s, and he would also have come to Mauny's attention after being granted a licence in 1359 to discharge victuals at Calais. He was already well established and in 1360 he was appointed 'disposer' of the fabric of the king's two palaces in London, at Westminster and the Tower. His greatest works were the nave of Canterbury Cathedral and the reconstruction of Westminster Hall. As well as being an accomplished master mason and architect, Yevele also acted as a designer and probably designed the tombs of both Edward III and Richard II in Westminster Abbey. It was entirely characteristic of Mauny that he should appoint as mason someone who was so prominent in his profession, held a position from the crown and carried out commissions for senior members of the court.

The start-up costs of the priory were higher than those which Northburgh would have anticipated, and so were the subsequent recurrent expenses.[6] Part of the outlay was met by wealthy sponsors from London, who each paid for a monk's cell. The direct involvement of citizens had been the pattern at the re-endowment of the charterhouse at Valenciennes almost fifty years earlier. The principal benefactors for the early cells were Mauny himself, who donated the prior's cell, which was the largest, Sir William Walworth, a fishmonger, who sponsored the first cell, and Adam Fraunceys, a mercer, who, like Walworth, twice served as Mayor, in 1352 and 1353, and sponsored five cells. Walworth made further contributions as the executor of his former master, the wealthy fishmonger and merchant John Lovekyn, who served four terms as Mayor and represented London in four parliaments. He died in 1368, having bequeathed his mansion and other wealth to Walworth, who used some of that legacy towards the cost of founding four cells.

The priory's name of the House of the Salutation of the Mother of God derived from the service of dedication of the cemetery chapel on the Feast of the Annunciation in 1349. That chapel was adopted as the priory's church and the burial ground became the outer precinct, remaining open to the laity. The small size of the chapel was not a problem, for Carthusian churches, although not entirely exclusive, did not need space for large lay congregations.[7] Londoners were expected to worship at their parish churches, not at the Carthusian one. Most of the new buildings lay on its north side, away from the burials, but in the early stages of the priory's existence not physically separated from them. Monks from existing Carthusian houses in England transferred to the London priory. The earliest of those houses were at Witham and Hinton, both in Somerset, founded respectively in 1178 and 1227, followed over a century later by Beauvale in Nottinghamshire (1343). Later foundations were at Kingston-upon-Hull (1377, by Michael de la Pole, Earl of Suffolk from 1385), Coventry (1381, by William, Lord Zouche), Axholme (1397-98, by Thomas Mowbray, Earl of Nottingham), Mount Grace (1398, by Thomas Howard, Duke of Surrey) and Sheen (1415, the establishment of which was overseen with keen interest by its founder, Henry V). Richard II laid the foundation stone of the Coventry charterhouse's chapel in 1385, and he added to its endowment. Only London and Sheen were double houses.

The time taken to erect the buildings of the London Charterhouse was the result of financial difficulties, despite the apparently generous endowment and further bequests made before the end of the fourteenth century towards the cost of the monks' cells and other buildings. Mauny allocated to the priory debts of £4,000, of which £1,000 was 'an old debt' due to him from the king 'by bills of his wardrobe', and the Black Prince should have paid him £66 13s 4d per annum for his salary as governor of Harlech Castle, but none of those sums were ever received. The priory was not alone, for the Black Prince owed £2,972 to various creditors when he died in 1376; the king undertook to pay those debts but died in the following year and by his will his personal estate was bequeathed to St Stephen's chapel, King's Langley priory and the monastery of St Mary Graces. The London charterhouse was creditor of both the Black Prince and Edward III and was left lamenting.

According to the chronicler of the house's early history, nothing was obtained from some other grants, including property in Calais bequeathed by Mauny but appropriated by the king.[8] The manor of Knebworth was assigned by Mauny to the endowment, yet at his death it was still in his possession and did not come into the priory's ownership subsequently, and receipts from the manor of Ockholt in Romney Marsh were seriously impaired by flooding. Had Mauny not died so soon after the foundation, then perhaps he could have prised some of the unpaid sums from his creditors or increased the endowment. His estate passed to his daughter Anne, then eighteen years old and the wife of John, Earl of Pembroke, and not to his wife or the priory.

By 1402 part of the Charterhouse's annual income of £133 that should have been generated by the endowments had been lost and the residue was more than accounted for by outgoings on annuities and pensions. The buildings were still not completed: the frater, parlour, barns and circuit wall were not built and the cloister had still to be paved and ceiled, work it was estimated would cost £1,730. The financial situation became so serious that in 1403 the house's affairs were taken over by Henry IV and entrusted to four administrators. But the king was unable to give direct aid on the scale required because of the crown's own parlous financial position and its fundamental commitments. The opening years of the fifteenth century saw a sharp decline in the exports of both wool and woollen cloth, reducing customs duties, and loans, which had been used to supplement the inadequate receipts from taxation, were declining, partly because repayments were falling into arrears. Coupled with the increased debts of the household and exchequer, and an intransigent parliament which met in January 1404, this produced a financial crisis and the king was in no position to aid a monastic house with grants, however much he admired the objectives of its order. He especially favoured the contemplative orders of the Carthusians and the Carmelites; he donated wine to five Carthusian houses in 1405-6, out of fourteen monasteries which benefited from such gifts.[9]

Although long-term direct aid was impossible, his agents may have had some success in reforming the priory's financial management, for construction work was resumed in the following years, bringing the house close to a 'full set' of the buildings which a Carthusian priory required. Activity in 1405-6 saw the addition of a chapel to the church, the construction of the Little Cloister, and probably the guesthouse on its west side, and the building of the south boundary wall and gatehouse, which was so placed as to give the laity convenient access to the church. The altar in the chapter-house was not consecrated until 1414 and the building of the cells continued for a few years after that.

The prior's cell was in the south-west corner of the Great Cloister and also opened into the Little Cloister, so that he could receive visitors, who were prohibited from entering the Great Cloister. The lay brothers, who attended to the monks' needs, were accommodated in a building to the south-west of the Little Cloister, which had other service buildings ranged around it. The Carthusian monks' cells were detached two-storey houses, arranged around the Great Cloister and each built in an enclosure, the greater part of which was used as a garden. The cells on the east side of the Great Cloister, including those at the north-east and south-east corners, had access to an orchard which lay between them and the highway. Internally, the Carthusian arrangement was to have two chambers on each floor, serving as oratory, dining-room, bedroom and workshop. The need to provide those separate cells contributed to the relative expense of establishing a

Carthusian priory, both in terms of the land required and the building costs.[10]

The outer precinct contained the flesh-kitchen, a two-storey structure which provided cooked meat for guests; the Carthusians themselves were vegetarians. It was placed there partly to keep the aroma of cooking meat away from the monks to avoid odoriferous temptation and partly to reduce the risk of fire. Some indication of the balance between fish and meat (which included salted beef and bacon) comes from the accounts for 1492-3, with fish costing almost twenty times the £5 5s spent on flesh.[11]

The difficult early phase was followed by one marked by a considerable financial recovery and by 1426 rents from the Charterhouse's London properties alone were worth almost £190 per annum.[12] The improvement in the priory's finances was helped by a burst of charitable donations in the early fifteenth century, especially gifts and bequests from Londoners. The contributions included a new water supply from springs at Islington assigned to the priory in April 1430 by John Feriby and his wife Margery. The construction of the pipes from the springs to the priory and the conduit there was paid for by William Symmes, who gave more than £200, and Anne Tatersale. Symmes gave a further £146 as an endowment to generate funds for repairing and maintaining the system. The conduit was in the centre of the Great Cloister, from where pipes flowed to each of the monks' cells and latrines in their gardens, with the overflow, described as 'waste' water, piped away along Charterhouse Lane and drawn upon by inns there.

From the drawing on the water-supply plan of the mid-fifteenth century it appears that the conduit house was a handsome ornament to the cloister, with its octagonal stone base beneath the timber chamber containing the cistern. A door at ground level provided access to the pipes, which ran to each side of the cloister, with a tank part of the way along each line. The branch to the south side of the cloister fed a cistern serving a laver, built into the cloister wall, which was ornamental as well as functional, having a hexagonal stone base beneath a stone canopy supported on both sides by pilasters or buttresses.

Carthusian houses in the larger cities may have been vulnerable to malpractices and interference by outsiders. They did not allow women into the precincts, yet in 1405 Henry IV saw the need to forbid women from entering the London priory, including the church, and would hardly have needed to do so if they had not been encroaching on the priory's space. The General Chapter's Visitors to the English Province incorporated that ban into an ordinance, also directing the prior and the proctor to construct a wall between the church and the cemetery. That created a boundary on the south side of the priory to restrict access and to mark the perimeter beyond which the monks could not pass, except for the prior and the proctor. The custom of meeting the burial parties at the gate to the outer precinct thereby came to an end, as did that of delivering sermons to the laity from the pulpit house, which was contrary to Carthusian practice and was strictly forbidden in 1405.[13]

The south-west area of the Great Cloister was used as a burial ground. Guy de Burgh, who had joined the order at Beauvale in 1354 and was one of the first monks at the London Charterhouse, was interred there, as was John Luscote, the first prior, who died in 1398 and requested to be buried at the feet of de Burgh. Excavations have revealed five graves in this area. Graves beneath the cloister alley north of the chapel included those of Symmes, who died in 1439, and his wife, and of Richard

Lessy, notary and Chamberlain to the Pope, who was buried in the cloister in 1498. They were marked by limestone ledger slabs.[14]

The laity, including women, maintained that they still had a right of entry to the church, which had been built for services for those buried in the cemetery. Not until 1405 was an addition to the building erected on its west side, extending the church by 30 feet. A screen separated the new ante-chapel from the original building. The ante-chapel was designated the chapel of St Anne and the Holy Cross and was built in response to the orders to exclude women from the church. Nevertheless, it remained accessible to men, and benefactors continued to found and build chapels attached to the church, and to erect tombs, some of which were lavishly decorated.[15]

The problem of lay access to the church continued and, in a further attempt to curb that practice, in 1481 a chapel was built in the outer precinct near to the priory's inner gateway. Endowed by Robert Hulett and dedicated to the Virgin Mary and All Saints, it was a simple rectangular brick building with a pitched tile roof. In the 1490s an organ was installed.[16] It served as a gate-chapel for those visiting the burial ground. Some plague victims were interred there during the fifteenth century, but it generally ceased to be a plague cemetery; the dead were buried elsewhere.

The additional contributions from donors did not entirely solve the house's financial problems. In 1442 it was again pleading poverty and in the late fifteenth century was still not wealthy, even with the support of so prominent a patron as Cicely Neville, Duchess of York and mother of Edward IV and Richard III. For twenty-four years, with two brief interruptions, Cicely was the mother of the reigning king. In 1482 the buildings were said to be greatly in need of repair.[17] The priory's receipts fluctuated considerably.[18] In 1492-3 they were £589, including arrears of rent, but at the end of that accounting year the house was £101 in debt. Philip Underwood then became Procurator and under his careful management income rose sharply, so that by the end of 1495 the debts had been cleared. When Underwood completed his last account, in 1500, receipts had reached £1,150 per annum and the annual surplus was £150.[19]

Many benefactors included their request for burial in the Charterhouse in their wills and bequeathed properties within the city, not in themselves very valuable but cumulatively of some significance in maintaining the priory's income. The bulk of its rental income came from the properties in London and Middlesex, which produced £508 per annum by the mid-1530s, when the Charterhouse's regular, rather than occasional, receipts were £736 per annum, reduced by annuities and fixed outgoings to £642. But the Charterhouse's prosperity had begun to wane by then, as a fall in charitable receipts coupled with rising prices created difficulties.

Some Londoners chose to be buried within the priory church, rather than in their own parish, throughout its existence. A chapel added to the church and dedicated to St John the Evangelist was consecrated in 1437, and two more, consecrated in 1453, were built and endowed by Sir John Popham, an experienced soldier who was appointed Treasurer of the Household in 1437. The chapel of SS Michael and John the Baptist contained Popham's tomb. Its smaller neighbour was dedicated to SS Jerome and Bernard. On the north side of the church, the chapel of St Agnes, dedicated in 1475 and endowed by William Freeman, clerk of the Order of St John of Jerusalem, was built on the site of the *domus colloquii* or parlour, where the sacristy had been. In the early sixteenth century the chapel of St Katherine was endowed by Sir Robert Rede, an eminent lawyer, fellow of King's Hall, Cambridge, and from 1506 Chief Justice of the Common Pleas. He died in 1519, specifying in his will that he should be buried in the chapel.

Additions and alterations to the buildings and an increase in the number of monks indicate that the early sixteenth century was a relatively prosperous period. The priory attracted the patronage of Henry VII as one of eighteen religious houses he selected to perform anniversary services interceding for him and his family; the agreement with the Charterhouse was made in 1504. This brought in a small annual fee and the priory was allocated a bequest of £40 in his will; he died in 1509.[20] The increased income and the king's legacy produced a burst of building activity, with substantial work to the chapter-house in 1512. Its height was increased and tall new windows were built, one in the east wall and three in the south one; at the same time the lower two stages of Chapel Tower were vaulted and a third stage added. The lower two stages of Chapel Tower were vaulted and a third stage added as part of the work; the new roof of the chapter-house butted up to the wall of the third stage. This work possibly used the bequest from Henry VII; the majority of the king's bequests had been paid within three years of his death in 1509.

Somewhere between 1490 and the early 1530s a new cell for the prior was built to the east of the church, and a group of three cells was also added, probably along the south side of the Great Cloister. A small court to the west of the guest-house was enclosed by ranges of service buildings in the early 1530s. There was a low doorway on the ground floor of the outer face of the west range, now filled in, although the four-centred brick arch remains, as do the jambs, which are not rebated for doors. The doorway is wide enough for a hand-cart to pass through and this part of the building was used in the sixteenth century as a fuel store and in 1614 was referred to as having been coalhouses.[21]

The London Charterhouse was a flourishing and respected Carthusian community during the early Tudor period, evidently having no problem attracting new monks during the late 1520s and early 1530s. The young Thomas More took part in their spiritual exercises between 1499 and 1503, while he was studying law. William Roper, his son-in-law and biographer, wrote that More was 'religiously lyvinge' in the Charterhouse, implying that he lodged within the precincts, but according to Erasmus he lived 'near the Charterhouse'. More's companion while he was studying at the Charterhouse was William Lilly, who had attended Oxford University and specialised in Latin and Greek, spending time at Rhodes and Rome before returning to London, where he was appointed by John Colet, Dean of St Paul's, as the first high master of St Paul's School. Erasmus described him as 'a man unusually well-versed in Latin and Greek and an expert in the education of the young'. As well as attracting scholars such as More and Lilly, the Charterhouse was also able to increase the number of its monks and lay brothers.

Half of the monks were under thirty-five years old when John Houghton became prior in 1531. By 1534 there were the prior, procurator, twenty-five monks, twenty-one priests, three professed religious (who had taken their vows but were not ordained), and thirteen lay brothers.[22] The Carthusians also had a good reputation within London for their charity, providing 'plentye of brede, and ale, and fyshe, gevyn to strangers, in the butterye, and at the butterye door, and as large distributions of bread and ale, to all ther servants, and to vagabunds at the gate'.[23] The priory's achievements and reputation at this time were attributable in large part to the influence and leadership of William Tynbygh, who had been a member of the house for perhaps thirty years before becoming prior in 1500, a position which he held until 1529.

9

MAUNY'S SUCCESSORS

Those who outlived Lord Mauny would have been aware of his achievements and aspirations, and taken notice of how events impacted upon them, as well as pursuing their own interests. His widow Margaret concentrated largely on her affairs and status rather than consolidating Walter's achievements.[1] In 1368 their daughter Anne married John Hastings, Earl of Pembroke; he was twenty-one and she was thirteen. His first wife was Margaret, daughter of Edward III. They married in 1359 and she died two years later. John and Anne had one child, another John, born in 1372; he never saw his father, who died in 1375. The boy succeeded his father as Earl of Pembroke but died as a result of a mishap at a tournament in 1389, ending the Hasting family's tenure of the earldom. His mother had died in 1384 and so Mauny's bloodline came to an end.

Anne's husband was a prominent soldier, as befitted a son-in-law of the king; that gave him considerable status and according to Froissart he was someone whom Edward's sons 'also called their brother'.[2] In January 1369 he went with one of the royal princes, Edmund of Langley, Earl of Cambridge, on an expedition from St Malo through Perigord with a force of men-at-arms and archers. That was essentially a *chevauchée* to relieve pressure on Edward the Black Prince following his return to Aquitaine from his campaign in Spain, which had produced a spectacular victory but also innumerable and long-lasting political problems.

Edmund and Pembroke captured the castle of Boudeilles and Pembroke was knighted. In the following summer he was again with Edmund, as well as the experienced soldier Sir John Chandos, at the siege of La Roche-sur-Yon in the Vendée, which fell to the English. But Pembroke felt that Chandos, despite his stature as a soldier, was socially too junior to be his commander and he was unwilling to serve under him; the subsequent campaigns of both men suffered from the antagonism which had developed because of that. Chandos died after being wounded in a rather bizarre incident during a minor skirmish on 1 January 1370; he was well respected and admired on both sides and his death was a serious loss to the English forces of his military experience and judgement.

With Edmund, Pembroke joined the Black Prince, already suffering from the wasting complaint which was to take his life, and John of Gaunt, Edward's third son to survive infancy, who was of increasing importance in England's strategy and campaigns. Pembroke had earlier been created a Knight of the Garter by the king. An operation through Anjou culminated in October 1370 with the siege of Limoges, which was taken by storm, followed by a massacre of some of the inhabitants, although modern historians have judged that the extent of the carnage was overstated by contemporaries. Froissart described 'pillagers, active to do mischief, running through the town, slaying men, women and children, according to their orders'. He also mentioned a combat during the fighting for the town in which three English knights fought three French ones, with Pembroke up against Roger de Beaufort 'who was but a simple esquire'. The Black Prince watched the struggle from his carriage, in which he had to travel because of his illness, and 'looked on the combat with great pleasure'; eventually the French knights surrendered. At the end of the campaign the Black Prince returned to England while Edmund and Pembroke remained in Aquitaine under Gaunt's command, before Pembroke, too, went back to England, attending Parliament in February and March 1371. Thus far his career was similar to Mauny's in his early days, and the English forces were more-or-less maintaining their position in western France, despite a determined French resurgence.[3]

Pembroke was in London during the early months of 1372 and so probably was at Mauny's funeral. All of Mauny's lands in England and the Low Countries passed to Pembroke, who sent two knights to Hainault to secure the property there: with that influx to add to his existing estates Pembroke had become a very wealthy man.[4] His standing as a soldier was also high and in April he was appointed to succeed John of Gaunt in command in Aquitaine. According to Froissart, the Gascons and Poitevins had asked that Pembroke be appointed, and the king concurred.

The Council pursued the policy that the defence of Aquitaine should be carried out and supported locally, and so Pembroke was ordered to raise an army there, being entrusted with £12,000, enough to pay the wages of 3,000 men for a year. In June his fleet of three warships and a dozen smaller vessels sailed, aiming to land at La Rochelle, which was in English hands. But France had earlier negotiated an alliance with Castile by which the Castilians provided a fleet of galleys, which posed a real threat to English control of their seaborne communications with western France.

The position was complicated by Gaunt's marriage in 1371 to Constanza, daughter and heir of the murdered Pedro I of Castile, who claimed the throne and was in exile. Gaunt could thereby claim to be king of Castile and indeed issued documents with that title. He was aware of the threat posed by the Castilian fleet but nothing had been done to counter it before Pembroke sailed.[5]

The French court had prior knowledge of Pembroke's expedition and its objectives and the Castilians were awaiting his flotilla off La Rochelle. They had a more powerful force than the English fleet, and their galleys were not only larger but had greater manoeuvrability in the confined waters off the town than did the English vessels. The Castilian ships had tall towers at prow and stern, giving them the advantage of height over the English ones, and Froissart believed that they carried some cannon. Furthermore, the English force was a small one that probably consisted of just the 160 men of Pembroke's household, besides the sailors. The fight lasted into a second day and during the night the citizens of La Rochelle were entreated to assist the English with their own vessels, but they refused. The outcome was a complete victory for the Castilians; the English ships were destroyed, most of the sailors were killed and the money for the new army was lost. Just a few prisoners were taken, including Pembroke.[6]

As Edward III's son-in-law, Pembroke could have been expected to be worth a substantial ransom, which the English would be glad to pay: the news of the defeat and the capture of the earl had 'greatly afflicted' the king. But the Castilians took him and the other prisoners to Santander, where they were put in chains and held in poor conditions, which Froissart condemned and compared to practices in Germany. There was no haste to negotiate a sum for his release and the prominent French soldier

Bertrand du Guesclin, who had been made Constable of France after campaigning in Castile, obtained the rights to Pembroke late in 1372, in exchange for two lordships in Spain which he had received as part payment for his services. He negotiated with the English court and an agreement was reached for a ransom of 120,000 francs, part of which was paid in advance to some merchants of Bruges.

Du Guesclin had moved Pembroke from Santander to Paris and with the agreement in place and the contract sealed he arranged for him to be taken to Bruges to complete the exchange, but Pembroke died on the way of 'a fever, or some other sickness', on 16 April 1375. Edward III then requested the return of the advance, which was duly paid him by the merchants, and although Du Guesclin sued them for the money, his claim, which he pursued for three years, was not conceded; after all the earl had not been released according to the agreement and so the ransom could not be paid.[7] Pembroke's capture and imprisonment contrasted with Mauny's career, who through military judgement and experience had come out on top, as a receiver and not a payer of ransoms.

The subsequent death of Pembroke's widow in 1384 and son John five years later ended the line of descent of Mauny's estate; the earldom became extinct, but the Barony of Hastings was successfully claimed by Reynold Grey, third Baron Grey of Ruthin. That was on the basis that his paternal grandmother Elizabeth, wife of Roger Grey, was the daughter of John, first Lord Hastings. Not only did Reynold, Lord Grey, obtain the title, but he also inherited many of the Hastings family estates to add to his inheritance from his father's death in 1388 of lands in several counties, centred on Bedfordshire and Buckinghamshire. They included Mauny's lands. Reynold died in 1440.[8]

The defeat at La Rochelle left England's possessions in south-west France badly exposed; the loss of the money to pay the soldiers meant that the new army could not be raised and because of the situation elsewhere military resources were stretched and control of them was uncertain. Within a few months of the debacle at La Rochelle French forces had occupied Poitou, most of Saintonge and the county of Angouléme, and the rest of the English possessions in the west seemed to be in danger. A part of the military response was a *chevauchée* by a force of 6,000 men under John of Gaunt, which left Calais on 4 August 1373. It proved to be a long and difficult campaign during which the army encountered stiff and shrewdly organised French resistance, which lengthened its march, and the remnants of the force arrived in Bordeaux in December in a distinctly bedraggled state, with some of the knights on foot, having been forced to leave their horses behind.

The expedition had covered 800 miles, which was impressive, but there was precious little to show for the cost of £80,000. Without the strategies and military leadership required, further territory was lost to the French until only Bordeaux and a narrow strip of land around it remained in English hands. This caused them to pursue peace negotiations more seriously and talks began in Bruges in March 1375 and continued for a year, but without agreement being reached; the main stumbling block remained the question of sovereignty over Aquitaine. Gaunt had effectively taken the senior position in directing military strategy as the king became elderly and increasingly ineffectual; he died in 1377 and the Black Prince, his heir, had predeceased him the previous year. On Edward III's direction the new king was Richard, the Black Prince's son, who was ten years old when he came to the throne on his grandfather's death.

Gaunt's military reputation had suffered badly as a result of the campaign in 1373 and he became more closely involved in government and administration, adopting a strong line against those who seemed to challenge royal authority. He was widely held responsible for the policies of the young Richard II and the taxation levied. That helped to make him especially unpopular in London, where political stability was threatened by the high costs of the war and the lack of military success; Gaunt was the chief scapegoat for the government's failings. Offsetting Gaunt's unpopularity was William Walworth, who was a key figure in the early years of the Charterhouse through his expert knowledge of London's affairs and its financial operations, and his connections with senior figures, probably through lending to them; he was also a prominent lender to the crown. Walworth was elected Sheriff in 1370 and chosen as an MP for London in the following year and was again selected as MP in 1377.

After Edward III's futile attempt to lead a successful campaign in France, in 1372, war finance was handled not by the royal wardrobe but by a separate war-treasurer. The system lapsed in 1375 but the House of Commons pressed for its revival and in 1377 Walworth and John Philpot, another London merchant, were appointed as joint war-treasurers. Between December 1377 and February 1379, they accounted for £145,651 received, which was disbursed wholly on the war, and they probably continued to act in the role for some time longer. This required Walworth to satisfy the government, the Commons, the taxpayers and the military, which he apparently achieved.[9] That he was entrusted with such a sensitive and demanding position reflected his standing and probity, and goes some way to explaining why he had been given the honour of being the founder of the first cell to be built at the Charterhouse, Cell B. He also shared the cost of the larger prior's cell, Cell A, with Mauny and used some of the wealth he had inherited from John Lovekyn towards the cost of founding Cells D, G, H and J. Walworth also assisted the Charterhouse by acquiring parcels of land to convey to the king, who transferred them to the priory to supplement the original site. He acted in the priory's interests throughout its formative years of the 1370s, while maintaining his role in London's government, succeeding Lovekyn as alderman of Bridge Ward and becoming prominent in opposing the government's interference in the City's affairs. He served as Mayor again in 1380-1, which was to prove a most difficult time to hold the post.

Partly in response to the innovative poll taxes imposed by Richard II's government, the Peasants' Revolt erupted in 1381. The rebels from Kent assembled on Blackheath on 12 June and then entered London when the gates were opened for them; those from St Albans arrived at the city on the 14th. They gained control of much of London and summarily executed those political leaders who they held responsible for policy and high taxation; Gaunt was absent in the north. In addition, Flemish residents were picked out and many of them were killed, including thirteen who had fled into the church of the Austin Friars seeking sanctuary, yet were dragged out and slain. The rioters beheaded one Roger Leget in Cheapside and set fire to two of his buildings, which later became the site of Barnard's Inn. The rebels wrecked the Marshalsea prison in Southwark, as well as a 'house of stews [brothel] hard by London bridge'. The Temple was attacked. John Stow, writing at the end of the sixteenth century, commented that the rebels 'plucked down the houses and lodgings' and burned documents and books in the street. They especially vented their anger upon the Middle Temple gatehouse, the lodgings of Sir Robert Hales, prior of the Hospitallers' house of St John in Clerkenwell, who was most unpopular for his role in the imposition of the poll tax. Hales was seized in the Tower, which the rebels were able to enter without any resistance, as was Simon Sudbury, Archbishop of Canterbury, who had supported the proposal to establish the Charterhouse when he was Bishop of London. Both men were summarily beheaded, together with a Franciscan friar and one of the king's serjeants-at-arms.

St John's priory at Clerkenwell was burnt, picked out for its connection with Hales, although the Charterhouse was not mentioned as having suffered, even though it was closer to the city than was St John's. Perhaps the rebels were respectful of the Carthusians, or its still relatively few buildings were spared because of their association with Mauny and Walworth, who was generally popular despite being a member of one of the two factions vying for predominance among the City's elite. When the gates were opened to allow the rebels in he had acted with the agreement of 'the rich men of the city', who were fearful that keeping the gates closed would so enrage the rebels that they would then burn the suburbs.

John of Gaunt's unpopularity made his Savoy Palace a prime target. The rebels forced an entry there and having been told that they ought not to benefit from his ill-gotten wealth by looting his valuables, they burned many of the palace's contents and threw gold, silver and precious objects into the Thames. Mistakenly thinking that some boxes contained gold, they set them on fire, unaware that they held gunpowder and the ensuing explosion wrecked the great hall. The flames and smoke trapped thirty-two men in the duke's wine cellar, and they died there. The Chronicle of London recorded that the rebels 'brenden the dukes place of Lancastre called Saveye, and wold fayn an had the duke of Lancastre, but as grace was he myghte not be founden'. The buildings then 'lay in Ashes and Rubbish' and were not rebuilt, its ruins remaining as a visible reminder of the revolt.[10]

The rebels were eventually subdued at Smithfield, with the death of Wat Tyler, one of the Kentish insurgents' principal leaders. After a meeting between Richard II and the rebels at Mile End on the 14th, another was held on the following day at Smithfield. Tyler outlined the rebels' demands to the king, but his behaviour infuriated members of the royal entourage, one of whom insulted Tyler, perhaps acting on a prearranged plan to provoke him. Tyler tried to attack the courtier and Walworth then attempted to seize Tyler, who struck him with his dagger. Walworth was wearing armour and was unhurt and he stabbed Tyler in the neck. Tyler, wounded, took refuge in St Bartholomew's priory, but was dragged out and executed in Smithfield. The king defused a potentially serious situation by riding ahead of the rebels, telling them to follow him to Clerkenwell, which they did. Walworth returned to the City, where he had ordered the citizens' armed bands to be ready, and he now directed them to follow the king, surrounding the rebels at Clerkenwell before escorting them through London and away into Kent. The rebels could have vented their anger on the Charterhouse buildings, which were so close, but they did not and apparently were so cowed by the loss of their leader that they followed the king's instructions. The revolt then petered out. Walworth was knighted there and then by the king, together with three other aldermen.

Walworth died early in 1386 and was buried in St Michael, Crooked Lane, which he had enlarged, and not at the Charterhouse. Adam Fraunceys died in May 1375; as well as sponsoring five cells at the Charterhouse, he was co-founder of a college of chantry priests at Guildhall, in 1356, and he left money for the establishment of two chantries in St Helen, Bishopsgate church. John Luscote remained the prior through the testing times of the revolt and the apparent cooling of interest in sponsoring the building of more cells which followed. Thomas Hatfield, Bishop of Durham, sponsored two cells before his death in 1381 (their occupants were to say masses for the bishop and his family) and John Buckingham, Bishop of Lincoln from 1363, founded a cell towards the end of the century; he also sponsored one at the Coventry charterhouse and was a benefactor of the Carthusian priory at Hull. Luscote died in 1398 and Buckingham in 1399; they were almost the last members of the generation who had known Mauny and had been enthused by his vision of establishing the Carthusian priory.

The death of John of Gaunt in February 1399 can be taken to mark the end of Mauny's military connections. Gaunt's brothers Thomas of Woodstock and Edmund of Langley died in 1397 and 1402 respectively. When Froissart died around 1410 the last direct memories of Mauny's versions of his exploits came to an end, although they were not lost because Froissart had done him full justice in the pages of his chronicles, which he had continued to revise in his later years.

English control of Calais was one of the significant achievements of Mauny's career, in its capture, holding against attack, fortification, settlement and administration in the aftermath of its occupation. It became an English town, sending two MPs to Parliament and having parallel civil and royal administrations, a recognition of its strategic importance. It served as a base where armies could be assembled before setting off on a campaign or a raid into enemy territory, and as a haven to which they returned to be disbanded. In 1380 an expedition under the Earl of Buckingham left the town on a destructive campaign which ended in Brittany, but with little achieved. The strategy, so effective in the past, no longer produced the anticipated results.

Calais was given another role in the approach adopted in the early stages of Richard II's reign, when it became one of the ports regarded as 'barbicans', designed as coastal strongholds from which English naval forces could defend seaborne communications and counter French preparations for an invasion of England. The others were Cherbourg, Brest and the Gascon ports. The area around Calais, known as the Pale, covered some 150 square miles and was defended by a number of subordinate fortifications, the chief of which were of Guisnes, Hammes, and 'a great fort called Marc, which is situated in the midst of the district'. Calais itself was very well fortified, with strong walls punctuated by towers and a wide moat, with two moats on the south side. The castle stood in the north-west of the town, from which it was separated by a ditch. Other towers were mounted with artillery covering the town, harbour and surrounding countryside. Calais was costly to maintain; as well as the garrison, stocks of provisions and military stores were held there, requiring frequent voyages from London and the ports of south-east England, especially Sandwich. Calais took about 29 per cent of the money spent on the war between 1369 and 1375 and when it was designated as one of the barbicans costs settled down at about £20,000 a year.

Calais's commercial economy was enhanced when it was designated as the staple for the export of English wool. The staple was a centre of distribution to which merchandise was taken for sale, and it was given a monopoly status; all ships carrying English wool for export in 1380-1 went to Calais, and in 1397-8 only two ships with cargoes of wool did not go there. Those who operated the staple were mostly London merchants and their business contributed to the town's commercial character, for it was not solely a garrison town and the port from which voyages to and from England were undertaken. But its trade changed somewhat as the volume of wool exports declined; in the late fourteenth century the number of ships going to Calais fell from roughly 200 in 1370 to fewer than 100 by the end of the century.

Its military role also diminished during the period following the truce between England and France agreed in 1396, which was intended to last for twenty-eight years. When the war was resumed in 1415 under Henry V, English ambitions came to be centred on the conquest and occupation of Normandy. The English had considerable success in the early years of that phase of the war, during the late 1410s and 1420s, but the tide subsequently turned and France not only re-conquered Normandy by 1450 but also took England's long-held territories in the south-west. The war effectively came to an end in 1453 with the French victory at Castillon and the surrender of Bordeaux, leaving only Calais and the Channel Islands in English hands.

Calais had endured a siege in 1436 when the French deployed formidable artillery batteries against it; the terrain and fortifications which had made Edward III's capture of the town such a major operation again favoured the defenders and the French were compelled to draw off. A further attempt to take the town in 1442 was also unsuccessful. The English government renovated the defences and added two new bastions, as well as enhancing its artillery with the deployment of twenty-four new cannon. During the Wars of the Roses it was both a place of refuge for those out of favour and a town where forces could be gathered with which to invade England. Its garrison and those of the Tower of London and Berwick-upon-Tweed was the only standing army and so the position of Captain of Calais was an important one. The

Earl of Warwick held the post from 1455 and used it as his base for both interventions in English politics and opening connections with European rulers. He maintained the garrison by raising money from piratical activities in the Channel, preying on French and other vessels. The size of the garrison varied but it generally consisted of at least 500 men; in 1356 it numbered about 950 and in 1383 just over 1,000. A Venetian diplomat at the end of the fifteenth century wrote that 'there are always about 800 chosen men, including horse and foot, on guard at Calais'.[11]

In 1459 Warwick took 600 of its soldiers to fight in England for the Yorkist cause and a Lancastrian force failed to enter the town later that year, when Warwick kept it as a Yorkist stronghold. After the successful Yorkist campaign in 1460 which culminated in the capture of Henry VI, Warwick's position as Captain of Calais was renewed and he held the position until his death at the battle of Barnet in 1471. In 1475 the town's former role as a base for operations was revived when Edward IV assembled a large army there for an invasion of France, but the campaign culminated in a treaty, not a military conflict. Henry VII and Henry VIII both assembled forces there for military campaigns and showy diplomatic missions; Henry VIII was based there in 1544 before his capture of Boulogne.

In the early sixteenth century Antonio de Beatis, a chaplain of Luigi d'Aragona, the Cardinal of Aragon, complained that Calais 'for all its strength is not a very fine town'. But the defences were strong, with walls 'extremely thick and the broad ditches full of water'; he thought that it was impregnable because of three or four water channels 'sunken like sewers', which ran from the sea and were controlled by sluices, so that the land around the town could be flooded. He noted that 'All the merchandise from England is discharged there, and all who want to go to that island embark there. Being of the highest importance to the King, as his only port on the mainland, he guards it ... with great fondness and jealousy.'[12] The French continued to harass the Pale from time to time; the chronicler Edward Hall included a detailed account of a French raid in 1524.

In 1554 an investigation was held in Calais prompted by the suspicion that a conspiracy was being hatched to betray the town to the French. The Emperor was informed that 'the plan to fall upon Calais is being put into execution. The French have brought up boats on carts to make pontoons and cross over the rivers and swamps on one side of Calais. The King of France has given pensions of 100, 200, 300 and 500 crowns to English refugee gentlemen, with instructions to levy troops for his service, which forces are to meet together at Compiègne.'[13]

Philip of Spain, Mary's consort, had taken England into a war with France which had seen a spectacular success by his forces at St Quentin, where a French army which was to relieve the town's beleaguered garrison was soundly defeated and the town was taken by storm. Philip's generals had then disbanded some of their forces anticipating a sluggish winter campaign and probably thinking that the war was all but over, but the French under the Duc de Guise saw an opportunity to strike at Calais. They began to filter troops through Picardy, to assemble outside Calais.

Giovanni Michiel, the Venetian ambassador to France, passed through Calais in March 1557. He considered that for all its fortifications the town was vulnerable on the sea side because there were 'neither moats, flanks, nor platforms within, the town being thought secured by the sea, from which it is only separated by the width of the road'. A sharp frost towards the end of 1557 froze the marshes around the town and Guise took the opportunity to send his men across the ice and seize Rybank, at the entrance to the harbour. The French also moved their artillery across the frozen ground and began to batter the walls, but the Duc 'could not make any effect, and was compelled, on the contrary, to retire'.[14] An English flotilla arrived the next day, but the crews refused to attack the harbour area in the face of the French artillery.

On the following day Surian reported that 'the French have taken the Castle of the harbour of Calais, which is a very small one, and fronts the town, nor is it more than 80 or 100 paces from it, and it is not strong ... the townspeople were battering it, having first burnt and levelled a suburb of houses, which impeded the fire of the artillery, so that the French will be compelled to abandon it'. But they were able to hold on and eventually capture both town and castle. The fortifications in the Pale, Hammes and Guisnes, were untenable once the principal fortress had been taken and the French were able to capture them in mid-January. Three days after his previous report Surian summarised the situation: 'Today, at noon, news arrived of the entry into Calais of the French, which ... is of greater importance than any other intelligence that could be heard at this present time.' This was very troubling news,

> ...both on account of the actual loss and the subsequent detriment; the French, on the other hand, having made the greatest possible acquisition in these parts, well nigh expelling the English from Flanders, and depriving them of that port which rendered them masters of the Channel, and of a fortress which they held in such great account, and giving them such vast repute, they being thus enabled to harass France and Flanders, and all these States at any time.[15]

Not for the first time or the last, a supposedly impregnable fortress had fallen to an assault and what had taken Edward III eleven months to accomplish was achieved by Guise within a few days.

Resentment at the failure to obtain any benefit from the property in Calais which Mauny had assigned to the London Charterhouse had lingered until at least the late fifteenth century, but the priory had been dissolved almost twenty years before the loss of Calais. Those two events ended the direct connection between Mauny, his monastic legacy and the continental wars against France, although that thought would not have so much as passed across the mind of contemporaries, who wrestled with the more immediate consequences of the French capture of Calais. The reaction in London was shock: the queen famously said, 'When I am dead and opened you shall find Calais lying in my heart.' The diarist Henry Machyn's reaction was that this was 'the hevest tydyngs to London and to England that ever was hard of'.[16]

10

THE DISSOLUTION

Despite its prosperity and the respect in which it was held, in the mid-1530s the Charterhouse faced the threat of the closure of the monasteries and appropriation of their assets by the crown. That was advocated by Thomas Cromwell, Henry VIII's chief minister, and supported by the king, as part of the wider reformation of the English church, by which it broke from Rome with the king as its head. The dissolution of the monasteries would remove doubts about their members' religious affiliation and loyalty to the monarch, as well as providing a financial windfall which would considerably enhance the royal coffers.

Respect for the Carthusians may have been on the wane before then. Erasmus's corrosive satire *Praise of Folly* was written when the author was staying with Thomas More in London in 1509. It mocks monks and theologians mercilessly and says of the Carthusians that they were the order 'amongst whom alone piety lies hidden and buried, hidden in fact so well that you can scarcely ever get a glimpse of it'. He would have had knowledge of the London Charterhouse through More. In 1516 Erasmus commented that the Carthusians, and two other orders, were less likely to grant individual freedoms to one of their order than were the popes. He added the disapproving remark that they 'do not even accept the pope's authority on such a point, though when he gives them wide-ranging privileges and prerogatives they count his authority sacrosanct and almost set it above Christ Himself'.[1]

Erasmus's *New Testament* appeared in 1516 and was criticised by John Batmanson, a member of the Carthusian order who was then prior of the house at Hinton, Somerset, and was to become prior of the London Charterhouse in 1529. Thomas More responded on Erasmus's behalf, addressing Batmanson as 'My old, dear friend', before attacking not only his lack of learning but also his background, with the acerbic comment that 'as if to reside for ever in the same spot and, like a clam or sponge, to cling eternally to the same rock were the ultimate of sanctity'. That could be read as a criticism of the Carthusians, cloistered away in their priories, or of monastic life generally. Either way, it seems to be a damning indictment from someone who had experienced the system at first hand. Erasmus, too, had found the monastic life to be uncongenial, writing in 1514 that 'I never liked the monastic life; and I liked it less than ever after I had tried it'.

On the other hand, their fellow humanist John Colet, Dean of St Paul's, was allowed to build a house within the Charterhouse at Sheen and, frequently harassed by the Bishop of London, Richard FitzJames, he wrote that 'every day I look forward to my retirement and retreat with the Carthusians'.[2] While some of the intelligensia were becoming so uneasy with the Carthusian order that they were openly disapproving, the London Charterhouse was still attracting donations, but that support was not enough to allow them to resist the royal will.

As Cromwell gathered evidence to support his plans, a critical report on the London Charterhouse was to be expected. Its compilation was entrusted to Jasper Fyllol, one of the king's assistant commissioners, an MP in the Reformation Parliament and an evangelical. He was lodged in one of the monks' cells so that he could gain a thorough understanding of the priory's life and operations at first hand.

One of Fyllol's criticisms was that the priory was continuing to dispense the usual level of alms despite inflation eroding the value of its revenues. In the past, when there had been fewer members in the priory, the shortfall between revenue and expenditure had been covered by 'the benevolence and charitye off the cite of London'. The implication was that this could no longer be relied on and so, with rising prices, some cuts to the budget were necessary. They could be resolved only by reducing the numbers in residence, the scale of the provisions and the quality of the diet, described as 'dainty fare'. Provisions could be served more economically if the monks sat in the refectory four to a mess, so that the food which was currently serving twelve people would then serve twenty of them 'honestlye'. More controversially, he challenged the monks' commitment to a vegetarian diet by commenting that if any of the monks 'luste to eate fleshe, yt were pitie to constrayn hym to eat fishe, for such constrayned abstinence shall never be merytorious'. Two lay brothers managed the buttery and it was recommended that they should be replaced by two laymen, for 'in those ii offyces lye waste of the howse'. And there was little security for the priory's provisions, for there were as many as twenty-two keys to the buttery door and they were held by twenty-two people.

Fyllol raised a similar point regarding the supposed isolation of the monks, who 'wold be callyd solitary, but to the cloyster door ther be xxiiii [24] keys, in the hands of xxiiii persons', so that there was coming and going to the monks' cells by people 'with tales and tydings'. In the original layout, the prior's cell had overlooked the door into the cloister, but with his accommodation now being to the east of the church he could not have oversight of the visitors.[3]

The treatment of the London priory was significant for the whole Carthusian community in England, because of its size and standing; its annual revenues were £642, almost a fifth of the £2,947 received by the nine Carthusian houses. The Henrician changes to the English church met with stiff resistance from some members of the order. In 1534 the monks at the London house subscribed to the first Act of Succession. Nevertheless, their misgivings were such that John Houghton, the prior, and Hugh Middlemore, the procurator, were briefly incarcerated in the Tower of London before they were persuaded to swear. Regarding the annulment of the king's marriage to Katherine of Aragon, Houghton was said to have told the king's commissioners that 'it pertained not to his vocation and calling nor to that of his subjects to meddle in or discuss the king's business, neither could they or ought they to do so, and that it did not concern him whom the king wished to divorce or marry, so long as he was not asked for any opinion'. But in front of the whole community he made the more dangerous comment that 'he could not understand how it was possible that a marriage ratified by the Church and so long unquestioned should now be undone'.[4]

It required three visits to the Charterhouse by the commissioners to obtain the oath from all the monks. The third visit was by Bishop Roland Lee, as a commissioner, and Sir Thomas Kytson, one of the sheriffs of London, who were accompanied by a detachment of men-at-arms. The corporation had no jurisdiction at the Charterhouse as it lay outside the City, but in a wider dispute which was substantially about jurisdictions, the intimidating presence of armed men more than offset the niceties of who could exercise authority.

Fyllol had managed to gain access to the prior's and procurator's cells, where he found 'three or four foreign printed books of as foul heresies and errors as may be. As one or two books are never printed alone, but hundreds, their cells must be better searched, for I can find few. They have great pleasure in reading such erroneous doctors and little or none in reading the New Testament or other good books.' When twenty-four copies of a reformist book were given to be distributed among the monks 'many took them, saying they would read them if the president licensed them. The third day they sent them back, saying that the president had commanded them so to do.' One of the monks, John Rochester, took a copy 'and kept it four or five days and then burnt it'.

As well as such blatant defiance, the government's probing also revealed unhappiness and dissent among some of the brethren. Cromwell went to the priory several times to interview the monks and urge their compliance. They included Thomas Salter, who castigated Houghton as 'this undiscreet prior'. After an interview with Cromwell, he was apparently held incommunicado within the priory, 'more like an infidel than a Christian man', although eventually he was allowed some degree of freedom, if only to go as far as the Great Cloister. He had written to Cromwell describing his problems, which included fear of going to confession because the Brothers would betray his revelations, so that, as he was unconfessed, he could neither attend mass nor take the sacrament. He pointed out that he and a fellow monk, John Darley, would both 'like to be out of the Cloister'. It seems that Salter not only achieved that before the priory was dissolved, but had attracted the government's favour, so that he received an annual pension of £5 from 1542 until his death in 1558, which was paid by the Court of Augmentations, the body entrusted with the revenues and lands of the dissolved monasteries.[5]

Cromwell gave considerable attention to the London Carthusians; in December 1535 he was said to be 'now much busied with the monks of the Charterhouse'. It seems that he had hopes of saving the monastery, if not as a Carthusian priory then as a scholarly evangelical community, with the life of its members based upon intensive Bible study. He even felt confident enough to suggest that there would be a royal pardon for the remaining monks 'for all heresies and treasons by any of them committed before that day'. But many members of the community felt unable to acknowledge the king as head of the English church, expressed in the Act of Supremacy of 1535, and gave Cromwell no support in his efforts to save the priory. One of his agents, the Catholic-turned-evangelical John Rastell, who like Fyllol was an MP in the Reformation Parliament, was arrested after delivering a sermon there in 1536; he had been assiduous in his efforts to convert the monks, visiting the house daily during the spring of 1535. He died in the Tower in the summer of 1536, after complaining that he was 'oppressed by extreme poverty and long imprisonment, forsaken by his kinsmen, destitute of friends'. He had made little or no impression on the Carthusians, nor had others who preached there or tried to debate with the monks.

That practice was systematically applied, with an order that 'there should be three or four times every week during this visitation, a sermon made by some discreet, well learned man, and all the monks, officers, and servants, to be caused to be present; none exception, save only sickness; and the said preachers to have their chambers there, and meat and drink, that they might quietly study therefore during that time'. All those efforts were to no avail. Cromwell's agent Thomas Bedell reported to his master that some members of the priory 'be minded to offer them self in sacrifice to the great idol of Rome' and in the summer of 1535 Dr Ortiz, a professor of theology at the University of Paris, told the Empress that nine Carthusians were in London 'determined to die'. It was noted that 'the lay brethren be more obstinate, and more forward, and more unreasonable than the monks'.[6]

The Carthusians' attitude provoked a sharp response from the king, who complained that 'the Charterhouse in London is not ordered as I would have had it'. He said that he had told Cromwell 'a great while ago to put the monks out of the house', yet Cromwell was telling people that they had been acquiescent. The king would have none of it and insisted that 'seeing that they have been so long obstinate, I will not now admit their obedience'. That effectively was the end for the house; the king had not forgotten and would not forgive.

Houghton was the first to be imprisoned and tried, for treason. He was convicted and was executed on 4 May 1535; his body was dismembered and one of his arms fixed above the gateway to the London Charterhouse. Also executed at the same time were the priors of the Carthusian monasteries at Beauvale and Axholme. During that summer three other senior members of the London house were imprisoned and executed. In 1536, fourteen monks and lay brothers were removed to other Carthusian houses and the Bridgettine abbey at Syon and two who had been transferred to the Charterhouse at Hull were subsequently executed; in the following year twenty of the brethren took the required oath while ten more still refused and were imprisoned in Newgate, where five of them died within a month. At the end of June a letter from John Husee in London to Lord Latimer on current affairs mentions, almost incidentally, that 'eight of the monks of the Charter House are dead in Newgate'. Two more were executed in 1540.

Those who died in Newgate probably were the victims of gaol fever, or typhus, in the prison's squalid conditions; the antiquarian and historian John Stow later wrote that they had 'died in prison with stink and miserably smothered'. They would have been vulnerable to infection. One of the monks, Nicholas Rawlins, had earlier written asking to be released from his vows so that he could return to the status of a secular priest and now told Cromwell that he had been sick for nine weeks and while in the priory he had

> ...never had my health a fortnight together. If I continue here I shall die; it is so hard, what with fasting and watching. There are not six whole monks in this cloister but they have one infirmity or other, which will be their death sooner than God would that it should be.

A year after the deaths in Newgate, Hugh Latimer, Bishop of Worcester, was complaining not about the harshness of their treatment but rather the mildness of their conditions in prison 'in a fair chamber'.[7]

The Emperor's ambassador, Eustace Chapuys, explained to his master that the leading Carthusians had been executed 'for no other cause than their having said and maintained that the Pope was the true chief and sovereign of the universal Christian Church, and that, according to God, reason, and conscience, it did not appertain to this King to usurp the sovereignty of the Church and supremacy over the English clergy'. He indicated the importance of the process by describing the presence at the executions of leading figures among the nobility and court, including the king's illegitimate son Henry Fitzroy, the Duke of Norfolk, Thomas and George Boleyn (the queen's father and brother) and Sir Henry Norris, who, rather bizarrely, wore masks and were dressed as if they were 'going on an expedition to the Scotch borders'.[8] When Anne Boleyn fell out of favour with the king, her brother George and Norris were both tried, convicted and in 1536 they, like the Carthusians, were publicly executed.

The keen interest in the Carthusians' fate did not necessarily reflect sympathy for them; their support had ebbed away, despite their previous high standing in London. In June 1537, when attention was again focused on the London priory, the Court of Aldermen reversed an earlier resolution to press for the continuance of the house and decided 'that no labour shalbe made by thys Cytye yn that bihalf'.[9] Edward Hall provides some indication why effective support for the Carthusians did not emerge. He was a lawyer at Gray's Inn and a chronicler of English history who was in good favour with the court; in 1533 the City 'at the request of the King's letters' elected him common serjeant, and in June 1535 the king wrote again, this time for 'our well-beloved subject Edward Hall to be now promoted to the office of under sheriff', which was done the following day. So his account of the proceedings concerning the Charterhouse is not wholly impartial, although it may be authentic.

Reporting the trial of William Exmewe, Sebastian Newdigate and Humphrey Middlemore, Hall wrote that in court,

> They behaved them selfes very stifly and stubbornly, for hearying their inditement red how trayterously they had spoken against the kynges Majestie his croune and dignitye, they neyther blushed nor bashed [were abashed] at it, but very folishly and hipocritically knowledged their treason whiche maliciously they avouched, havynge no lernying for their defence, but rather being asked dyvers questions, they used a malicious silence.

When they were later interrogated in the Tower of London they explained that they had refused to answer because 'they thought those men whiche was the Lorde Crumwell and other that there satte upon them in judgement to be heretiques and not of the Churche of God, and therfore not worthy to be either aunswered or spoken unto'. Others would have drawn the same conclusion as Hall, that 'therefore as they deserved, they received'. In other words, they refused to acknowledge the authority of the court and so could offer no defence and the obdurate manner with which they had treated the crown's commissioners earlier had damaged their case.[10]

In all, ten monks and six lay brothers lost their lives. Despite the forcible removal of many of the community, the priory continued in being, and some monks co-operated with Cromwell's agents. Those who had not been removed to gaol eventually accepted the king's headship of the church and in 1536 William Trafford, from Beauvale, replaced Houghton, becoming the thirteenth and last prior. The house was surrendered to the king on 10 June 1537, but the remaining occupants, with an influx from other houses, were allowed to stay until it was suppressed in November 1538. The prior received an annual pension of £20 and the remainder £5 per annum; sixteen monks who were to be paid were listed in December 1538.[11]

After the dissolution of the priory its plate and ornaments were appropriated by the king's commissioners, glass was taken down 'for fear of stealing' and filled twenty-two cases, and cisterns and new lead pipes were also removed for safe keeping. The contents of the church must have been valuable, for a certain richness to the interior is revealed in the report prepared by Henry VIII's commissioners in March 1539. At the high altar was a reredos of carved bone, possibly ivory, with the story of the passion, flanked by images of SS John the Baptist and Peter. The front of the high altar was decorated with an alabaster carving with the trinity and other images. The other altars were also embellished with painted and gilt images and those in the choir were separated by wainscot partitions. The chapels of St John the Evangelist, St Jerome and St Katherine were partly wainscoted. In his will, proved in 1515, Sir Thomas Thwaites, a mercer, had bequeathed to the priory all the 'jewels and stuff' from his own chapel, to be used in the chapel of St Jerome, where he was to be buried.[12]

The monks were authorised to remove 'suche thynges as was meyte for them', the contents of the cells, and by November 1537 some cells were 'deffasyd' and 'spolyd'. Much of the wainscoting was taken away; one man persuaded the caretaker to deliver to him the wainscot from one cell 'as it stood' and one Gerrard Haydon, who was described as the 'receiver of the Charterhouse', had filled a house full of wainscott 'and has since carried it off'. Wainscot from 'one great cell' was sold for £1 6s 8d and the caretaker re-used enough glass to repair a dozen windows in the porter's lodge. Other items were sold to help defray the commissioners' costs, including seven seats from the church and the great clock; all the new timber in the woodyard was taken for the proprietor of The Splayed Eagle in Gracechurch Street, the wainscot in 'the corner cell', boards from the bakehouse, and thirty-two lead pipes and six lead cisterns were also among the items removed.

The furniture and furnishings were not overlooked and were taken away, including four 'great painted tables standing in every four corner' of the cloister (presumably altars), as were the 'hangings' and a plan described as 'a paper called mappa mundi'. Nor were the gardens and orchard forgotten, perhaps not surprisingly because the orchard had a reputation for producing fine apples. One of Thomas Cromwell's agents sent him a dish of apples from the Charterhouse, with the comment that 'if they like you they shall be kept for you as long as they last, and provide for the convent almonds and figs accordingly'. The king's gardener took cuttings from at least ninety-one trees and removed three loads of bay trees to the royal garden at Chelsea.[13]

Despite those depredations, in March 1539 the bells and some of the lead remained, and the buildings themselves were intact in the years immediately after the priory was dissolved.[14] They included the guest-house and former pulpit house, a kitchen and buttery, 'certain lodgings' with a hall, a wine cellar, the old brewhouse with four vats, a horse mill, three stables, a sawpit, the washing-house, a place called the fish-hall with four privies beneath it, two chambers and the water conduit, and a new brewhouse with three vats.

Twenty of the monks' cells remained in the custody of the Court of Augmentations, two of which were 'spoiled', and five more were assigned to Sir Marmaduke Constable, a soldier and a Knight of the Body to the king, together with two houses. There were two more cells, one of which was occupied by the caretaker, who was paid 8d per day and described himself as 'a poor man'.[15] Despite his presence, and he denied any wrong-doing, there is a sense that the depredations were carried out piecemeal, in addition to authorised sales, to help pay the court's expenses.

The church was also retained by the crown and was used for storing and repairing the king's tents and pavilions, and as a workshop for making new structures for his use during military campaigns. When he was preparing to go abroad, that part of the site was a hive of activity; in the spring of 1544 almost 450 men were at work there and suppliers of materials and tools were arriving in large numbers. The operation was under the control of

Sir Thomas Cawarden, a courtier who came into prominence in the late 1530s and who was appointed a gentleman of the privy chamber in 1539/40. In 1544 he was appointed keeper of the pavilions, hales and tents, and – a separate appointment – Master of the Revels, and he organised the Boulogne expedition that year. His efforts brought him a knighthood.[16] The king's pavilions were stored at the Charterhouse after his return to England. In 1545 the priory's flesh kitchen and the adjoining granary in the outer precinct, with the kitchen garden, were granted to John Bernard on his appointment as Clerk Comptroller of the king's tents, halls and pavilions 'and of the revels, masks and masking garments'.[17]

Members of the Bassano family, musicians and musical instrument makers from Venice, were assigned the eastern part of the former priory, perhaps because of the presence of those entrusted with paraphernalia for the king's masques and revels; it would have been a practical arrangement to place the musicians and organisers of such court events together. The Bassanos occupied five cells on the south side of the Great Cloister and four on its east side, as well as the prior's new cell and other buildings around the east end of the church, with the pulpit house of the Black Death burial ground on the church's south side. The family, possibly of Jewish origin, had lived in Bassano del Grappa in north-east Italy and later in Venice. They had come to England during the 1530s, when war between the Venetian republic and the Ottoman empire made Venice less than ideal for them, which coincided with an enticing offer from Henry VIII's court, skilfully timed by Cromwell. They had settled in the city by the end of the decade and were living at the Charterhouse before June 1542, where they remained until 1552.

In 1540 the brothers obtained appointments as 'the King's servants', forming a royal recorder consort. The recruitment of the brothers may have been intended to enhance the royal music consort in time for the wedding of Henry and Anne of Cleves, and for her coronation, which was anticipated in the spring of 1540, although it did not take place. A factor in their move to London may have been an assurance that a development of the range and capability of Henry VIII's court musicians was planned. In 1540 a group of five violists also arrived, two of whom were fellow Venetians and the others were from Milan and Cremona. A sixth member was added to that consort in 1545, with the arrival of another violist, Mark Anthony Galliardello from Brescia, within Venice's mainland territories. Those musicians probably brought with them, or soon adopted, violins as well as viols; by 1545 they were documented as having violins, which were then evolving into a recognisably distinct instrument. The two groups of players surely would have invigorated the musical life of the court and beyond. They also influenced the next generation of English composers.

The Bassanos certainly seemed to have given satisfaction, for in 1545 they were granted letters of denization, as were the five children born to two of them, including Alvise's eldest son Augustine, who joined the consort five years later. That entitled them to stay in England and permitted their children to inherit their property. Meanwhile Jacomo had returned to Venice, perhaps to take over the family business after the death of their father, Jeronimo. John also returned but moved between Venice and London until his death in 1570, maintaining contact between the two branches of the family.

In 1545 Alvise was described as having a 'working house' and he wished to expand the brothers' activities by adding the three cells on the east side of the cloister not already in their occupation. A few years later the Bassanos stated that they had invested approximately £300 in improving the buildings. Clearly, they were prospering, in instrument making as well as performing. A tabor-pipe made of boxwood and bearing the Bassanos' mark has been recovered from the wreck of the *Mary Rose*, which sank in the Solent in July 1545.[18]

Despite their success, the Bassanos' stay in the Charterhouse buildings was curtailed by Sir Edward (later Lord) North, who bought the former priory in 1545. The Bassanos came under considerable pressure from North to vacate the premises; his grant required him to permit them 'to enjoy their houses, &c, as long as they remain in the King's service'. After Henry's death he argued that the stipulation no longer applied; they had left by June 1552 and their cells were then demolished.[19]

Despite their expulsion from the Charterhouse, the Bassanos remained in London and prospered, as musicians and musical-instrument makers. All the members of the second generation who have been traced were court musicians and a half of the third generation followed the same path.[20] They conformed to the English church and evidently were able to weave their way through the vicissitudes in religious practices during the later years of Henry VIII and the reigns of Edward VI, Mary and Elizabeth.

The Bassanos made a significant contribution to the development of music and musical instruments in England over the following decades, maintaining their contact with Venice during the long period in the late sixteenth century when there was no diplomatic contact between the two countries, and so continuing to bring music and playing techniques to England. Evidently, they had been content in the environment provided by the buildings of the priory established by Walter Mauny more than 150 years before.

11

MANSION, ALMSHOUSE AND SCHOOL

Edward North was a lawyer, the son of a London merchant, who in 1531 became joint Clerk of the Parliaments, with Sir Brian Tuke. Because of Tuke's other commitments and ill-health, North carried out much of the routine work. He also attracted the attention of Thomas Cromwell and, perhaps through his influence, in March 1539 he was appointed as treasurer of the Court of Augmentations; in 1544 he became Chancellor of the court. North was well regarded by Henry VIII, who appointed him as one of his executors. He was knighted in 1542, was created first Baron North in 1554 and became a Privy Councillor. He successfully steered a course through the changes of reign and swings of regime, despite having briefly lost his touch by supporting Jane Grey's claim to the throne, before swiftly changing tack and favouring Mary. His position at the Court of Augmentations put him in a good position to assess the former monastic property before pulling out the ripe plum which was the Charterhouse.

Soon after North had acquired the property, in the autumn of 1545 many of the priory buildings were demolished, including the church. Mauny's tomb was broken up and removed and, like the rubble from the other demolished buildings, its materials were incorporated in North's new house. That was an impressive courtyard mansion which forms the core of the present buildings, most of it newly built, although some of the priory buildings were retained by North's builders. The service buildings were preserved, ranged around a smaller courtyard (now Wash-house Court) that was enclosed by the west range of North's new house. They also kept the gatehouse and adjoining stretch of the boundary wall, the inner arch, the chapter-house, which subsequently was adapted as the chapel, and the western cloister walk of the Great Cloister. The principal courtyard that was created (now Master's Court) was flanked by ranges containing a great hall, great chamber, long gallery and domestic quarters. The Little Cloister was demolished and its ruins subsumed within the area of Master's Court, and its outline and scale were wholly lost. The house encroached upon the south-west corner of the Great Cloister, but the greater part of that space was laid out as a formal garden.

North was not alone in converting former monastic buildings in London into a mansion. Sir Thomas Cawarden, a courtier created Keeper of the Tents and Master of the Revels in 1544, came into possession of the former monastic buildings of the Dominicans, or Blackfriars, in 1550, using the church as a store for the king's tents after they were removed from the Charterhouse. Cawarden developed the area and built himself a house there and later in the century Sir Henry Carey, Lord Hunsdon, Privy Councillor under Elizabeth I and a patron of the theatre, also lived there.

St Saviour's priory at Bermondsey was acquired by Sir Thomas Pope after the dissolution; he was treasurer of the Court of Augmentations, He built a house on the site, which he was occupying by 1546. Most of the abbey buildings were demolished, although some of the monastic fabric was incorporated into the new building, which John Stow described as 'a goodly house built of stone and timber'. In 1555, Pope sold the house, known as Bermondsey House, to Sir Robert Southwell, solicitor-general of the Court of Augmentations. Sir Thomas Audley was granted the Augustinian priory of Holy Trinity, Aldgate, by Henry VIII in 1534, two years after it became the first monastic house in London to be surrendered to the king. Audley demolished the church, steeple and other buildings to erect a mansion. After his death it passed to his daughter Margaret, Lady Audley, who married Thomas Howard, 4th Duke of Norfolk, and after she died it came into his possession and became known as Duke's Place. But by then he had acquired the mansion at the Charterhouse, which he made his principal London house.

After the closure of the Carthusian priory, during the sixteenth and seventeenth centuries the outer precinct was variously described as Charterhouse Yard, Charterhouse Churchyard or Charterhouse Close. It was colonised by senior figures; building had been taking place within it since at least 1490, as the Carthusians released plots of land on the east side for building. Among the houses there by the 1530s was one which was let to John Neville, Lord Latimer, who in 1537 wrote that 'the getting of a lease of it cost me 100 marcs [£67]' and that he had improved the property. He liked it 'because it stands in good air, out of press on the city', yet to help minimise his punishment for support of the rebellion known as the Pilgrimage of Grace he was forced to hand over the house to Thomas Cromwell's friend Sir John Russell, who had proved his loyalty and was later created first Earl of Bedford. Latimer was Catherine Parr's second husband; they married in 1533 and he died in 1543. Catherine Parr became

Henry VIII's sixth queen later that year. In 1537 her brother William Parr was recorded as living in the house in Charterhouse Square.

Another house on the east side was occupied by John Leland, a topographer and the 'King's Antiquary', who was recorded there between 1538 and 1546. A licence to alienate a property was granted by the Court of Augmentations in 1546, for a 'Tenement, &c., in the parish of St. Botolph without Aldersgate, London, within the site of the late Charterhouse, and now in tenure of John Lelande, and the adjoining tenement in tenure of Wm. Wylkynson, and the water course from the great conduit of the Charterhouse to the said two tenements'. The journeys around England during which Leland collected the materials from which he compiled his 'Itinerary' were carried out mostly in 1534-43, although it was not published until 1710, and in an authoritative edition not until the early twentieth century, edited by Lucy Toulmin Smith and issued as *The itinerary of John Leland in or about the years 1535–1543*.[1]

The square attracted such residents not only because of its proximity to the City, while being just outside its jurisdiction, but also for its social standing and the security which it offered, as an enclave with gateways at its two entrances. It provided safety if there was social unrest and isolation during an epidemic and it was judged to have comparatively clean air.

The Charterhouse was sold in 1565 to Thomas Howard, 4th Duke of Norfolk, and became known as Howard House. His plotting with Mary, Queen of Scots, to depose Elizabeth and place Mary on the throne, with himself as her consort, were known to the government for some time before he was detained under house arrest at Howard House in 1571. With time on his hands and money to spend, the duke spent quite lavishly in making alterations and additions to the property. The west cloister walk of the Great Cloister had been retained by North's builders and Norfolk now set about creating a recreational feature there by building a tennis court at its north end and forming a gallery by replacing the roof of the cloister walk with a semi-circular brick vault. The long gallery above, built after the sale to North, was removed to create an open terrace. Norfolk thereby made two features overlooking the gardens on the site of the cloister garth: a long gallery for recreation in bad weather with a terrace above for use during fine weather. It may be that this was part of a more ambitious scheme which had to be abandoned when the duke was arrested; the terrace which forms the upper level was an unambitious element not characteristic of the elaborate features he was creating.

When Dudley, Lord North, sold the Charterhouse to the Duke of Norfolk in 1565 he retained a mansion erected on its east side and described in 1563 as 'new builded'. Roger, 2nd Lord North, died there in 1600, and the house passed to Dudley North, his grandson, who spent much of 1601 and 1602 with the English forces in the Netherlands and thereafter attracted attention mainly for his extravagances at court. From at least November 1602 Roger Manners, 5th Earl of Rutland, was his tenant there and in 1630 Francis, the 6th earl, bought the property, which thereafter was known as Rutland House. An inventory of 1634 shows that it had over forty rooms, including a hall, great chamber, gallery, dining-room, drawing-room, and rooms for the 'Gentlemen' and 'Gentlewomen'. Francis died in 1632, when it passed to his second wife Cicely, who occupied it until her death in 1654. The property should then have passed to George, 2nd Duke of Buckingham, but his estate had been seized for his delinquency as a royalist and so Rutland House was confiscated and sold to two speculators, who rented it to tenants.

Rutland House was noted during the 1650s as the setting for productions staged by Sir William Davenant, who had succeeded Ben Jonson as Poet Laureate in 1638. Following an involvement in the Civil War and a period of exile in Paris in the late 1640s, he was imprisoned in 1650. Soon after his release two years later he was arrested for debt and spent a further spell in prison. He went to France in 1655 and on his return moved into Rutland House. In the following year he staged a 'Morall Representation' consisting of dialogues on various historical topics, with music by Henry Cooke, Henry Lawes, Charles Coleman and George Hudson. This he entitled *The First Days Entertainment at Rutland-House*. Later in 1656 Davenant's *The Siege of Rhodes* was performed there. The programme describes the venue as being 'At the back part of Rutland House in the upper end of Aldersgate Street'.[2] That may have been the first performance of an English opera, although Richard Flecknoe's *Ariadne Deserted by Theseus: a dramatick piece for recitative music* was printed two years earlier. Performances of such works were prohibited during the Interregnum and Davenant sailed perilously close to the wind with his productions at Rutland House. Indeed, no other theatrical performances were recorded there before the Duke of Buckingham gained possession of the property following the Restoration.

Buckingham probably did not occupy the house, but he did initiate a project to manufacture crystal glass on a part of the site and he engaged the Frenchman John de la Cam to provide the expertise. In November 1661 Martin Clifford, the duke's secretary, and Thomas Paulden were granted a licence to manufacture crystal glass, confirmed by a patent in 1662. The project failed and the duke soon granted the property to John Eaton, a mercer, in settlement of debts. Following that grant, the property came into multiple occupation and the gardens and Glasshouse Yard were developed with small houses, subsuming the remains of the monks' cells on that side of the former Great Cloister. Much grander houses were built fronting the square, including two which survive as Nos 13 and 14. The process took a long time and not until 1825, when Rutland Place was laid out, were the last sections of the former mansion of the North and Rutland families demolished.

The demolition of the priory and especially of Mauny's tomb removed a major physical reminder of the priory's origins and the connection with the great pestilence. But the name 'the Charterhouse' was retained after the dissolution, outliving the presence of the Carthusian monks and the priory as an institution. Its origins were still acknowledged in 'an inscription fixed on a stone cross' in the outer precinct, the translation of which is: 'A great Plague raging in the Year of our Lord, 1349, this Churchyard was consecrated; wherein, and within the Bounds of the present Monastery, were buried more than 50,000 Bodies of the Dead: besides many other from thence to the present Time: Whose Souls God have Mercy upon. Amen.' That was recorded by John Stow in his *Survey of London* published in 1598. His phrasing suggests that the cross was no longer there when he wrote and only the memory of the space as a burial ground remained.

A second edition of his *Survey* was published in 1603, a plague year, as was Henry Chettle's broadsheet entitled *A true list of the whole number that hath died*, which gave information on previous plague outbreaks in London and elsewhere. Chettle wrote that 'in one yeere, in a little plot of ground of 13 acres compasse, then called Spittle-croft, and now the Charter-house, was buried fifty thousand persons, besides all them that were then buried in the Churchyards, and divers places in the fields'.[3] It may be that Stow was Chettle's source, or perhaps the basis for Chettle's statement was a tradition maintained by the inscription. The comments and figures given by Stow and Chettle indicate that into the seventeenth century the area was still known to have been a plague burial ground.

Stow described Mauny as 'Sir Walter Manny, Knight, a Stranger born, Lord of the Town of Manny in the Diocese of Cambrey, beyond the Seas, who for Service done to King Edward the Third, was made Knight of the Garter'. And he summarised his role with the observation that he had

> ...caused first a Chapel to be built, where for the Space of twenty-three years offerings were made; and it is to be noted, that above one hundred thousand bodies of Christian people had in that churchyard been buried; for the said knight had purchased that place for the burial of poor people, travellers, and other that were diseased, to remain for ever; whereupon an order was taken for the avoiding of contention between the parsons of churches and that house; to wit, that the bodies should be had unto the church where they were parishioners, or died, and, after the funeral service done, had to the place where they should be buried. And the year 1371 he caused there to be founded a house of Carthusian monks, which he willed to be called the Salutation, and that one of the monks should be called prior; and he gave them the said place of thirteen acres and a rod of land, with the chapel and houses there built, for their habitation.[4]

In 1572 the Duke of Norfolk was executed for his part in the plot centred around the Florentine banker Roberto Ridolfi and the Charterhouse passed to his eldest son, Philip Howard, who held the courtesy title of Earl of Surrey and succeeded his grandfather as Earl of Arundel in 1580. He did not occupy the house, which was used as the Portuguese embassy between 1571 and 1577. Thomas Lord Paget, a prominent Roman Catholic, also lived there in the late 1570s; he fled to France in 1583 after being suspected of plotting on behalf of Mary, Queen of Scots. Following Arundel's attainder for treason in 1589, he was condemned to death. The sentence was not carried out, but he remained a prisoner for the rest of his life, and the house passed to the crown. Elizabeth restored it to the Howard family in 1601, when she granted it to Philip's Protestant half-brother Lord Thomas Howard, who was created Earl of Suffolk by King James.

Suffolk's main building activity was the erection of his very large and expensive new mansion at Audley End in Essex and, to help finance that prodigious undertaking, in 1611 he sold the Charterhouse to Thomas Sutton for £13,000. Sutton had quite different plans for the Charterhouse, which he proceeded to put into action. Since the mid-1590s he had been planning to establish a charity, consisting of an almshouse and a school, which was to be at his manor of Little Hallingbury in Essex; that was the place specified in the foundation documents. But he changed his mind early in 1611 and the purchase went along swiftly enough for the charity to be established at the Charterhouse in June that year. Sutton's legacy created the most lavishly endowed charity established since the Reformation. The almshouse housed eighty male pensioners, known as Brothers, and the school provided for forty scholars. In terms of a residential charity in early modern England, that was a huge establishment.

Thomas Sutton was said to be the wealthiest commoner in England. He was born in 1532 and so by the standards of the time was an elderly man when he died in December 1611.

Certainly, longevity was one reason which could be suggested for accumulating great wealth, which naturally attracted envy and anxious concern on the part of those who hoped to be among the beneficiaries of such a rich man's estates.

Sutton's patrons were the brothers Robert Dudley, Earl of Leicester, and Ambrose Dudley, Earl of Warwick, 'to the first of whom he was a steward and to the second a secretary'. In 1569 he was granted rents from the manor of Walkington in Yorkshire, which gave him a dependable income from land, to add to the fees and other perquisites which doubtless came to him from his position with two such influential figures of the Elizabethan establishment. Through the Dudleys, Sutton entered the service of Richard Cox (Bishop of Ely, 1559-81), for whom he may have acted as under-steward. Warwick was Master General of the Ordnance and arranged for Sutton to act as his deputy and Warwick and Leicester also secured for Sutton the post of Master of the Ordnance in the North Parts. He was appointed to that post in February 1570 and held it until 1594, although he stayed in the north of England only until 1582.

Such an appointment did not preclude the holder from private dealing and Sutton engaged in trade on his own account. More profitably, he obtained, again through Leicester's influence, a lease of coal mines in County Durham that were formerly part of the bishopric of Durham's estates. His post with the ordnance and his income from the burgeoning output of the coalfields, which increasingly were supplying London's fuel, were the makings of his fortune. On his return to the south it was said that he carried two horse-loads of money with him. He then made an advantageous marriage, to Elizabeth Dudley, the widow of John Dudley of Stoke Newington, a distant cousin of Leicester and Warwick, which brought him an additional annual income of £670.

In 1583 Sutton sold the lease of the coal mines for £12,000 and in his later years it was through his activities as a moneylender that he increased his assets by lending on mortgages and recognizances, which carried an annual rate of interest of 10 per cent. In the last sixteen years of his life he lent £220,000, with £37,000 advanced in 1604 alone, in sums that ranged from £1 to the £8,800 on a mortgage held by Sir Oliver Cromwell of Hinchingbroke in Huntingdonshire.

Sutton was not a part of the London merchant community and did not become a citizen of the City, nor would he accept honours from the crown. After his wife's death he sold her house at Stoke Newington and bought one at Hackney, but did not invest in property in London, preferring to accumulate country estates in Cambridgeshire, Suffolk and Essex, and when in London he lived in rooms above a shop in Fleet Street. According to John Aubrey,

> The later end of his dayes he lived in Fleetstreet at a Wollen draper's shop, opposite to Fetter-lane; where he had so many great Chests full of money, that his chamber was ready to groane under it; and Mr Tyndale, who knew him ... was afrayd the room would fall.[5]

In the last years of his life he regarded Castle Camps, which he acquired in 1608, as his country seat.

Sutton accrued an unenviable reputation for being miserly. One of his later biographers and apologists explained that his wealth 'got by industry and ingenuity improved its selfe by thrift and frugality'. He was said to have been Ben Jonson's model for the principal character of his play *Volpone*, first performed in 1606, although Jonson himself denied this and he reportedly said that he 'understood well enough that his mushrome playes could never disparage or outlast Mr Suttons good workes'. Yet Volpone's tactic of taking gifts from a succession of self-seeking suitors with the promise that they would be made his sole legatee was also attributed to Sutton, with the allegation that:

> He served himselfe soe much of the hopes soe many entertained of being his heires; receaving hooked gifts of some who looked to have them returned with advantage, and buying easy purchases of others that expected their land that they passed away by their own deed should come again to them by his will.

It was hotly denied that he would use 'soe poore and crosse a peice of sordidnesse' to make money, and other accusations that he engaged in sharp practices were also refuted. Yet Aubrey was not to be dissuaded and asserted that "twas from him that B. Johnson tooke his hint of the Fox: and by Seigneur Volpone is meant Sutton'.[6]

Attention was focused on Sutton not only because of the way in which he had made his money but also how he intended to dispose of it. He had an illegitimate son, Roger Sutton, but did not give him financial support after 1592, and the death of his wife Elizabeth in 1602 further increased curiosity as to his plans. The fact that he had not made a will did nothing to damp down eager speculation and his heir, his nephew Simon Baxter, had considerable expectations. So, too, did Elizabeth's daughter by her first marriage, who had married Sir Francis Popham in 1590; they anticipated that a part of Sutton's fortune would come their way. His intentions to use much of his wealth to establish a charity may not have been widely known until he made the legal arrangements in 1610 and then bought the Charterhouse as its home in 1611.[7]

Even after Sutton had bought the Charterhouse he did not make a will and drew one up only a few weeks before his death, and to ensure that there should be no doubt about its legitimacy, he had it beside him on his deathbed. Baxter and the Pophams were both so disappointed with the amount bequeathed to them that they challenged the will; Baxter claimed that he was entitled to the whole of Sutton's estate, including the endowment of the charity. This went to the courts and the Privy Council instructed Sir Francis Bacon to prepare a paper for the king. He chose to question not the descent of ownership but the whole basis of the charity, recommending as an alternative the establishment of several smaller charities, so that the endowment reached a wider range of needy people than just the school and almshouse, and the risk of large-scale fraud was reduced. It is likely that Bacon represented a wider concern about the use of charitable donations, and not a conspiracy to thwart Sutton's plans.

Baxter's claim failed and was dismissed in the summer of 1613, but the governors did draw upon Bacon's terminology to specify the kind of almsmen who should be admitted. He suggested that because of the scale of the endowment, the charity should benefit 'maimed soldiers, decayed merchants and householders, aged and destitute churchmen, and the like; whose condition being of a better sort than loose people and beggars, deserveth both a more liberal stipend and allowance, and some proper place of relief not intermingled or coupled with the basest sort of poor'. Sutton had been less precise and had specified who should benefit only in the Letters Patent, which referred to 'poor, aged, maimed, needy and impotent people'.[8] That lack of clarity produced some misunderstanding; John Chamberlain, an assiduous collector and communicator of information and gossip, wrote a few days after Sutton's death that his 'college or hospital at the Charterhouse' was intended for 'the maintenance of eightscore [160] soldiers, sober men who are to have pensions according to their degrees, as they have borne places of captains, lieutenants, or ancients and the like. There is a school likewise for eightscore scholars.' He greatly exaggerated the numbers who could be provided for, and the almshouse was intended for poor men, not only those who had served as soldiers.

Their qualifications laid down by the governors were that they should be bachelors or widowers over fifty years old (but if they were maimed, they could enter at forty), who had been servants to the king 'either decrepit or old Captaynes either at Sea or Land', maimed or disabled soldiers, merchants fallen on hard times, those ruined by shipwreck, fire or other calamity, or held prisoner by the Turks. The Statutes issued in 1627 included the phrase 'gentlemen by descent and in poverty', the definition of poverty being generously set at an income of no more than £24 per annum or an estate worth less than £200.[9] They were required to provide testimonials of their good behaviour and 'soundnes in religion'. Further stipulations were that they should be free from any infectious disease, they were not to have long hair and could not keep or carry weapons within the hospital.

The charity was the single biggest beneficiary of Sutton's wealth, receiving £5,000 to convert the buildings and a further £1,000 for its initial costs, 'to begin their stock with, and to defend the rights of the House'. He had already assigned an endowment which produced an annual income, initially, of £3,872 and as residuary legatee it received a further £23,000 from his estate. His careful preparations when setting up the charity had been worthwhile, as had his fussy attention to his wealth, for within six months of his death his executors had received more than £25,000 and the total eventually collected was £51,420.

Sutton had begun the process of adapting the buildings for his charity, but he died with the alterations barely under way. They were completed by the governors appointed by him and the buildings were brought into use in 1614. The work was carried out in 1613-14 by Francis Carter. The Dutch artist William Schellinks was greatly impressed when he paid a visit in 1662, describing it as 'a very large building and grand in its conception, halls, chambers, kitchen, school, and many other rooms, besides galleries, [and] a beautiful church'.[10] His opinion was echoed by John Strype in the early eighteenth century, who explained that Sutton's purchase 'was sufficiently known to be a very large and goodly Mansion, beautified with spacious Gardens, Walks, Orchards, and other Pleasures, enriched with divers Dependencies of Lands and Tenements thereunto belonging, and very aptly seated for wholesome Air, and many other Commodities'. He also noted that this was 'in the very Place where Sir Walter Manny, in the time of K. Edward III, founded a House of Carthusians, called now corruptly The Charterhouse'.[11]

There were curious similarities between the foundations of the two charities on the site. Although their respective founders had seemingly long had the intention of establishing their charity and were well enough off to make them spectacularly large in the context of their time, they did not do so until just before their deaths. Of course, neither man could know that he had such a short time to live and did not intend to run it so close, and presumably planned not only to establish the charity but to see it successfully installed in its premises and functioning efficiently. Both men provided what should have been adequate, if not lavish, endowments, yet both the priory and the almshouse and school ran into difficulties and the buildings took longer to complete than would have been expected. Both charities required royal intervention because of their financial problems: Henry IV acted to sort out those of the priory, and Charles, Prince of Wales, intervened to install a new master from his own household on the death of Francis Beaumont in 1624. His nominee was Sir Robert Dallington, whose careful management of the charity until his death in 1638 restored its financial position and reputation, indeed secured its very existence, which had been threatened.

The imputation that the founders of new charities were wealthy men who acted from 'a late repentance' does not really hold, and it seems more likely that both men, more than two centuries apart, deferred such a major undertaking until they thought that they could give enough time to their project to ensure that it was a success. Both miscalculated, but the problems which ensued were subsequently overcome.

The author of an account of the charity written in 1669 pointed out that Sutton was born during the decade when the priory was closed, together with all other English monasteries, but that although 'others demolished *Publicke* places built upon Popish *foundations*; this man came into the world who was to erect a most famous one out of the ruines of the other upon *Protestant grounds*'.[12] Retaining the name Charterhouse did indicate that the strength of favourable opinion towards the title of Mauny's foundation was enough to overcome doubts about the use of a designation with such clear Catholic origins. The usage continued through the coming century, both formally and colloquially, despite the religious tensions and sectarian divisions, fears of Popish plots and civil wars. It is still applied to the almshouse, which remains on the priory's site and is now designated 'Sutton's Hospital in Charterhouse', and to Charterhouse School, which was moved to a site at Godalming in 1872. The adoption of the term Poor Brothers to describe the almsmen, and regulations which did not allow them or the officers to be married, or any women, even the scholars' matrons, to live within the precincts, were other ways in which the connections with the priory were acknowledged by the charity's Jacobean governors.

12

ASSOCIATIONS

The chivalric culture of Mauny's time continued through the fourteenth century and into the fifteenth. But already there was a harking back to past times, with a touch of nostalgia. The author of the *Livre des Faits* of Jacques de Lalaing, a Hainaulter with a formidable reputation as a fighter at tournaments, declared that 'once upon a time in the county of Hainaut [sic] and its surroundings resided the flower of chivalry'. Its knights 'would earn and accomplish so much by their prowess that their renown spread and blossomed across every reign'. He stated that such a society still existed when he wrote, but that may not have been entirely true. Hainault came under the rule of the Duke of Burgundy in 1432 and after the deaths of de Lalaing in 1453, at the siege of Poeke Castle, and that of Charles the Bold, Duke of Burgundy, in 1477, at the Battle of Nancy, its distinctive chivalric culture declined. Individual combat skills were becoming less significant in warfare as the deadly efficiency of gunpowder projectiles increased; it was ironic that de Lalaing was killed by a splinter which had broken off a piece of wood when it was struck by a cannon ball.[1]

In English society, fighting ability became less important in the establishment of social credentials, with increasing emphasis placed upon lineage: family descent and connections were given greater credence than military proficiency. Edward IV did attempt to revive a court culture which gave prominence to the Arthurian legend and indeed rebuilt the chapel of St George at Windsor Castle to match the image, but that was a nostalgic rather than rational phase and when he took an army to France in 1475, he withdrew without fighting, having come to terms with Louis XI.[2]

Although brief and unconvincing, Edward's sentimental flirtation with the chivalric past did help to maintain interest in the fourteenth century and its leading figures. That was also encouraged by printed books, which were imported in larger numbers than were issued by the printers William Caxton, his successor Wynkyn de Worde and de Worde's rival Richard Pynson. Among Caxton's output was Ramon Lull's *Book of the Ordre of Chyvalry*, which he published in 1488 and mentioned Mauny in a short list of those chivalrous knights who since the Norman Conquest had performed 'noble actes'. The others from before the fifteenth century he named were Richard I, Edward I, Edward III and his sons, Sir Robert Knollys, Sir John Hawkwood and Sir John Chandos, so Mauny was in distinguished company. In 1480 Caxton issued the chronicle known as the *Brut*, with the title *The Chronicles of England* and followed that two years later with Ranulf Higden's *Polychronicon*. But it was probably Froissart's *Chronicles* which did most to keep alive an awareness of Mauny's achievements.

The *Chronicles* circulated in manuscript copies during the fifteenth century and were a popular source for book producers after the advent of printing, with ten editions printed between 1495 and 1520. In England the chivalric and history texts were favourites of Prince Henry. After he had come to the throne as Henry VIII he commissioned from John Bourchier, Lord Berners, an English translation of Froissart's *Chronicles*, which was published in two volumes in 1525 and long remained the version read in England. The antiquary John Stow wrote in the late sixteenth century that Berners's translation became 'common in mens hands'.[3]

Interest in the chivalric tradition then waned, reflected in the number of tournaments held, which fell from twenty-four in the 1510s to just four in the 1540s. Yet the late sixteenth century saw a revival of interest, linked to the cult of the ageing Queen Elizabeth as the Virgin Queen, and promoted by Edmund Spenser in his *The Faerie Queene*. Jousts and tournaments continued to be held through Elizabethan's reign and such chivalric ideals as maintaining a vow once taken and respect for one's lady were still admired. There were seventeen tournaments during the 1590s and the interest in chivalric matters did continue briefly into the Stuart period, but not beyond the death of Prince Henry, King James's heir, in 1612. Court culture had moved away from those ideals and in truth none of the Stuart monarchs could provide an appropriate figurehead for a revival of them.

Other texts besides those of Froissart became available in published editions during the nineteenth and twentieth centuries and a new translation of his *Chronicles* was made by Thomas Johnes and published in 1803. Historians of Lord Mauny's times were greatly indebted to the chronicles, and hence to Mauny's contributions to them. Although the chronicle of Raphael Holinshed, in fact a collaborative effort, was the most commonly used source for British history by playwrights in the 1590s – a folio edition of the work was issued in 1587 – they were also aware of Froissart: in Shakespeare's *Henry VI part 1* the French nobleman the Duke of Alençon refers to 'Froissart, a countryman of ours'.

Both Christopher Marlowe and Shakespeare depicted scenes from Mauny's lifetime. In *Edward the Second* Marlowe depicts 'good Sir John of Hainault' offering the queen and the young Edward a refuge in Hainault where 'doubt ye not We will find comfort, men and friends' with which to challenge Edward II. This the queen accepted, believing that the Count 'is a noble gentleman; [who] I dare presume, will welcome me'. Sir John is subsequently depicted as a military leader during the invasion of England.[4]

Sir Walter Mauny features, although as 'the Earl of Salisbury', in the drama *The Reign of King Edward III*, published anonymously in 1596, but probably written in 1592-3 by Shakespeare and others. The earl is engaged in the campaigns in Brittany and later in the journey across France to join the king at Calais, suggesting that the character's actions were based on those of Mauny. The episode of the safe-conduct forms one of the strands of the play, no doubt because the playwright saw it as exemplifying aspects of chivalry regarded as still being of interest.

The knight who obtained the safe-conduct from the Duke of Normandy is named as 'Villiers, a French lord'. In the play he explains to the sceptical duke that he is requesting the pass so that he will be discharged from his ransom, to which the duke replies 'Art thou not free? And are not all occasions/That happen for advantage of our foes /To be accepted of and stood upon?' To which Villiers's responds, 'Profit must with honour be commixed, Or else our actions are but scandalous.' He insists that he must abide by his oath and acquire the pass from the duke or voluntarily return himself to custody. The duke is persuaded and provides the required document. When Salisbury is apprehended and taken before the king, the duke then, in his turn, argues that the honourable course must be followed and his safe-conduct respected, while the king is all for executing the earl on the grounds that his own authority overrides the duke's undertaking: he goes so far as to order that the earl should be hanged from a bough, 'for I do hold a tree in France too good/To be the gallows of an English thief.' Yet the duke wins his point, honour is upheld and Salisbury is released to continue his journey to Calais. When he reaches the English encampment he conveys to Edward III the bad, and in reality false, news of the heavy defeat of Edward, the Black Prince, as he had been told to do on his release. The chronology is much altered from reality, to fit in the various events which the playwrights regarded as forming a dramatic frame for the play. They include the siege of Calais and its surrender. #

The king's implacable wrath is expressed in a speech which surely was derived from Froissart: 'I will accept of nought but fire and sword,/Except, within these two days, six of them, /That are the wealthiest merchants in the town, /Come naked, all but for their linen shirts, /With each a halter hanged about his neck, / And prostrate yield themselves, upon their knees, /To be afflicted, hanged, or what I please.' A stage direction marks the entrance of 'sixe Citizens in their Shirts, bare foote, with halters about their necks'. The queen's intercession on their behalf is included, but Salisbury (alias Mauny) does not appear in that scene at all, which is not as developed as when it was treated by later writers.[5] With all of Froissart's *Chronicle* to draw upon, the playwright chose two episodes which were derived from Mauny's experience to represent the chivalric code of the time, the overwhelming importance to the individual of maintaining his word and so his honour, and the mercy shown by both kings when they had the power to execute those they regarded as their enemies. Other sources would have provided similar background information. Geoffrey le Baker's opinion on the keeping of oaths was clearly expressed in his chronicle, with the phrase, 'One ought to keep one's word even when given to an enemy.'[6]

Mauny's career and his charitable legacy were also acknowledged by historians writing about the fourteenth century, notably Joshua Barnes in his vast biography of Edward III, published in 1688 as *The History of that most victorious monarch Edward IIId, King of England and France and Lord of Ireland, and first founder of the most noble Order of the Garter*, by Sir William Dugdale's history of English monasticism, and also by the historians of Sutton's charity. In 1677 Samuel Hearne published a history of the Charterhouse in which he gave due attention to the priory, which he described as the Old Foundation, as well as to Sutton's charity. So did Philip Bearcroft in his *An historical account of Thomas Sutton, esq.; and of his foundation in Charter-house*, which was published in 1737. He described the acquisition of the burial ground and Mauny's proposals, explaining the failure to establish a college in the splendid phrase, 'Going abroad soon after to the Wars, the Saint seems to have been lost for a Time in the Soldier, and these Religious purposes forgotten amidst the Din and Clash of Arms.' As Mauny grew older and 'the Heroe reassumed the Saint', he again turned his attention to the site and established the Carthusian priory. Bearcroft printed transcripts of the foundation documents and included a brief biography of Mauny, with Froissart as his source. The anonymous fifteenth-century account of the priory's foundation was as yet unknown.[7]

Bearcroft's account came as renewed interest in the fourteenth century was just beginning to develop during the later eighteenth century and prompted visits to the ruins of castles and monasteries from the period to absorb the atmosphere of past times. John Byng, Viscount Torrington, wrote in his travel journal for 1790 that priory ruins 'are my first pursuits, as filling my mind with noble ideas of former religion and architecture'. He was also attracted by castles, ruined or still inhabited, and was very impressed by Warwick Castle, which the Beauchamp Earls of Warwick had rebuilt during the fourteenth century. He wrote that one evening, while staying at Warwick:

> We walked down at my desire to the bridge, where we gazed for half an hour at the stupendous magnificence of the castle, which is probably the most perfect piece of castellated antiquity in the kingdom. During our stay I was enwrapt in all the chimeras of chivalry and romance and could have wished to have seen an armed knight issue from the castle to lead us to a banquet prepared by the governor, who had seen us from a turret and who was famed for his hospitality to pilgrims and travellers.[8]

Not all travellers would have had Torrington's vivid imagination, but the association between the chivalric culture and ruins was clearly a strong one.

Interest in all things medieval was enhanced by Sir Walter Scott's novels with historical backgrounds, especially after the publication of *Ivanhoe* in 1819, which used the 1290s as a setting and was 'received with a more clamorous delight than any of its predecessors'. It and its successors, *Quentin Durward* and *The Talisman*, have been credited with increasing interest in romance and medievalism; for John Henry Newman's generation, Scott 'had first turned men's minds in the direction of the Middle Ages', while Carlyle and Ruskin made similar assertions of Scott's overwhelming influence over the revival, based primarily on the publication of *Ivanhoe*.[9] Scholarly opinion became less accepting of its actual influence, partly on the ground that 'all it has to tell us of England in the reign of Richard I ... might be inscribed "Scene – a forest. Time – as you like it."'

It may be that the Middle Ages in England were losing interest for the intelligentsia just as they were becoming more widely seen as romantic in 'an unblessed union of ignorance and fascination'.[10] That 'romantic' popularity was reflected in George IV's remodelling of parts of Windsor Castle and in events such as the costume ball hosted by Queen Victoria at Buckingham Palace in May 1842 on the theme of Edward III and Queen Philippa. Prince Albert was dressed as Edward III, the queen as Philippa, and, among the other participants, the Marquess of Normanby attended as Walter Mauny. The occasion was recorded by a double portrait of the royal couple by Edwin Landseer, the queen's favourite painter.

Interest in and enthusiasm for the age of chivalry continued through the nineteenth century and when the young composer Edward Elgar was commissioned to supply a work for the Three Choirs Festival at Worcester in 1890 he produced a concert overture which he entitled *Froissart*. Elgar's attention had been drawn to the *Chronicles* when he read Scott's *Old Mortality*, in which one of the characters hopes to inspire a young man with the comment: 'Did you ever read Froissart? ... His chapters inspire me with more enthusiasm than even poetry itself' and commending 'a gallant and high-bred knight' for his 'loyalty to his king, pure faith to his religion, hardihood towards his enemy, and fidelity to his lady-love!'[11]

While attention was focused on the wars of the fourteenth century, a concise name came to be applied to those between

England and France which ran from 1337 until 1453. Not until the mid-seventeenth century did historians begin to regard the conflicts of that period as having any coherence; wars between the two countries had occurred both before the 1330s and after the 1450s, and Calais was not recovered by the French until 1558. David Hume, in 1762, wrote that the wars lasted 'more than a century' and in 1818 Henry Hallam regarded them as 'a struggle of one hundred and twenty years'. Henri Martin's *Histoire de France* of 1855 was influential in this respect and within a few years of its publication the term 'La Guerre de cent ans' was coined. In 1869 Edward Freeman wrote that French historians were correct to describe the 'whole time from Edward the Third to Henry the Sixth as the Hundred Years War'. Thereafter the usage became common. Freeman, a political liberal and religious independent, was widely read and, as he said himself, he contributed to 'all possible quarterlies', modestly admitting that 'my parish is a big one, taking in all civilized Europe and America'.

The term the Black Death also became current in the mid-nineteenth century, chiefly through its use in Elizabeth Cartwright Penrose's *History of England from the First Invasion by the Romans to the End of the Reign of George III*, published by John Murray in 1826. Writing under the pseudonym of Mrs Markham, Penrose adopted the approach of a book ostensibly written for the instruction of her children, in an accessible style and with question-and-answer sections at the end of each chapter. In her account of Edward III's reign she wrote: 'Edward's successes in France were interrupted during the next six years by a most terrible pestilence – so terrible as to be called the black death – which raged throughout Europe, and proved a greater scourge to the people than even the calamities of war.' The book proved to be the most popular textbook on English history through the mid-nineteenth century, with twelve editions issued by 1846. And so 'popular' terms for two of the dominant events of Mauny's lifetime, the war and the pestilence, were brought into use.[12]

Through Froissart's chronicles and a new edition of Holinshed's *Chronicles of England, Scotland, and Ireland*, issued in 1807-8, in the nineteenth century Mauny's exploits reached a wide audience. For example, in John Murray's *Handbook for Travellers in Holland and Belgium*, the battle of Cadzand in 1337 is described as 'a glorious victory gained by the valiant Sir Walter Manny and Henry Plantagenet Earl of Derby' and the action is briefly described. In contrast, the naval victory at Sluis is dismissed in a sentence, although it was recognised by contemporaries and historians as a far more significant battle: 'Off the town of Sluys ... Edward III gained a great naval victory over the French fleet in 1340.' George Gleig included a chapter on Mauny in his *Lives of the Most Eminent British Commanders* (1835), as 'a specimen of the military commander during the chivalrous age'. Gleig had been a soldier in Wellington's army in the final years of the Napoleonic Wars and then became a cleric, novelist and historian, publishing his memoirs and several works on military history, and serving as chaplain of the Royal Hospital at Chelsea from 1834 and as Chaplain-General of the Forces from 1844. Mauny's adventures also occupied 68 of the 173 pages of a book of extracts from the *Chronicles*, published in 1841, which were presented as though his life was being told to two children.[13]

George Frederick Beltz, Lancaster Herald, included a short biography of Mauny, drawn from Froissart, in his *Memorials of the Most Noble Order of the Garter, from its foundation to the present time*, of 1841. Froissart's praise of his fellow-Hainaulter certainly made an impression on Beltz, who wrote that the name Sir Walter Mauny was

> ...associated with all that is bright and pleasing in the knightly character, revives, with talismanic power, the feats of prowess, combats of generosity, and examples of self-devotion and loyalty of heart, exhibited by the 'preux chevaliers' of his time, and for which none more than that hero was pre-eminently distinguished.

The biography is almost entirely given over to Mauny's military exploits, although the purchase of Spitalcroft as a plague burial ground is mentioned and the Charterhouse is given a short space at the end of the essay.[14]

The credibility of Froissart's characterisation of Mauny gave the novelist and short-story writer Sir Arthur Conan Doyle enough to go on to include a description of him in his novel *Sir Nigel*, written in 1906. Mauny is a minor character in the tale, in which the eponymous hero is the son of a landowner on the Hampshire-Surrey border, who, after his father's death, is being harassed by a nearby abbey which is trying to deprive him and his mother of their property. Nigel's attempts to thwart the monks land him in prison, but he is rescued by an archer who takes him to meet Edward III and his retinue. Alongside the king 'and so near to him that great intimacy was implied' was Sir Walter, who appeared to be roughly the same age as Edward. Conan Doyle describes him as having the 'broad face, the projecting jaw and the flattish nose which are often the outward indications of a pugnacious nature'. He adds that his complexion was 'crimson, his large blue eyes somewhat prominent, and his whole appearance full-blooded and choleric. He was short, but massively built, and evidently possessed of immense strength.' But his appearance was belied by his voice, which was 'gentle and lisping, while his manner was quiet and courteous'. In a separate passage the author mentions his 'choleric face'. Mauny is acknowledged by the author as having 'as high a reputation for chivalrous valour and for gallant temerity as [Sir John] Chandos himself'. Of course, Conan Doyle represented him as the kind of belligerent martial hero which he himself admired.

In France, attention in the eighteenth century came to be focused on the burghers of Calais, who were hailed as French patriots. That was how they were presented by the dramatist Pierre-Laurent De Belloy in his play *Le Siège de Calais*, performed in 1765 in the aftermath of the Seven Years War between France and England, during which France lost many of her overseas territories. He acknowledged Froissart as his source and included extracts from the *Chronicles* in the first printed version of the text. The play was not only a drama depicting an actual event, but also a vehicle projecting its author's vision of French bravery and patriotism. The mayor and civic leader, Eustache Saint-Pierre, is a bourgeois hero, his duty to his country overcoming his grief at losing his son in the fighting. Edward III is a harsh enemy, depicted as being prepared to burn the city unless its civic leaders, headed by Saint-Pierre, swear their allegiance to the English crown. He required them to walk to the gallows to atone for the citizens' opposition to him, before he would accept their surrender.

Mauny is portrayed as being a merciful adversary and having a kind regard for the citizens of Calais. He questions the king's proposed punishment of the civic leaders, weeping during the scene, and again later in the play, as he is cast as the compassionate counterpart to Edward's intransigent conqueror. Mauny could be regarded as representing a conciliatory stance in the aftermath of victory, an approach that was wished for following the Seven Years' War. His empathy with Saint-Pierre and his fellow citizens is highlighted when he jibs at the king's order that they should be hanged; such insubordination is a serious step for any officer to take in any war. Edward does eventually relent, in the play as he did in fact, having been subjected to emotional appeals. In De Belloy's drama the queen has no part in this change of heart; she is not even listed in the cast of characters, while Mauny plays a significant role.

The play was criticised by the Enlightenment *philosophes*, who challenged the basis of De Belloy's representation, and examination of the contemporary records prompted by the 400th anniversary of the siege produced evidence which also led to a questioning of the generally accepted interpretation of the event. But its emphasis on patriotism helped to make *Le Siège de Calais* immensely successful in France until the revolution in 1789, although it was not performed thereafter. It does reflect the importance attached to Froissart's account of the siege and the fate of the six burghers, while providing much scope for debate; Voltaire claimed that the halters which the burghers had around their necks when they were presented to the king were merely symbolic.[15]

The English also gave much attention to the submission, humiliation and reprieve of the burghers of Calais at the surrender of the town in 1347. So much so that it became one of the best-known episodes in English history. The American artist Benjamin West settled in London in 1763 and attracted the approval and patronage of George III, who commissioned him to paint eight canvases depicting the reign of Edward III for St George's Hall at Windsor Castle. The episode of the king pardoning the burghers was one of the subjects chosen.

Completed in 1789, it shows three men standing behind the king, one of whom presumably is the Black Prince and one of the others may have been intended to be Walter Mauny. The French artist Jean-Simon Berthélemy had depicted the episode seven years earlier, with a larger group behind the seated king, who is being entreated by the queen to show mercy.

In her account of Edward III's reign, Elizabeth Penrose (Mrs Markham) in her *A History of England* included a brief account of the Crécy campaign and the siege of Calais, devoting 450 words to the siege, of which 200 are on the surrender and the reprieve of the six burghers. She described how Edward was

> ...so much enraged against the people of Calais for holding out so long against him, that he ordered these six men to be executed. Queen Philippa then fell on her knees before him and besought him to pardon them. The king granted her request, and she had them conducted to her apartment, where she entertained them honourably, and sent them back to the town, bestowing on them many rich presents.

Mauny was not mentioned, but the author's account was based on Froissart and therefore owed much to le Bel's description of those events, derived from Mauny.

In 1836, George James gave a full account of the surrender of Calais in his biography of Edward the Black Prince, mentioning Mauny's role, and including passages in direct speech, taken from Froissart. This he justified:

> All the other authorities of any import confirm the statements of that writer in every material point ... Nevertheless, I do not believe myself, and do not wish others to believe, that these speeches

> contain the precise words used by the individuals to whom they are attributed; but in all probability they are such as persons so situated would have spoken in that day; and I give them as substantially if not verbally correct, and as furnishing an accurate picture of the manners of the time, as well as of the emotions under which the principal characters acted.

This was both a summary of the faith placed in Froissart's account and an explanation for his use of direct speech. The distinguished Victorian scholar J.R. Green was also bold enough to give the exchanges during the siege in direct speech. In his account, 'the gentle knight' Sir Walter Mauny said, 'Ha, gentle sire! bridle your wrath; you have the renown and good fame of all gentleness; do not a thing whereby men can speak any villainy of you! If you have no pity, all men will say that you have a heart full of all cruelty to put these good citizens to death that of their own will are come to render themselves to you to save the remnant of their people.' The king's response was an angry one: Hold your peace, Master Walter! it shall be none otherwise. Call the headsman! They of Calais have made so many of my men die, that they must die themselves!' The queen then intervened on her knees and prevailed with the king to spare the lives of the six citizens. Later in his narrative Green mentioned Mauny again, referring to his piety in purchasing the Black Death burial ground 'whose site was afterwards marked by the Charter House'.[16]

The episode of the burghers of Calais was singled out by writers on English history addressing 'popular' and 'young' readerships. Sir Edward Parrot gave the surrender a section of his chapter on the first three king Edwards in his *The Pageant of British History* (1908). He did not mention the Black Death. The author tells the tale of the events at Calais in what had become the conventional manner, describing how Mauny 'braved the royal wrath' to plead for the citizens and how, as 'the good Sir Walter', he acted as the go-between during the negotiations.[17]

The surrender also warranted a mention in guide-books, as the British travelled abroad in increasing numbers during the late nineteenth century, often beginning their journeys at Calais. Murray's guide to Holland and Belgium sensibly began its perambulation there, remarking that 'no one needs to be reminded of the siege of Calais by Edward III ... and of the heroic devotion of Eustace de St. Pierre (whose house is marked by a marble slab and Latin inscription) and his five companions'.[18] It has remained an item which the guide-book writers feel is worth a mention, and not only those writing on Calais and its region. A recent guide to Mons, where the contract for the marriage of Philippa and Edward was sealed on 27 August 1326, includes a section headed 'Philippa of Hainault', which notes that she was 'widely admired and popular for her kindness and compassion', going on to give a brief description of her role in persuading the king 'to spare the six courageous men who volunteered to sacrifice themselves'.[19] Mauny is not mentioned, but the connection is correctly made; Philippa was from the independent county of Hainault and Mons was a city within it.

The process by which France used war and diplomacy to push back its north-eastern frontier culminated in her occupation of the former county of Hainault together with the whole of the Netherlands during the Revolutionary War in the 1790s and their integration into France. When the country was divided into new départments in 1795 the former county of Hainault was split, with Mons designated as the capital of the départment of Jemappes, named for a town in the region where the French army had defeated the Austrians in 1792. The former Austrian

Netherlands, earlier the Spanish Netherlands, was incorporated in the kingdom of the Netherlands in 1814 but broke away to become Belgium in 1830. The name Hainault was adopted for one of the new country's provinces, which contains Mons and the north of the former county, while Valenciennes and the south had been ceded to France by the Treaty of Nijmegen in 1678 and remained part of the country thereafter. Hainault was adopted during the seventeenth century as the name of a place in Essex known by the fourteenth century as Hineholt, meaning 'wood belonging to a religious community', in that case Barking abbey. The change of name to Hainault seemingly came about because of some supposed – but in fact fictitious – connection with Queen Philippa.[20]

The treatment of the burghers was deployed by Edward III's nineteenth-century biographer William Longman to criticise the king.

> That he was cruel and revengeful is far from doubtful when his conduct to the burgesses of Calais is considered; for he either intended to put them to death in revenge for their courageous defence, or else, with cat-like wantonness, cruelly disregarding their misery, tortured them with the fear of a punishment he never intended to inflict.[21]

Longman's two-volume biography was published in 1869, when Edward III's reputation, once so high, was under a stiff assault from Victorian historians who came to view the king's military career with disfavour, for pursuing campaigns without justification and for the tactics of raiding, plundering and burning, and the killing of non-combatants. Longman was representative of his age in presenting a critical account of the king and he did not consider the possibility that the treatment of the burghers had been negotiated in advance.

During the nineteenth century an interpretation of the episode which gained favour represented the burghers as having displayed civic loyalty, in being prepared to sacrifice themselves for their city rather than their king, who had not attempted to relieve it despite his army being so close. Awareness of the event and the six burghers as individuals was increased by the sculptor Auguste Rodin's set of bronze figures 'The burghers of Calais'. In the aftermath of the French defeat in the Franco-Prussian War of 1870-1, and in a republican age, he was commissioned in 1884 by the town council of Calais, encouraged by the mayor Omer Dewavrin, to produce a memorial to Eustace de Saint-Pierre. Rodin was so moved by Froissart's account that he decided to represent all six men who were handed over to Edward, who included two brothers. He depicted them in the style of what he described as 'the sublime Gothic age ... in the idiom of Froissart's time'. They are larger-than-life figures, thin, although not to the point of emaciation, dressed in the robes of condemned men, barefoot and joined together by a rope around their necks. One of the men carries the key to the city.

The commission was only for a figure of Saint-Pierre, presumably to be shown in a heroic mould, and so Rodin's depiction of the whole group, identifiable by name, and in a naturalistic form with the bodies cast as naked and then covered by their clothing, was unconventional to say the least. The group was completed in 1889 but because of financial problems and some disquiet over Rodin's treatment of his commission it was not unveiled in Calais until 1895, after Dewavrin had returned to office in 1892. It came to be recognised as one of the most powerful and influential sculptures of the century, not least in conveying movement and the emotions of the burghers, for Rodin depicted the moment when the group was preparing to leave the city. He hoped that the set would be placed outside the town hall so that the men would seem to be leaving the building to walk to Edward III's camp, although it was well into the twentieth century before it was positioned there.[22]

Rodin created a second set of the figures for the Musée Rodin at the Hôtel Biron in Paris and in 1911 the National Art Collection Fund purchased another set, which was sited in Victoria Tower Gardens adjoining the Palace of Westminster, where it remains. Those figures, with Froissart's account, inspired George Bernard Shaw to write a one-act play entitled *The Six of Calais: A Medieval War Story*, first performed in 1934 and dealing with the surrender of the burghers. Sir Walter Mauny appears on stage with the earls of Derby, Northampton and Arundel as the burghers reach the king's pavilion, but he does not have a speaking part and the soldiers' point of view is not expressed; much of the dialogue consists of exchanges between Edward and Philippa, with contributions by Eustace de Saint-Pierre and a defiant burgher named Peter Hardmouth. Shaw commented that his work was chiefly 'to correct Froissart's follies and translate Rodin into words'.

The various reactions to the story of the surrender and the impact which it made upon, for example, an eighteenth-century dramatist and a nineteenth-century sculptor, show how persuasive a narrator Froissart was. That can also be said of Mauny, who had told his tale in such a way that le Bel and then Froissart could set out such a powerful and convincing version of it. Mauny was surely aware of what would make a 'good story', at the same time reflecting favourably on both himself and, more especially, on the queen, a fellow Hainaulter, and his patron the king, for his clemency. He should be given some acknowledgement for that uplifting tale of compassion overcoming cruelty, the characteristic which no doubt explains the attention which it has attracted.

An academic assessment of Walter Mauny was provided by James Tait in his short biography of 1893 for the *Dictionary of National Biography*, in which he summarised Mauny as 'clearly one of the ablest and boldest of Edward III's soldiers of fortune', while admitting that 'his merits certainly lost nothing in the hands of his countrymen, Jean le Bel, Jean de Kleerk, and Froissart'. Admiration of his 'chivalrous daring' should be offset by 'his vengeance on Mirepoix, as related in the *Chroniques Abregees'*, when the besiegers had killed the members of a garrison after it had surrendered. The conduct of the men under his command at Cadzand also suggested that 'he could on occasion be cruel'. Jonathan Sumption's article for *The Oxford Dictionary of National Biography*, published in 2004, was also generally favourable, describing Mauny as 'in some ways the model soldier of his age. He was gallant and courageous. He observed the chivalrous conventions of his class. He was one of the few prominent figures in the early part of the Hundred Years' War to receive unqualified admiration from both sides.' But to that statement he added the judgement that he was 'a poor commander with little strategic grasp, whose military achievements were more spectacular than useful', pointing out that he made a large personal fortune from war and citing a contemporary observation that 'an excessive interest in ransoms made a poor soldier'. In his history of the Hundred Years' War Sumption mentions 'That arch-spoliator Walter Mauny', although elsewhere referring to him as 'the aged paladin', which means 'a brave and chivalrous knight'. His perspective and allegations of avarice were carried over into the early twenty-first century, albeit by historians whose focus was on the conduct of the wars and who were not writing a considered biographical sketch.[23]

Mauny's organisational abilities, disposal of his fortune and piety should be considered in any assessment, as well as his humane concern for others on some occasions and brutal disregard for them on others. That was the approach followed by Gleig in recognising that Mauny's acquisition of the burial ground of Spitalcroft was 'unquestionably a generous and by the notions of the age a pious deed, yet the piety of the "good knight" ended not here. He caused a chapel to be erected within the cemetery, which he liberally endowed, in order that masses might be continually said for the souls of the departed.' In another passage he wrote that 'his purchase of the burial ground, and his erection of the Carthusian monastery, have obtained for him the reputation of liberality towards the poor, and piety towards God'. He regarded the priory as 'the rudiments, if we may so express ourselves, of the present excellent Charter-House'.

Mauny was indeed not only a soldier and accumulator of wealth but also a philanthropist on a large scale. But in some quarters his role had been overlooked, for when a coat-of-arms was uncovered in Wash-house Court around the middle of the nineteenth century the Preacher referred it to a friend at the College of Heralds for identification, and received the rather strange reply: 'The coat is undoubtedly that of Sir Walter Manny, a knight of the time of Edward III.; but what in the world had he to do with Charterhouse?' The association with the plague remained nevertheless and in 1856 H.T. Riley reported in *Notes and Queries* that a 'plague plant' still grew in the Charterhouse's grounds. It was distinctive, with a small yellow flower, and 'it was a current tradition that it only grew on that spot, owing its nutriment to the bodies interred there during the great plague of

1348-52'. His bizarre account was not followed up by a more accurate description or verification.[24]

During the period of Catholic revival in the late nineteenth century Dom Lawrence Hendriks, a monk at the recently founded Carthusian priory at Parkminster in Sussex, produced a history of the London priory. He drew heavily on Bletz's work for his account of Mauny and gave attention to Mauny's funeral and will. Aware that Mauny had requested that his tomb should resemble that of Sir John Beaumont in St Paul's, he mentioned the engraving of that monument in William Dugdale's *History of St Paul's* and described it as 'an altar-tomb supporting the recumbent effigy of the knight in armour, with escutcheons of the family on the sides'; the original was destroyed in the Great Fire.

In 1925, the papers of William St John Hope on the priory's history were published posthumously, and they contained his transcription and translation of the Charterhouse register of the fifteenth century, which contained an account of its foundation and early years. A reviewer who welcomed the book drew attention to 'two of the most familiar of the great captains of Froissart, Sir Walter de Manny and that brave but sinister figure Sir Robert Knolles'. He quoted a description of Mauny from Froissart and another from the unknown author of the manuscript's portrayal of the founder as 'full of sanctity and grace, devoted to God and the Holy Church, for he desired to hear two masses daily, if nothing stood in the way, and he reckoned it great gain to help those who were in need'. The reviewer was aware of the apparent incongruity of two prominent soldiers being involved in the establishment of the monastery, for, as well as Mauny's role, Knolles 'who spent his life in savage destruction, was the founder of one of the "cells"'.[25]

Nor had Mauny's significance been forgotten at the Charterhouse and when the school was moved to Godalming in 1872, he was described as 'That accomplished knight ... at once the first soldier and diplomatist of his day', and his roles as purchaser of Spitalcroft and founder of the priory were acknowledged. When the third centenary of the foundation of Sutton's charity was celebrated in 1911, he again received his due: 'Charterhouse owed its foundation to the Black Death and Sir Walter Manny, a knight famed for his prowess in the reign of Edward III.' Gerald Davies wrote a booklet to commemorate the anniversary and later a full-length account of the Charterhouse from the mid-fourteenth century into the nineteenth. Davies's life and loyalties were focused on the Charterhouse. He attended Charterhouse School and returned there as a master after university, eventually becoming Head Master, and after his retirement he was appointed Master of the almshouse.

Davies faced reconciling the contrast between the brutality and pillaging during Mauny's campaigns and his charity. In his booklet he pointed to Froissart's *Chronicles* when claiming that Mauny had been 'the foremost in ability and chivalry' during Edward III's wars: 'He had won honour at Berwick, at Sluys, and on many a field in France. He won fame in his chivalrous relief of Hennebont, and, above all, in his noble protest to Edward for the Burghers of Calais.' In his history Davies gave attention to Mauny's career as a soldier, describing him as 'the best and bravest of Edward's knights'. He did admit that Mauny 'may, indeed, have sunk on some occasion to the level of the warfare of his day – for chivalry to the conquered was by no means the hall-mark of war in Europe ... But the testimony, in the case of Manny, is but slight at best, and the charge fits ill with his character.' He again cited in Mauny's favour his pleas for the lives of the burghers of Calais, commenting that if the story was true it was difficult to understand how he could have used the argument with the king that he 'would sully his knightly fame for ever if he put to death defenceless men whom he had taken prisoners' if he himself had recently been guilty of a similar act at Mirepoix. In Davies's judgement Mauny had been 'a very noble not entirely faultless man'. Davies quoted from Mauny's will, noted the discovery of a section of his tomb in the fabric of the later Charterhouse buildings and described his funeral, based on Froissart's account.[26]

Writers on London drew attention to the Charterhouse and its history, within that of the city. Walter Thornbury assigned two chapters to it in his four-volume history and description of the city published in the 1870s. He acknowledged Mauny's role in providing the burial ground and establishing and endowing the priory, describing him as 'that brave knight whose deeds are so proudly and prominently blazoned in the pages of Froissart'.[27] Sir Walter Besant described the almshouse as 'the most beautiful and venerable monument of old London' and when the celebrations for the third centenary of Sutton's charity were announced *The Times* explained to its readers that, although the school had been moved away, 'a goodly portion' of the old buildings remained, forming 'one of the most picturesque spots in the City of London'. It referred to 'the medieval calm of the old monastery', which contrasted with the bustle of the nearby meat market in Smithfield. Mauny's role was described. The Charterhouse qualified for inclusion in *Unnoticed London*, whose author described it in similarly glowing terms as 'one of the most lovely and gracious things in all London', He added, 'One does not like to think of the number of people who leave London without ever having seen the Charterhouse.'[28]

The lessening of interest may have been connected to the changed nature of Charterhouse Square. The former outer precinct had undergone several alterations of character, as its relative seclusion was gradually lost by the opening in 1687 of Charterhouse Street (from 1871 Hayne Street) to Long Lane and, more drastically, the building of the Metropolitan Railway in a cutting in 1865-6 and the widening of the south side and the opening of Charterhouse Street in 1874 as part of the improved access to the new Smithfield Market buildings. The creation of that thoroughfare was followed by the proliferation of butchers' carts and drays, organ grinders, horse-dealers using the square to exercise their horses, and commercial travellers loitering outside hotels. Showrooms and warehouses were built, occupied by milliners and clothiers. By 1900 the square was no longer primarily residential, let alone socially desirable. Householders designated 'esquire' had gone, only one clergyman remained, there were four hotels and two staff hostels of commercial companies, and most of the other buildings were occupied by businesses, the printing trade predominating.

The Charterhouse itself had also changed. When the school was moved away in 1872 its part of the site was sold to the Merchant Taylors' School, which remained until 1933, when it was acquired for St Bartholomew's Hospital medical school. From the late 1870s the general agricultural recession had a deleterious impact on the charity's finances; falls in the prices of farm produce were followed by declining rents and increasing problems retaining tenants. Throughout the 1920s and 1930s Sutton's Hospital experienced such serious financial problems that the number of Brothers had to be reduced. With less money available for maintenance and improvements, the buildings became increasingly shabby and stood alongside a rather unappealing square in a commercial part of central London. Perhaps not surprisingly, writers of guides to the city who set out to inform their readers of its attractive aspects no longer mentioned the Charterhouse or the square. That was true of Paul Cohen-Portheim in his description of the city published in 1935 as *The Spirit of London*. The connections between the Black Death, Mauny, the priory and the present had not been lost, but certainly by the outbreak of the Second World War they were less well known than hitherto.

13

REDISCOVERIES

Walter Mauny and his legacy attracted attention in a most unexpected way in the mid-twentieth century. The outbreak of the Second World War, with the imminent threat of air-raids, posed a dilemma for the governors: should the Brothers be moved away from London for their safety and the buildings guarded by fire-watchers, or should that disruption be avoided by keeping them at the Charterhouse, where they could do the fire-watching themselves? The decision taken was that the Brothers should remain, thereby avoiding the cost of employing fire-watchers from outside. That worked very well until the particularly heavy air raids on the night of 10-11 May 1941, which caused extensive damage in the City. An undetected fire-bomb on the roof of the range next to the chapel started a blaze which was driven by a north-easterly wind, so that the flames spread southwards and westwards. The ranges around Master's Court and much of Wash-house Court, the kitchens and the Registrar's house were all gutted. The chapel was undamaged and the Brothers' accommodation in Pensioners' and Preacher's Courts was not affected, but without the service areas the buildings were no longer usable and so the Brothers were evacuated to Godalming.

Among the governors was Sir Charles Peers (1868-1952), who had been educated at Charterhouse School. He was an expert in the conservation of historic buildings and in 1903 was appointed architectural editor to the *Victoria History of the Counties of England* and in 1910 became inspector of ancient monuments in the Ministry of Works, and three years later took the post of Chief Inspector, which he held until his retirement in 1933. His approach at monastic and other sites was to remove post-medieval accretions to reveal their 'historic core'. That produced the uncluttered ruins with exposed masonry characteristic of the historic buildings in the custody of the Ministry, and many restoration architects adopted his principles. For the Charterhouse, Peers submitted a report advising that the Tudor and Stuart buildings be reinstated and recommended the partnership of the Hon. John Seely (from 1947 Lord Mottistone, 1899-1963) and Paul Paget (1901-1985) as architects to carry out the restoration. Seely and Paget had been contemporaries at Trinity College, Cambridge, and had gone into partnership in 1926. By the early 1940s their reputation rested chiefly on the restoration of Eltham Palace, where Peers had acted as consultant, and the construction of the adjoining house for Stephen and Virginia Courtauld, which was carried out between 1933 and 1936. Their previous work had also included the remodelling of the old chapel at Charterhouse School as a music school.

The architects investigated the history of the site and its occupiers, as well as the evolution of the buildings. They prepared a timeline showing the development of the Charterhouse and contemporary events and formed impressions of the individuals who had contributed to the erection of the buildings and the organisations and individuals which had occupied them. They were in no doubt about the significance of their task; Paget described the Charterhouse as being 'generally regarded, like the Tower of London, as one of the sights of the City though not actually within the jurisdiction of the Corporation'. Paget's notion of Mauny was that he was 'just the kind of person who in the last war, might have been in command of "Combined Operations" for he was continually engaged in coastal attacks of a commando character upon the shores of France at the time of Crécy'. He imagined Mauny saying during the Black Death: '"Really something must be done to give these wretched victims of this horrible disease a decent burial" from which he proceeded to provide the necessities of burial ground and mortuary chapel at his own expense.'[1]

Although Peers's report and Seely and Paget's initial plans were approved by the governors, there was a considerable delay before the restoration could begin. The charity's uncertain financial position, the need for approval from the War Damage Commission, which funded the reinstatement, the licensing system controlling building materials, and the low priority given to an almshouse, meant that little work could be carried out other than that which qualified as remedial and urgent. That included the removal of the floor in the Great Hall, which had been damaged by dry rot. Finds made while preparations were under way in 1946 to lay a concrete sub-floor began a trail of discoveries that led to the reinterpretation of the layout of the monastic buildings.[2]

The correct location of the priory church, where Mauny was buried in 1372, had been lost and it was not realised that the chapter-house had been adapted as the chapel for the Tudor mansion and then Sutton's charity. Interpretations of the priory site were based upon the assumption that the south aisle of the present chapel was the choir of the priory church, the ante-chapel was equated with the lay brothers' choir and the church was thought to have had a nave to the west, on the site of Chapel Cloister, which had been demolished during the Duke of Norfolk's ownership *circa* 1571. That conflicted with the evidence of a plan drawn sometime between 1431 and 1457 to illustrate the water supply to the priory from Islington, which has plan-views of many of the buildings. That was available to scholars after it was first shown to the Society of Antiquaries in 1746 and donated to the Charterhouse shortly afterwards.[3]

The excavations in 1946 uncovered what was recognised to be one of the drains of the priory, the south-west corner of the Great Cloister and the remains of a monastic cell, which the fifteenth-century plan indicated was cell A, originally the prior's cell. Interpretation of the site from at least the early nineteenth century had placed the corner of the cloister further north, despite the evidence of the plan. The new discoveries in the Great Hall made this untenable and raised the possibility that the plan was indeed accurate. Further evidence came when the floor of the room on the north side of Chapel Cloister was lifted, revealing floor tiles, ledger slabs over monastic burials and the footings of walls indicating that it lay on the line of the south cloister walk.

The plan shows that the chapter-house stood to the north-east of the church and so on the site of the south aisle of the present chapel. The discrepancy between its evidence and the accepted interpretation of the layout of the site was explained by the assumption that the medieval cartographer had made a mistake. Yet the medieval plan had been given detailed consideration by Sir William St John Hope, who was later recalled to have 'scoffed' at it on his visits to the Charterhouse.[4]

Doubts about the interpretation of the site should have been raised when, in 1894, a fragment of Mauny's tomb was discovered in the fabric of the range overlooking Entrance Court. This was correctly identified and was mounted in a case, with an inscription; in 1885 *The Times* had reported that Mauny's remains 'are believed still to rest under the choir of the old church'. As the mid-sixteenth century had been a period when many tombs in London churches were destroyed for their materials, the newly found fragment did not in itself provide conclusive evidence that the chapel itself had been pulled down. But it should have prompted a reconsideration of the accepted arrangement of the buildings at the south end of the Great Cloister. There was, too, an entry in the *Chronicle of the Grey Friars* for September 1545 which states that in that month 'was the Charterhowse pulde downe, and the watter turned to dyvers places ther to gentylmens placys'. That chronicle was published by the Royal Historical Society in its Camden Society series in 1852 and ought to have caused doubts about the validity of assigning so much of the layout to the priory period, when its buildings were stated in a contemporary source to have been pulled down.[5] Admittedly, much of the potential evidence within the fabric was covered by later accretions, the internal walls were panelled and plastered and most of the external ones were covered by render and brickwork, while smoke blackening made detailed analysis of the outside walls difficult. Those problems were overcome after 1941 by the ruinous state of the buildings and the need to expose the fabric before the restoration work could be carried out.

Seely and Paget were contemplating the implications of the findings during the excavations when even more startling evidence came to light. A workman clearing old plasterwork from the walls of the Treasury on the first floor of Chapel Tower inadvertently opened a void which on investigation was found to angle downwards to a circular hole in the external wall. The hole had been hitherto noticed but neither investigated nor explained. The architects now realised was that it may have been a squint which looked down on the high altar, to allow the sacrist to take part in the mass without leaving the Treasury; it could have served no purpose if it were an external feature. If that was indeed the case then 'the sight line through this squint would impinge on the very spot where the original altar had stood, and some distance west of this, where the choir would have been, we might hope to find the burial place of Sir Walter de Manny'.

Excavation of the site indicated by the alignment of the squint did indeed reveal the footings of what was surely the high altar. According to the chronicler of the priory's history Mauny's tomb was at the foot of its steps and so an excavation was undertaken there, which, sure enough, revealed a grave. That was opened and found to contain 'a leaden coffin shaped in the rough effigy of a man'.[6]

A licence was granted on 2 May 1947 by the Consistory Court of London permitting the lifting and opening of the coffin. It was removed from the grave and placed on a long and stout table, which now stands just within the main doorway. Watched by a select group that included the Master, Edward Schomberg, the Duke of Wellington and other governors, the Medical Officer, Sir Alfred Clapham (Secretary of the Royal Commission on the Historical Monuments of England), and the architects, the coffin was opened. Within it were human remains, which were those of Lord Mauny.

The skeleton was 1675 mm (5ft 7ins) long, the head was wrapped and had 'an ample length of scalp hair' with a 'full beard ... in a fair state of preservation'; the cranium and lower jaw were almost intact. The experts' examination drew attention to the 'extremely broad head', which they associated with the population of northern France and Belgium. From an analysis of the remains it was concluded that the skeleton was that of a man probably over sixty years old who was at least 5 feet 7 inches tall, the average height for a man in medieval London, and 'all the bones point to the conclusion that the individual was of muscular and sturdy build'. Fragments of the cere-cloth had survived, as had enough of a narrow band to show that it was a braid of plain weave and made of flax, with a blue line running near one edge. Within the coffin was a circular lead disk which proved to be the seal of the bulla granted by Pope Clement VI in 1351, permitting Mauny to select a confessor for a deathbed absolution. Not even a fragment of the document itself had survived: 'All of the loose material that remained had been put through a sieve but nothing was discovered resembling vellum.' The disk was taken to be additional proof that the body was that of Lord Mauny. And so the excavations had quite unexpectedly led to the discovery of the remains of the priory's founder, although the architects' chief objective had been establishing the plan of the monastic buildings.[7]

There was no evidence of fractures or disease in the remains; the lack of fractures may be surprising given Mauny's years of combat. His contemporary and fellow soldier-cum-diplomat Bartholomew Burghersh, who died in 1369, was 5 feet 10 inches tall and his skeleton, inspected in 1961, showed evidence of his service in action or at tournaments, for he had a well-developed right arm (which was longer than his left one) and strained elbow joints, and at some stage he had sustained broken ribs and a twisted ankle. Some of Mauny's joints did have a 'very slight arthritic appearance', but less than is usually found in persons of that age.

The skeleton was replaced in the lead coffin, which was re-interred in the original grave on 3 June 1947; a stone slab was placed over the grave with the simple inscription 'Lord de Manny KG. Died 1372'. Aware that the coffin was 'now somewhat mutilated', Seely and Paget wished to cover it with a pall during the ceremony. As Paget later pointed out, that was not easy because of 'the difficulty of clothes rationing'. They approached their neighbour adjoining their offices in Cloth Fair, who was 'the one surviving cloth merchant' in the street and asked whether he had 'any remnant of old stock which he could let us have without coupons. Before we had time to explain the whole of the circumstances he said, "Well there is some stuff which we used to supply before the war to some monks in Ireland for making their habits," and there and then he produced some fine white cloth of exactly the same texture as that which Carthusian monks wear today.'

That precisely suited their purpose and the architects made a further connection with Mauny's burial in 1372 by distributing coins. Mauny had directed that everyone who attended should be given a penny, and Seely and Paget, allowing 'something' for inflation between 1372 and 1947, 'obtained some freshly minted half-crowns and presented one to each of the workmen, who warmly appreciated this memento of the search with which they had been associated and in which they had become most keenly interested'. A half-crown was worth 2s 6d, so the mark-up since 1372 was a thirtyfold increase.[8]

The discovery of the site of the 1349 chapel prompted a full excavation of the whole of the exposed area within the historic buildings. The architects recognised that it required a more professional approach than they could offer and so it was carried out, in 1948-49, by W.F. Grimes, a distinguished archaeologist who had been appointed as the director of the London Museum in 1945 and in the following year as honorary director of excavations for the Roman and Medieval London excavation council. His findings established the plans of the monastic church and its chapels, the southern end of the Great Cloister and the Little Cloister. They confirmed that the ranges around Master's Court were built after the dissolution and that the materials from the priory church had been re-used in North's new house. As Maurice Chauncy, one of the monks, had stated, albeit in a Latin phrase which was somewhat ambiguous, he 'used the church to make a Dining Hall'.

The work also indicated beyond doubt that the water-supply plan was topographically correct. The excavations showed that the northern part of the east wing of Master's Court rested on the west wall of the 1349 chapel, and its southern part was built upon the footings of the east and west walls of the Popham Chapel, a mid-fifteenth-century addition to the 1349 building. That had preserved the wall lines of the west end of that chapel, but the survival of those on its south side was extremely fortuitous, for Edward Blore's new range of *circa* 1840 for the Master's Lodge, separating Chapel Court from Charterhouse Square, had a full-depth basement with an area in front, which its predecessor did not have, yet its new north wall had not encroached on the archaeology of the chapel and so its evidence had not been destroyed.

A statue of St Katherine of Alexandria was recovered within one of the walls, headless and trimmed to serve as a building block but otherwise in good condition. It had come from the side chapel of the priory church dedicated to that saint and dated from *circa* 1500. Also removed from the stonework in good condition and retaining much of its original colour was another section of Mauny's tomb. With the section retrieved in the late nineteenth century and the depiction of Beaumont's tomb in St Paul's which Mauny cited as a model, it has been used as the basis for a conjectural drawing of the side elevation of Mauny's tomb, depicted as an arcade of vaulted niches. When reporting the renovation of the Charterhouse, *The Times* had no hesitation in declaring that the 'most notable' of all the discoveries made during the work was Mauny's coffin, which contained 'indisputable proof' that the remains within it were his.[9]

In the Norfolk Cloister the doorway of Cell B, the first to be built in 1371, survived and was protected by being sealed behind brickwork, which Seely & Paget removed; they then restored the doorway. Other vestiges of the cell fronts on that side of the cloister also survived. Bomb damage within the medical college required substantial new building work there and in 1949 that uncovered a cell doorway and the foundation trench of the inner wall of the cloister walk on the east side of the Great Cloister. On its north side the cloister wall was revealed in two places and its north-east corner was also exposed. The extent of the Great Cloister was then established as having been 340 feet from east to west and 300 feet from north to south. The doorways of two cells on the east side of the Great Cloister and the side wall of one of them had also survived, incorporated in the later buildings.

The results of the discoveries were recorded in three ways. Firstly, the lines of the principal walls uncovered during the excavations were marked as the restoration proceeded. Within the buildings brass strips were laid in the cork-tiled floors, with lighter tiles within the strips to distinguish the wall thickness, and externally they were marked by narrow lines of stone chips set in concrete. Secondly, parts of the medieval fabric uncovered during the work, such as the doorway and food hatches of the cells, were left exposed and the floor tiles and ledger slabs recovered were re-set in the new floors. Thirdly, on the advice of (Sir) Robert Birley, Headmaster of Charterhouse School, Professor David Knowles was invited to write the history of the priory, with a contribution from Grimes describing the findings of the excavations. Knowles was the leading post-war historian of English monasteries; he acknowledged the important role played by the architects in discovering the monastic plan, admitting that 'all the good ideas have come from Seely & Paget'. Knowles and Grimes's account was published in 1954 as *Charterhouse: The Medieval Foundation in the light of recent discoveries*. It incorporated the deductions by the authors, architects and Mabel Mills, the Charterhouse's archivist. Knowles pointed out that there was 'no life or study' of Mauny and that he had based his account on the fifteenth-century history of the priory, which he dubbed the Charterhouse Register.[10] Later work has amplified those findings, especially with excavations on the sites of the cells and cloister walk on the north side of the Great Cloister. The correct designations have been established for the cells for which fabric has survived.

While attention was focused on the rediscovery of the priory buildings, in May 1947 the Master pointed out to the governors that 25 March 1949 would be the 600th anniversary of Mauny's acquisition of the site. He suggested that a commemorative service should be held, to which the governors and the king and queen would be invited. That did not take place; it would have been possible because although the other buildings were still in ruins the chapel was intact, but, for whatever reason, no service or other commemoration was held, and so there was no high-profile recognition of Mauny's role.[11]

After a long delay, another episode from the priory's history was marked. Before the Second World War there had been a proposal for a memorial to the Carthusian martyrs of the 1530s, prompted by the 400th anniversary of their deaths. The narrative which Maurice Chauncy wrote in 1570 was published in 1935, adding momentum to the project. Fundraising was begun and a design was prepared.

Chauncy describes Prior Houghton delivering a sermon and then going from monk to monk, kneeling at the feet of each in turn and asking forgiveness for any wrongs which he may have done them. He then repeated this in 'the other choir', which presumably meant that of the lay brothers. According to the pre-war interpretations of the site the ante-chapel was where Houghton had completed his process of reconciliation and so provided the appropriate place for the commemorative tablet, which was to note that it was 'from this place' that the Carthusians went to their deaths. But the project faltered and the tablet was not made; when the scheme was revived in the late 1940s the Master realised that, because of Seely and Paget's discoveries, both the position and the wording were inappropriate. Not until 1957 was a stone tablet completed, to Seely's design, and placed not in the chapel but on the boundary wall behind the site of the monastic church's high altar, its inscription recalling that the monks and lay brothers who lost their lives 'worshipped at this altar'.[12]

The site of the priory is identifiable in the modern cityscape. Charterhouse Square is its outer precinct, although encroached upon by later buildings. An imaginary line drawn between parish boundary markers on No. 14 on the north side, adjoining the Charterhouse, and No. 41, on the south side, indicates the eastern boundary of the Black Death burial ground. The land to the west was part of Spitalcroft and that to the east was acquired in 1377; the discovery of a skeleton there during an exploratory excavation is evidence that it, too, was used for burials. Beyond the buildings on the south side of the square is Barbican underground station, formerly known as Aldersgate Street station. Much of the area of the station lies within Spitalcroft: passengers at the west end of both the eastbound and westbound platforms are within the area of the plague cemetery, although of course at a much deeper level than were the burials, which were cleared when the ground was excavated for the railway in 1865.

The priory's flesh kitchen probably was cleared after the dissolution; its site was tentatively identified by a resistivity survey, close to the centre of the open space, although that was not confirmed by excavation. The other medieval structure in the square was the chapel of the Virgin Mary and All Saints, pulled down in 1615-16 when a payment was recorded for levelling the grounds and causeway there. The improvements made the area (now Charterhouse Square) appear 'more neat and comely' and must have made it look less like an old burial ground.[13]

While attention in recent years has been largely focused on the buildings, a reminder of the original use of the site came when work was carried out in Charterhouse Square for the construction of the London underground network's Elizabeth Line. During the construction of a shaft in 2013 twenty-five skeletons were discovered, eleven of them from the Black Death period, two from a second phase of burials, probably the outbreak in 1361, and twelve from a third phase, dated to the fifteenth century. Burials from all three phases contained evidence of *Yersinia pestis*. The remains of ten people were suitable for analysis, four of whom probably had moved to London, one after the age of five, one after the age of eight and two after the age of sixteen, so that even during the difficult mid-fourteenth-century period London was, as usual, drawing in people from the regions around the city.[14] It also reminds us that Mauny intended that the cemetery should be for 'poor strangers and others'.

Several sections of the priory buildings remain, dispersed around the site, but many connected by Seely and Paget's practice of marking the wall lines of the Carthusian structures. Access is through Chapel Court, where Mauny's grave is marked by a slab within the outline of the walls of the chapel of 1349, with the site of the altar raised above ground level. On the north side of the chapel site is Chapel Tower, which is monastic, except for the bell-turret, bell and cupola. Two of the buttresses of the Black Death chapel remain, identifiable by their shape and their construction of ashlar; one is set in the west face of Chapel Tower, and the other stands against the tower's east face. The circular aperture on the south wall of Chapel Tower is the sacrist's squint identified by Seely and Paget. The memorial to the Carthusian martyrs is on the east wall of the court.

Until the clearance of the wartime damage, Chapel Court was enclosed on its south side by a range of the Master's Lodge fronting the square. Seely and Paget did not replace that range and changes in 2016 created a new access to the buildings through the court, which was set out to a new design. Those changes were part of a project designated Revealing the Charterhouse, which was funded by the Heritage Lottery Fund and other donors. That involved the creation of a public access through a new reception area and the establishment of an education centre and a museum. The reception area stands partly within the 1349 chapel, and the education centre is on its south side, occupying the site of Popham's chapel. The museum occupies a later room but straddles the cloister walk on the south side of the Great Cloister, where the graves of Symmes and Lessy were discovered by Seely and Paget. The display in the museum includes the skeleton of a man aged between eighteen and twenty-five, one of those uncovered by the excavations in 2013. Fragments of Mauny's tomb are also displayed, as is the mid-fifteenth-century water-supply plan, with its map of the priory.

The chapel is approached from Chapel Cloister, which despite its name was not built until 1614, through an ante-chapel, which is the lowest stage of chapel tower, built in the early fifteenth century as a two-storey structure with a third stage added later, perhaps in 1512, the date of the vault. The vault is formed of moulded stone ribs springing from carved angel corbels with blank shields. The carved bosses at the intersections of the ribs carry the instruments of the Passion: an angel holding a shield, a spear and hammer on a flower, two scourges on a shield, three nails and two bunches of hyssop. The boss against the centre of the west wall carries the monogram IHS. The ground floor served as a vestibule which allowed the monks to pass under cover between the cloister walk to the north, the church to the south and the chapter-house to the east. Its two altars were dedicated in 1414 to the Holy Trinity and SS Peter and Paul and to SS John the Baptist and Hugh of Lincoln. The south archway was blocked when the priory church was demolished. On the upper floor was the priory's treasury, cared for by the sacrist, whose squint was re-opened by Seely and Paget.

Beyond the ante-chapel is the south aisle, the monastic chapter-house, dating from the early fifteenth century; its altars were dedicated in 1414. It was reconstructed in the early sixteenth century, probably in 1512. The rebuilt chapter-house was higher than its predecessor and contained three deep windows on the south side and one in the east wall. The easternmost of the three windows has been filled in, and the lower sections of the others and the east window were filled in 1726. As the chapel occupying the former chapter-house was not large enough for the charity's needs, in 1613-14 a second aisle was added alongside it. Between the two aisles is a Tuscan colonnade, with three round arches decorated with strapwork and keystones carrying carvings of the Sutton arms. That marks the north wall of the chapter-house, immediately beyond which was the priory's Great Cloister walk, the site of which lies beneath the north aisle of the chapel and the museum room. Its outline to the west is marked by brass strips in the floors of the entrance hall and the Great Hall.

The entrance to the Charterhouse from the square is through an archway in the gatehouse of *circa* 1405. When the layer of render on the gatehouse was removed the original stone face was revealed with a chequerboard pattern in the stonework which is continued along the adjoining wall. The gateway and wall were those built in 1405 in response to the Carthusian Visitors' insistence that the priory should be physically separated from the graveyard. Above the gatehouse is part of the adjoining Physicians' House of 1716. Beyond the gatehouse, across Entrance Court is the inner archway of the priory. With the laity able to pass through the outer gateway, security was provided for the areas further into the priory by the construction of this inner gateway, perhaps in the early sixteenth century.[15] Alongside it is a water conduit house built in 1614 after the pipes of the priory's water supply had been re-directed; it was restored by Seely and Paget.

Through the inner gateway is the outer wall of the west range of Wash-house Court, with a blind archway and the letters IH among other diaper work. The range was built in 1531 and was the last of the priory buildings to be erected. Opposite is a high wall, the lower part of which is built of similar bricks to those of the Wash-house Court range and also contains diaper work. It was the west boundary wall of the Carthusian priory and can be followed for much of the length of the present boundary on that side of the site. Its thickness suggests that the brickwork is an outer layer covering an earlier wall, presumably of stone, which required a protective layer by the early sixteenth century. That earlier wall could well have been the one referred to when the site of Spitalcroft was acquired by Mauny and is therefore of mid-fourteenth-century date or earlier.

Wash-house Court itself is reached through a slype and is the most attractive part of the Charterhouse buildings. A passage through its south range has a section of rubble-stone wall on its east side, which is probably the west wall of the lay brothers' quarters. The building itself was demolished and replaced by the current range, almost certainly by North's builders. They were also responsible for the east range, which is the west range of Master's Court. The priory's guest-house was on a part of the site of this range, but was entirely replaced by North's new building. Master's Court is reached through a slype, a term which seems not to have come into use in post-dissolution times until the mid-nineteenth century, when interest in the monastic remains at the Charterhouse and elsewhere was revived. Its adoption may have been a conscious resumption of an expression which had been in abeyance since the sixteenth century. A description of the Charterhouse buildings in the early 1840s uses the word 'passage' when describing a slype.

Within Master's Court are the outlines of the Little Cloister, of 1405-06, and the chapel of St Anne and the Holy Cross, which was added to the Black Death chapel at the same date. In the wall of the east range is an area of ashlar within the ragstone wall, which is the side wall of the Popham chapel, added to the priory church in 1453. Until the 1840s a slype through that range connected Master's Court with Chapel Court.

On the north side of Master's Court stands the Great Hall of 1546, which obliterated the site of the first prior's cell, endowed by Mauny. That cell stood at the south-west corner of the cloister walk, which is shown by the brass strips in the Great Hall's floor. On its north side was the frater, now part of the Old Library, which opens into the Norfolk Cloister, a part of the west range of the cloister walk. Until 1872 the cloister was the full length of the cloister walk, almost twice its present length, but in that year a long section was pulled down by the Merchant Taylors' Company, to make space for its new school hall. That area had been altered when the school was created in 1614 and the tennis court was enlarged and converted into the schoolroom, with sleeping quarters built for the resident boys; a part of the monastic wall was then demolished to create a common wash-place for them. The rubble-stone west wall is that of the monastic cloister, while the brick east wall and vault were built for the Duke of Norfolk in 1571, creating an impressive approach to his tennis court. Decorative outer faces of brick were added on both the west and east sides in 1641. The doorway of cell B survives almost intact, as does its serving hatch (guichet), curved within the thickness of the wall, through which the monk's meals were passed. The hatches of cells C and D also survive on this side of the cloister, that of cell C being wrongly labelled as that of cell D. Wooden doors would have provided coverings for the outer openings of the hatches.

The doorways of cells S and T have been preserved *in situ*, in the east boundary wall of St Bartholomew's Medical College, and within its former Anatomy Department building. Like that of cell B, they are of Reigate stone and are very similar to it, although their decorative features are too damaged to permit any close comparison, and they were built roughly ten years later. The cells on the east side each had their own access to the orchard behind them. The layout of the north side of the cloister was excavated before being built over and the line of the main pipe of the water supply was recorded. It ran to a conduit house in the centre of the Great Cloister, the position of which has been tentatively identified but not confirmed.

On the opposite side of the site, the locations and sequence of buildings close to the west boundary wall have been found, together with a substantial dividing wall, approximately 2 feet thick, which was built from the western boundary wall to the rear wall of the monks' gardens, not before the early fifteenth century. It provided greater security to the yard on its north side, and perhaps to the great garden and fish-ponds. Presumably vegetables and fruit for the priory were grown in the great garden, and there was also a separate cook's garden.[16] Two buildings were erected close to the western boundary, probably in the early years of the priory. Both were subsequently demolished and a substantial stone building, at least 59 feet long, was erected against the boundary wall and the dividing wall across the site, perhaps in the late fourteenth or early fifteenth centuries. It may have been a barn or granary. At the dissolution three stables and a saw-pit were mentioned and there was also a 'great doveshouse' that was rebuilt in 1498-1500.[17]

* * *

Walter Mauny's success came from his ability to adapt to the English court and his prudent conduct as a member of the royal households, while his wealth derived from both royal favour and military service. Others who had profited from the wars employed their gains for building projects, notably Bodiam Castle in Sussex, built by Sir Edward Dalyngrigge in the late fourteenth century. Mauny did not erect such a building as the centre of the administration of his estates and other interests, or to express its owner's successful career, or reconstruct an existing prestigious building in the modern style, as John of Gaunt did at Kenilworth Castle. Perhaps Mauny regarded his inheritance at Masny as fulfilling that function, or he was reserving his wealth for the foundation of the priory, which marked his status in the way that a prestigious house or castle would have done had he chosen to spend his money differently.

The Charterhouse, with Mauny's grave, and Charterhouse Square remain to evoke his achievements through his deployment of his wealth to fulfil an urgent need during the Black Death and later create a large and prestigious monastery in London. The boundaries of Spitalcroft and various elements of the Carthusian priory are still readily traceable, providing tangible reminders of Walter Mauny, one of the most successful of Edward III's commanders, and his piety, generosity and social concern.

NOTES

Abbreviations

CM	Charterhouse Muniments
Froissart	Thomas Johns, *Chronicles of England, France, Spain and the adjoining Countries ... by Sir John Froissart*, London, William Smith, I, 1839
le Bel	*The True Chronicles of Jean le Bel, 1290–1360*, trans. Nigel Bryant, Woodbridge, Boydell & Brewer, 2011,
LMA	London Metropolitan Archives
ODNB	Oxford Dictionary of National Biography
RIBA	Royal Institute of British Architects
TNA	The National Archives

1 Hainault and England

1. Jean Derheims, *Histoire ... de la ville de Saint-Omer*, Saint-Omer, 1843, p. 179.
2. Ole J. Benedictow, *The Black Death 1346-1353: The Complete History*, Woodbridge, Boydell, 2004, pp. 111-14.

3. Chris Wickham, *Medieval Europe*, New Haven & London, Yale UP, 2016, pp. 132-3. Jane Gilbert, 'Valenciennes', in David Wallace, ed., *Europe: A Literary History, 1348-1418*, I, Oxford, OUP, 2016, p. 53.
4. Gilbert, 'Valenciennes', p. 55.
5. David Crouch, *Tournament*, Hambledon & London, Hambledon, 2005, pp. 3, 27-8, 208 n. 22. Elizabeth Morrison, *A Knight for the Ages*, New Haven & London, Yale UP, 2018, pp. 11-12. William StJohn Hope, *The History of the London Charterhouse*, London, SPCK, 1925, p. 9.
6. le Bel, p. 144.
7. William Langland, *The Book Concerning Piers the Plowman*, trans. Donald and Rachel Attwater, ed. Rachel Attwater, London, Everyman, 1957, Prologue p. 1.
8. E.B. Fryde, 'Parliament and the French War, 1336-40', in E.B. Fryde and Edward Miller, eds, *Historical Studies of the English Parliament, Volume I Origins to 1399*, Cambridge, CUP, 1970, p. 256.

2 *A new Reign*

1. H.S. Lucas, *The Low Countries and the Hundred Years War, 1326-1347*, Ann Arbor, University of Michigan Press, 1929, pp. 52-4.
2. Froissart, p. 9.
3. A.H. Thomas, ed., *Calendar of the Plea and Memoranda Rolls of the City of London: Volume 1, 1323-1364*, London, HMSO, 1926, 2 Jan. 1327.
4. Richard Barber, ed., *The Chronicle of Geoffrey le Baker of Swinbrook*, Woodbridge, Boydell & Brewer, 2012, pp. 33-4.
5. le Bel, p. 30.

6. Lucas, *Low Countries*, pp. 71-2. Michael Livingston and Kelly DeVries, eds, *The Battle of Crécy: A Handbook*, Liverpool, Liverpool UP, 2015, p. 211.
7. le Bel, p. 51. Richard Barber, *Edward III and the Triumph of England*, London, Allen Lane, 2013, pp. 58-60.
8. Kathryn Warner, *Philippa of Hainault*, Stroud, Amberley, 2019, pp. 99-100, 115, 123.
9. Nigel Saul, *For Honour and Fame: Chivalry in England, 1066-1500*, London, Bodley Head, 2011, p. 40.
10. W. Mark Ormrod, *Edward III*, New Haven & London, Yale UP, 2011, p. 142.
11. Chris Wickham, *Medieval Europe*, New Haven & London, Yale UP, 2016, pp. 212-13.
12. Juliet R.V. Barker, *The Tournament in England, 1100-1400*, Woodbridge, Boydell, 1986, pp. 46-8.
13. Rosemary Horrox, *The Black Death*, Manchester, Manchester UP, 1994, p. 131.
14. E.J.F. Arnould, 'Henry of Lancaster and his *Livre des seintes medicine*', *Bulletin of the John Rylands University of Manchester*, 21, 1937, pp. 383-4.
15. Ormrod, *Edward III*, pp. 133-4.
16. Michael Prestwich, *A Short History of The Hundred Years War*, London, I.B. Tauris, 2018, p. 78.
17. James Bothwell, *Edward III and the English Peerage: Royal Patronage, Social Mobility and Political Control in Fourteenth-Century England*, Woodbridge, Boydell, 2004, p. 41.
18. Prestwich, *The Hundred Years War*, pp. 78-80. Froissart, *Chronicles*, ed. Geoffrey Brereton, London, Penguin, 1968, p. 58.

3 Sir Walter Mauny: Soldier and Admiral

1. Henry S. Lucas, 'John Crabbe: Flemish Merchant, Pirate, and Adventurer', *Speculum*, 20, 1945, p. 344. Elizabeth Ewan, 'Crab, John, (c. 1280–c. 1352)', ODNB. Richard Barber, ed., *The Chronicle of Geoffrey le Baker of Swinbrook*, Woodbridge, Boydell & Brewer, 2012, p. 61.
2. *Calendar of Patent Rolls, Edward III, 1334-1338*, p. 90.
3. le Bel, pp. 61-2.
4. Thomas Wright, ed., *Political Songs and Poems relating to English History*, London, Longman, Green, 1861, I, pp. xii-xiv, 4-9, 13-15. David Green, *Edward The Black Prince*, Harlow, Pearson Education, 2007, pp. 30-1.
5. Froissart, p. 50.
6. Froissart, pp. 57, 58-9.
7. Jonathan Sumption, *The Hundred Years War Volume I: Trial by Battle*, London, Faber & Faber, 1990, pp. 554, 575.
8. Graham Cushway, *Edward III and the War at Sea: The English Navy, 1327-1377*, Woodbridge, Boydell, 2011, p. 70. Frederic Richard Barnes, 'The taxation of wool, 1327-1348', in George Unwin, ed., *Finance and Trade Under Edward III the London Lay Subsidy of 1332*, Manchester, 1918, p. 161. *Calendar of Close Rolls, 1337-1339*, p. 358.
9. Kenneth Fowler, *The Age of Plantagenet and Valois*, London, Ferndale, 1980, p. 11.
10. Craig L. Lambert, *Shipping the Medieval Military: English Maritime Logistics in the Fourteenth Century*, Woodbridge, Boydell, 2011, pp. 25, 36. *Calendar of Patent Rolls, Edward III, 1334-1338*, p. 580; *1338-1340*, pp. 71-2, 130, 189. *Calendar of Close Rolls, 1337-39*, pp. 349, 351, 364-5. Cushway, *Edward III and the War at Sea*, pp. 72-3, 155.

11. Froissart, p. 50.
12. Froissart, p. 56.

4 *The Battle of Sluis and After*

1. Froissart, pp. 72-3. This chapter is largely based upon Graham Cushway, *Edward III and the War at Sea: The English Navy, 1327-1377*, Woodbridge, Boydell, 2011, pp. 90-100.
2. le Bel, p. 86.
3. Clifford J. Rogers, ed., *The Wars of Edward III: Sources and Interpretations*, Woodbridge, Boydell and Brewer, 1999, pp. 94, 95. 'The French Chronicle of London: Edward III', in H.T. Riley, ed., *Chronicles of the Mayors and Sheriffs of London 1188-1274*, London, Trübner, 1863, p. 277.
4. Jonathan Sumption, *The Hundred Years War Volume I: Trial by Battle*, London, Faber & Faber, 1990, pp. 360-3. E.B. Fryde, 'Financial Resources of Edward III in the Netherlands, 1337-40 (2nd part)', *Revue belge de Philologie et d'Histoire*, 1967, p. 1158.
5. *Calendar of Patent Rolls, Edward III, 1338-1340*, p. 545.
6. *Calendar of Patent Rolls, Edward III, 1340-1343*, pp. 258, 261-2, 304, 561; *1343-1345*, pp. 177, 179. Sumption, *Trial by Battle*, p. 469. Douglas Richardson, *Plantagenet Ancestry: A Study in Colonial and Medieval Families*, 2nd edn, Salt Lake City, Genealogical Publishing, 2004, p. 638.
7. *Calendar of Patent Rolls, Edward III, 1345-1348*, pp. 445-6.
8. *Calendar of Inquisitions Post Mortem: Volume 10, Edward III*, London, HMSO, 1921, p. 427.
9. *Calendar of Patent Rolls, Edward III, 1340-1343*, p. 290; *1343-1345*, p. 304. William Farrer and J. Brownbill, *A History of the County of Lancaster*, IV, London, 1911, n. 40.
10. Le Bel, p. 69.

11. W.M. Ormrod, 'Montagu, William [William de Montacute], first earl of Salisbury (1301–1344)'; 'Ufford, Robert, first earl of Suffolk (1298–1369)', ODNB. Richard Barber, *Edward III and the Triumph of England*, London, Allen Lane, 2013, pp. 118-19, 121, 152.

5 Sir Walter Mauny: The Fighting Years

1. *Calendar of Close Rolls, 1341-1343*, pp. 504-5. le Bel, pp. 130-3.
2. le Bel, pp. 135-6.
3. le Bel, pp. 137, 144.
4. le Bel, pp. 139-42. *Cal Patent Rolls, Edward III, 1338-40*, p. 397.
5. le Bel, p. 157. Penny Lawne, *Joan of Kent*, Stroud, Amberley, 2015, p. 133.
6. Nicholas A. Gribit, *Henry of Lancaster's Expedition to Aquitaine, 1345-1346: Military Service and Professionalism in the Hundred Years War*, London, Boydell & Brewer, 2016, pp. 53, 81-2, 89, 91, 94, 98.
7. Froissart, pp. 138-9.
8. le Bel, pp. 158-60. Richard Barber, ed., *The Chronicle of Geoffrey le Baker of Swinbrook*, Woodbridge, Boydell & Brewer, 2012, p. 68.
9. Frank Sargent, 'The wine trade with Gascony', in George Unwin, ed., *Finance and Trade Under Edward III the London Lay Subsidy of 1332*, Manchester, 1918, p. 296. *Calendar of Inquisitions Post Mortem: Volume 13, Edward III*, London, HMSO, 1954, no. 174.
10. le Bel, p. 164. Froissart, pp. 149-50.
11. Michael Livingston and Kelly DeVries, eds, *The Battle of Crécy: A Handbook*, Liverpool, Liverpool UP, 2015, pp. 27, 141, 225, 297.

12. Barber, ed., *Chronicle of Geoffrey le Baker*, p. 69.
13. Froissart, pp. 170-1.
14. Robert McCullum and James Davis, 'Robert Gyen of Bristol: A 14th-Century Merchant, Crown Official and Swindler Extraordinaire', *Trans Bristol and Gloucestershire Archaeological Soc.*, 136, 2018, p. 244.
15. Friedrich W.D. Brie, ed., *The Brut; Or, The chronicles of England*, London, Early English Text Soc., 1906, p. 300. Livingston and DeVries, *Battle of Crécy*, pp. 441-3. Barber, ed., *Chronicle of le Baker*, p. 60.
16. le Bel, pp. 201-3. Michael Prestwich, *Armies and Warfare in the Middle Ages*, New Haven and London, Yale UP, 1996, p. 152.
17. Froissart, p. 131.
18. Barber, ed., *Chronicle of le Baker*, p. 80. Brie, ed., *The Brut*, p. 301.
19. Froissart, pp. 114-16.
20. G.A.C. Sandeman, *Calais Under English Rule*, Oxford, Blackwell, 1908, p. 84.
21. *Calendar of Inquisitions Post Mortem*, vol. 14, London, 1952, pp. 182-193, Item 175.
22. le Bel, p. 130.
23. Richard Barber, *Edward III and the Triumph of England*, London, Allen lane, 2013, p. 395.
24. Froissart, pp. 59-60.
25. E.B. Fryde and Edward Miller, eds, *Historical Studies of the English Parliament, volume I Origins to 1399*, Cambridge, CUP, 1970, p. 20.

6 *The Black Death*

1. Rosemary Horrox, *The Black Death*, Manchester, Manchester UP, 1994, p. 34.

2. Tim Mackintosh-Smith, ed., *The Travels of Ibn Battutah*, London, Macmillan, 2002, pp. 274-5.
3. Horrox, *Black Death*, pp. 46-7, 53-4.
4. Richard Barber, ed., *The Chronicle of Geoffrey le Baker of Swinbrook*, Woodbridge, Boydell & Brewer, 2012, p. 87.
5. Horrox, *Black Death*, p. 77.
6. Johannes Nohl, *The Black Death: A chronicle of the plague compiled from contemporary sources*, trans. G.H. Clarke, London, Unwin, 1961, pp. 45, 58.
7. Kathryn Warner, *Philippa of Hainault*, Stroud, Amberley, 2019, p. 196.
8. Horrox, *Black Death*, pp. 66, 68.
9. Horrox, *Black Death*, pp. 69, 81.
10. Horrox, *Black Death*, pp. 72, 74.
11. Barber, ed., *Chronicle of Geoffrey le Baker*, p. 87. Sir William St.John Hope, *The History of the London Charterhouse*, London, SPCK, 1925, p. 7.
12. Hope, *History of the London Charterhouse*, p. 8.
13. Barney Sloane, *The Black Death in London*, Stroud, History Press, 2011, p. 52.
14. David Knowles and W.F. Grimes, *Charterhouse*, London, Longmans, Green, 1954, pp. 53, 56.
15. W.H. Bliss and C. Johnson, eds, *Calendar of Papal Registers Relating To Great Britain and Ireland: Volume 3, 1342-1362*, London, 1897, pp. 462-9. John Stow, *The Survey of London*, ed. H.B. Wheatley, Dent, London, 1987, p. 385.
16. *Chronicle of London from 1089 to 1483*, London, 1827, reprinted Felinfach, Llanerch, 1995. p. 60. Brereton, ed., *Froissart: Chronicles*, p. 111.

17. Sam Pfizenmaier, *Charterhouse Square: Black Death Cemetery and Carthusian Monastery, Meat Market and Suburb*, London, MOLA, 2016, pp. 23-5, 30-40, 44, 46, 117-22.
18. Duncan Hawkins, 'The Black Death and the new London cemeteries of 1348', *Antiquity*, 64, 1990, pp. 637-42.
19. Barber, ed., *Chronicle of Geoffrey le Baker*, p. 86.
20. D.A.L. Morgan, 'The Charterhouse of Cadzand and the Serendipities of Empire', in Huw Pryce, John Watts and R.R. Davies, eds, *Power and Identity in the Middle Ages: Essays in Memory of Rees Davies*, Oxford, OUP, 2007, pp. 164-80.
21. 'The French Chronicle of London on the Battle of Sluys and the Siege of Tournai', De re miltari: The Society for Medieval Military History, deremilitari.org/2016.
22. Horrox, *Black Death*, p. 85.
23. Horrox, *Black Death*, pp. 88-92.

7 Lord Mauny: Diplomacy and Philanthropy

1. W.H. Bliss and C. Johnson, eds, *Calendar of Papal Registers Relating To Great Britain and Ireland: Volume 3, 1342-1362*, London, HMSO, 1897, p. 375.
2. Richard Barber, *Edward III and the Triumph of England*, London, Allen Lane, 2013, pp. 376-81.
3. Kenneth Alan Fowler, Henry of Grosmont, First Duke of Lancaster, 1310-1361, PhD thesis, University of Leeds, 1961, pp. 315-16, 446-50.
4. Richard Barber, ed., *The Chronicle of Geoffrey le Baker of Swinbrook*, Woodbridge, Boydell, 2012, p. 99.
5. G.A.C. Sandeman, *Calais Under English Rule*, Oxford, Blackwell, 1908, p. 36.
6. Barber, ed., *Chronicle of Geoffrey le Baker*, p. 109.

7. Fowler, Henry of Grosmont, p. 840.
8. Ralph H. Major, *Classic Descriptions of Disease*, Springfield and Baltimore, Charles H. Thomas, 1932, p. 76. Rosemary Horrox, *The Black Death*, Manchester, Manchester UP, 1994, p. 85.
9. Horrox, *Black Death*, p. 88.
10. Richard Barber, ed., *Fuller's Worthies*, London, Folio Soc., 1987, p. 257.
11. Jonathan Sumption, *The Hundred Years War Volume III Divided Houses*, London, Faber & Faber, 2009, pp. 42-4. Thomas Johnes, ed., *Sir Jean Froissart's Chronicles*, I, 1803, pp. 429-30.
12. Edith Rickert, *Chaucer's World*, ed. Clair C. Olson and Martin M. Crow, New York, Columbia UP, 1948, pp. 271, 292.
13. Mary Darmesteter, *Froissart*, London, T. Fisher Unwin, 1895, p. 16. Jane Gilbert, 'Valenciennes', in David Wallace, ed., *Europe: A Literary History, 1348-1418*, I, Oxford, OUP, 2016, p. 56.
14. David Green, *Edward The Black Prince: Power in Medieval Europe*, Harlow, Pearson Education, 2007, pp. 66, 170.
15. Barber, *Edward III*, pp. 333, 336. W.M. Ormrod, 'Henry of Lancaster [Henry of Grosmont], first duke of Lancaster (c. 1310–1361)'; Carole Rawcliffe, 'Stafford, Ralph, first earl of Stafford (1301–1372)', ODNB.
16. Philip Beresford and William D. Rubinstein, *The Richest of the Rich: the Wealthiest 250 People in Britain since 1066*, Petersfield, Harriman House with the Social Affairs Unit, 2007, p. 198.
17. Green, *Edward The Black Prince*, pp. 57-63.
18. Gerald Davies, *Charterhouse in London*, London, John Murray, 1921, pp. 18-19.

19. Barber, *Edward III*, pp. 337-8. Hope, *Charterhouse*, pp. 94-5.
20. Nigel Saul, *For Honour and Fame: Chivalry in England 1066-1500*, London, Bodley Head, 2011, pp. 294, 304.
21. Hope, *Charterhouse*, pp. 6, 15. Barber, *Edward III*, p. 278.
22. Saul, *For Honour and Fame*, p. 279.
23. le Bel, pp. 21, 51-2, 78, 186-7, 200.
24. Barber, *Edward III*, p. 13.

8 The Priory

1. Edouard Desplats, 'Des chartreux à Marly et Valenciennes (1297-1791)', *Cercle Archeologique et Historique de Valenciennes et de son Arrondissement*, 88, May 2013. Gerald Davies, *Charterhouse in London*, London, John Murray, 1921, pp. 323-5.
2. William StJohn Hope, *The History of the London Charterhouse*, London, SPCK, 1925, p. 11.
3. Hope, *Charterhouse*, pp. 9-10.
4. Hope, *Charterhouse*, pp. 12-13.
5. Hope, *Charterhouse*, pp. 19,26. *Calendar of Patent Rolls, 1377-81*, p. 238.
6. Hope, *Charterhouse*, p. 14.
7. Emma Capron, *The Charterhouse of Bruges*, London, Frick Collection & D. Giles, 2018, p. 27.
8. Hope, *Charterhouse*, pp. 56-8.
9. Hope, *Charterhouse*, pp. 44, 58. *Calendar of Close Rolls, 1402-5*, pp. 217-18. *Calendar of Patent Rolls, 1401-1405*, p. 174. Chris Given-Wilson, *Henry IV*, New Haven & London, Yale UP, 2016, p. 378.
10. Capron, *Charterhouse of Bruges*, p. 25.
11. TNA, SC12/25/55, m.4.
12. TNA, SC12/22/77.

13. Capron, *Charterhouse of Bruges*, p. 25. Hope, *Charterhouse*, p. 43.
14. Hope, *Charterhouse*, pp. 59, 148. David Knowles and W.F. Grimes, *Charterhouse: The Medieval Foundation in the light of recent discoveries*, London, Longmans, Green, 1954, p. 66. H.F. Owen Evans, 'Charterhouse, London', *Trans of the Monumental Brass Soc.*, IX, 1962, pp. 464-8. RIBA, S&P, AE drawings, 74.
15. *Calendar of Papal Registers, 1471-1484*, pp. 444-5.
16. LMA, acc/1876/D1/6. TNA, SC12/25/55, m.55.
17. *Calendar of Patent Rolls, 1441-6*, p. 104. *Calendar of Close Rolls, 1441-7*, p. 415. *Calendar of Papal Registers, 1471-1484*, p. 260.
18. BL, Cotton MSS, Cleop. E.iv, f.42.
19. TNA, SC12/25/55, mm.4-19.
20. Information kindly supplied by Margaret Condon, from her transcripts of the agreement with the Charterhouse in 1504 and the king's will, NRA, E33/13/1; E23/3.
21. LMA, acc/1876/F/9/48.
22. G.W.S. Curtis, ed., *The Passion and Martyrdom of the Holy English Carthusian Fathers: The Short Narration by Dom Maurice Chauncy*, London, Church Historical Soc., 1935, pp. 17-18.
23. *Valor Ecclesiasticus*, I, 1810, pp. 430-1. BL, Cotton MSS, Cleop. E.iv, f. 42.

9 Mauny's Successors

1. Rowena E. Archer, 'Brotherton [Marshal], Margaret, *suo jure* duchess of Norfolk (c. 1320–1399)', ODNB. Nigel Saul, *For Honour and Fame, Chivalry in England 1066-1500*, London, Bodley Head, 2011, p. 276.

2. Geoffrey Brereton, ed., *Froissart Chronicles*, London, Penguin, 1968, p. 176.
3. R. Ian Jack, 'Hastings, John, thirteenth earl of Pembroke (1347-1375), ODNB. Froissart, pp. 453-5.
4. Froissart, p. 468.
5. Simon Walker, 'John [John of Gaunt], duke of Aquitaine and duke of Lancaster, styled king of Castile and León (1340–1399)', ODNB.
6. Froissart, pp. 470-3.
7. Richard Vernier, *The Flower of Chivalry: Bertrand du Guesclin and the Hundred Years War*, Woodbridge, Boydell, 2003, p. 167. Froissart, pp. 501-2.
8. R. Ian Jack, 'Hastings, John, thirteenth earl of Pembroke (1347-1375)'; 'Grey, Reynold, third Baron Grey of Ruthin (c. 1362–1440)', ODNB.
9. Chris Given-Wilson, *The Royal Household and the King's Affinity*, New Haven & London, Yale UP, 1986, pp. 122-4.
10. *Chronicle of London from 1089 to 1483*, London, 1827, reprinted Felinfach, Llanerch, 1995, pp. 73-4.
11. Charlotte Augusta Sneyd, ed., *A Relation, or rather a true account, of the Island of England*, London, Camden Soc., 1847, p. 45.
12. J.R. Hale, ed., *The Travel Journal of Antonio de Beatis*, London, Hakluyt Soc., 1979, pp. 103-4.
13. Charles Whibley, ed., *Henry VIII by Edward Hall*, London, T.C. & E.C. Jack, 1904, II, pp. 2-12. *Calendar of State Papers, Spain, volume 12, 1554*, London, HMSO, 1949, Letter of Simon Renard, London, 13 May, 1554.
14. *Calendar of State Papers, Venice, volume 6, 1555-1558*, London, HMSO, 1877, items 1123, 1124.

15. *Calendar of State Papers, Venice, volume 6, 1555-1558*, items 1127, 1129.
16. David Loades, *Mary Tudor*, Stroud, Amberley, 2011, pp. 220-2. J.G. Nichols, ed., *The Diary of Henry Machyn, citizen and merchant-taylor of London, from A.D. 1550 to A.D. 1563*, Camden Soc., 42, 1848, p. 163.

10 The Dissolution

1. Desiderius Erasmus, *Praise of Folly*, ed. Betty Radice, London, Penguin, 1993, p. 112. R.A.B. Mynors and D.F.S. Thomson, eds, *The Correspondence of Erasmus*, vol. 4, Toronto, University of Toronto Press, 1977, pp. 24-5.
2. Peter Gwyn, *The King's Cardinal: The Rise and Fall of Thomas Wolsey*, London, Barrie & Jenkins, 1990, p. 476. Frederic Seebohm, *The Oxford Reformers*, London, Longman, Green, 1911, pp. 297, 306.
3. BL, Cotton MSS, Cleop. E.iv, f.42
4. F.A. Gasquet, *Henry VIII and the English Monasteries*, London, Bell, 1893, p. 208.
5. *Letters and Papers of Henry VIII*, 9, item 523. W.J.D. Roper, *Chronicles of Charter-house*, London, Bell, 1847, pp. 22-3.
6. *Letters and Papers of Henry VIII*, 7, 1534, p. 408; 9, item 523. Martha Carlin and Joel T. Rosenthal, eds, *Medieval London: Collected Papers of Caroline M. Barron*, Kalamazoo, Medieval Institute Publications, Western Michigan University, 2017, pp. 222-3.
7. Diarmaid MacCulloch, *Thomas Cromwell: A Life*, London, Allen Lane, 2018, pp. 280-5, 409-10. Cecil H. Clough, 'Rastell, John (c. 1475–1536)', ODNB. Alan Harding, 'Rastell, John (by 1468-1536), of London', in S.T. Bindoff, ed., *The History of Parliament: The House of Commons*

1509-1558, London, HMSO, 1982. *Letters and Papers of Henry VIII*, 9, item 1150.

8. Lauren Mackay, *Inside the Tudor Court*, Stroud, Amberley, 2014, p. 146.
9. Caroline M. Barron and Matthew Davies, eds, *The Religious Houses of London and Middlesex*, London, University of London, 2007, pp. 24, 87.
10. Edward Hall, *The Lives of the Kings: Henry VIII*, II, ed. Charles Whibley, London, T.C. & E.C. Jack, 1904, p. 264.
11. William StJohn Hope, *The History of the London Charterhouse*, London, SPCK, 1925, p. 151. *Letters and Papers of Henry VIII*, 14 pt 1, item 232/63b.
12. Hope, *Charterhouse*, pp. 185-6. Reginald R. Sharpe, ed., *Calendar of Wills Proved and Enrolled in the Court of Husting, London, A.D.1258-A.D.1688*, II, 1890, p. 621.
13. *Letters and Papers of Henry VIII*, 8, London, HMSO, 1885, item 601; vol. 13, item 903.
14. Hope, *Charterhouse*, pp. 178-83. David Knowles and W.F. Grimes, *Charterhouse: The Medieval Foundation in the light of recent discoveries*, London, Longmans, Green, 1954, p. 86.
15. *Letters and Papers of Henry VIII*, 13, item 903.
16. Philip Temple, *The Charterhouse*, Survey of London monograph 18, 2010, pp. 36-8.
17. *Letters and Papers of Henry VIII*, 20 pt I, 1545, p. 213.
18. Temple, *Charterhouse*, pp. 25, 34. Mary Rose archive, ID No. 81A1191.
19. TNA, C4/8/1. *Letters and Papers of Henry VIII*, 20 pt 1, p.303.
20. David Lasocki and Roger Prior, *The Bassanos: Venetian musicians and instrument makers in England, 1531–1665*, Aldershot, Ashgate, 1995, p. 39.

11 Mansion, Almshouse and School

1. TNA, SC6/H.VIII/2396. *Letters and Papers of Henry VIII*, 18 pt 1, 1543, p. 132; vol.21 pt 1, p. 767.
2. TNA, SP18/128/108.
3. TNA, C4/8/1.
4. John Stow, *The Survey of London*, ed. H.B. Wheatley, Dent, London, 1987, pp. 384-5.
5. Oliver Lawson Dick, ed., *Aubrey's Brief Lives*, London, Penguin, 1972, p. 453.
6. BL, Lansdowne MS 1198, f. 5v. Dick, ed., *Aubrey's Brief Lives*, p. 453.
7. Thomas Nash, *Christ's Tears over Jerusalem*, 1593, reprinted London, 1815, pp. 151-2.
8. James Spedding, *The Letters and the Life of Francis Bacon*, London, Longman Green, 1861-74, IV, p. 251. Danby Pickering, *The Statutes at Large*, VII, 1763, p. 43.
9. Elizabeth McClure Thomson, *The Chamberlain Letters*, London, John Murray, 1966, p. 43. *Charter, Acts of Parliament, and Governors' Statutes for the Foundation and Government of the Charterhouse*, private publication, 1832, p. 50.
10. Maurice Exwood and H.L. Lehmann, eds, *The Journal of William Schellinks' Travels in England 1661-1663*, Camden Soc., fifth series, vol.I, 1993, p. 71.
11. John Strype, *A Survey of the Cities of London and Westminster*, 1720, p. 205.
12. BL, Lansdowne MS 1198, f. 1r.

12 Associations

1. Elizabeth Morrison, ed., *A Knight for the Ages: Jacques de Lalaing and the Art of Chivalry*, Los Angeles, J. Paul Getty Museum, 2018, pp. 13-14.

2. Nigel Saul, *For Honour and Fame: Chivalry in England 1066-1500*, London, Bodley Head, 2011, pp. 338-44.
3. Chris Given-Wilson, *Chronicles: The Writing of History in Medieval England*, Hambledon & London, Hambledon, 2004, pp. xx-xxii. J.J.N. Palmer, ed., *Froissart: Historian*, Woodbridge, Boydell, 1981, pp. 1-2.
4. Christopher Marlowe, *Edward the Second*, ed. W.M. Merchant, London, A & C Black, 1967, Act IV sc ii, iv, pp. 69-72, 74-5.
5. Giorgio Melchiori, ed., *King Edward III*, Cambridge, CUP, 1998, pp. 9, 140-1, 152-4, 161-3, 208-9.
6. Richard Barber, ed., *The Chronicle of Geoffrey le Baker of Swinbrook*, Woodbridge, Boydell & Brewer, 2012, p. 90.
7. Philip Bearcroft *An historical account of Thomas Sutton, esq.; and of his foundation in Charter-house*, London, 1737, pp. 165-80.
8. John Byng, Viscount Torrington, *Rides Round Britain*, ed. Donald Adamson, London, Folio Soc., 1996, pp. 52, 166.
9. Wilfred Partington, 'Introduction', *Ivanhoe*, London, Daily Express Publications, 1935. Alice Chandler, 'Sir Walter Scott and the Medieval Revival', *Nineteenth-Century Fiction*, 19, 1965, pp. 315–32.
10. G.M. Young, 'Scott and the Historian' in Sir Herbert Grierson, Edwin Muir, G.M. Young and S.C. Roberts, *Sir Walter Scott Lectures 1940-1948*, Edinburgh, Edinburgh UP, 1950, pp. 86-8.
11. Alan Young, *Tudor and Jacobean Tournaments*, London, George Philip, 1987, p. 186. Jerrold Northrop Moore, *Edward Elgar: A Creative Life*, Oxford, OUP, 1984, p. 144.
12. Kenneth Fowler, *The Age of Plantagenet and Valois*, London, Ferndale, 1980, p. 13. Frank Barlow, 'Freeman, Edward Augustus (1823–1892)', ONDB.

13. *True tales of the olden time. Selected from Froissart*, London, William Smith, 1841, pp. 44-112.
14. George Frederick Beltz, *Memorials of the Most Noble Order of the Garter, from its foundation to the present time. Including the history of the order in the reigns of Edward III and Richard II*, London, William Pickering, 1841, pp. 110-22.
15. Pierre-Laurent De Belloy, *Le Siège de Calais*, ed. Logan J. Connors, London, Modern Humanities Research Association, 2014, pp. 9-14.
16. G.P.R. James, *A History of the Life of Edward the Black Prince*, London, Longman, Orme, Brown, Green & Longmans, 1836, II, p. 25n. *A Short History of the English People by John Richard Green*, London & Toronto, Dent, 1915, I, pp. 214, 233.
17. J. Edward Parrott, *The Pageant of British History*, London, Nelson, 1908, pp. 159-62.
18. *A Handbook for Travellers in Holland and Belgium*, London, John Murray, 19th edn, 1876, p. 105.
19. Anthony Mason, *Mons: European Capital of Culture*, Chalfont St Peter, Bradt, 2015, p. 15.
20. A.D. Mills, *Oxford Dictionary of London Place-Names*, Oxford, OUP, 2001, p. 99.
21. Cited in, Ian Mortimer, *The Perfect King: The Life of Edward III*, London, Cape, 2006, p. 7.
22. Dominique Jarrassé, *Rodin: A Passion for Movement*, Paris, Terrail, 2005, pp. 9, 13-14, 24, 30.
23. Jonathan Sumption, *The Hundred Years War Volume I: Trial by Battle*, London, Faber & Faber, 1990, p. 520; *Volume III: Divided Houses*, 2006, p. 36.
24. George Gleig, *Lives of the Most Eminent British Commanders*, London, 1835, pp. 43-4. *The Times*, July 1911,

p. 6. J.F.D. Shrewsbury, *A History of Bubonic Plague in the British Isles*, Cambridge, CUP, 1970, pp. 84-5.

25. Lawrence Hendriks, *The London Charterhouse, its monks and its martyrs, with a short account of the English Carthusians after the dissolution*, London, K. Paul, Trench, 1889, pp. 7-8, 44-5. *The Times*, 16 June 1925, p. 12.
26. *The Times* 24 May 1872, p. 7; 8 July 1911, p. 8. Gerald Davies, *Charterhouse London: A Historical Sketch*, London, John Murray, 1911, p. 8; *Charterhouse in London*, London, John Murray, 1921, pp. 21-3.
27. Walter Thornbury, *Old and New London*, II, London, Cassell, Petter & Galpin, 1878, pp. 380-1.
28. *A Pictorial and Descriptive Guide to London and its Environs*, London, Ward, Lock & Co., 1923 edn, pp. 213-14. *The Times*, 8 July 1911, p. 8. E. Montizambert, *Unnoticed London*, London & Toronto, Dent, 1923, pp. 148-9.

13 Rediscoveries

1. CM, Paul Paget, The London Charterhouse, typescript.
2. For this and the following paragraphs: David Knowles and W.F. Grimes, *Charterhouse: The Medieval Foundation in the light of recent discoveries*, London, Longmans, Green, 1954, pp. 41-50, and Royal Institute of British Architects (RIBA), Seely & Paget archive, box 36, 'Sequence of events...', 20 June 1950.
3. W.StJ. Hope, 'The London Charterhouse and its old water supply', *Archaeologia*, LVIII, 1902, pp. 293-312. It had been reproduced as an illustration in The Carthusian in 1839.
4. CM, AD/1/13, C. McNee to J. McLeod Campbell, 26 Oct. 1961.
5. *The Times*, 24 Dec. 1885, p. 12. J.G. Nichols, ed., *Chronicle of the Grey Friars of London*, Camden Soc., Old Series, 53, 1852, p. 49.

6. Knowles and Grimes, *Charterhouse*, pp. 47-8. Lord Mottistone, 'The Ancient Buildings of the London Charterhouse', *Journal of the London Soc.*, 1951, pp. 101-2.
7. Knowles and Grimes, *Charterhouse*, pp. 87-92.
8. CM, Paul Paget, The London Charterhouse, typescript.
9. Julian Luxford, 'Carthusian Monasticism and the London Charterhouse', in Cathy Ross, ed., *Revealing the Charterhouse*, London, The Charterhouse & D. Giles, 2016, pp. 48, 50. *The Times*, 6 May 1954, p. 8f.
10. RIBA, Seely & Paget archive, box 36, letter, Knowles to Mottistone, 17 Oct. 1950.
11. CM, G/2/19, pp.14-15.
12. Bruno Barber and Christopher Thomas, *The London Charterhouse*, London, MoLAS Monograph 10, 2002.
13. TNA, E164/45. LMA, acc/1876/AR/1/5/1.
14. Barber and Thomas, *London Charterhouse*, pp. 25-7, 38, 45-9. TNA, SC12/25/55, mm. 18-19, 55.
15. Royal Commission on Historical Monuments, *London, II: West London*, p. 22.
16. Barber and Thomas, *London Charterhouse*, pp. 41-2. TNA, SC12/25/55, mm. 4, 55.
17. Sam Pfizenmaier, *Charterhouse Square: Black Death Cemetery and Carthusian Monastery, Meat Market and Suburb*, London, MOLA, 2016, pp. 23-5, 30-40, 46, 117-22.

BIBLIOGRAPHY

Anon, *Charter, Acts of Parliament, and Governors' Statutes for the Foundation and Government of the Charterhouse*, private publication, 1832.

Anon, *True tales of the olden time. Selected from Froissart*, London, William Smith, 1841.

Anon, *A Handbook for Travellers in Holland and Belgium*, London, John Murray, 19th edn, 1876.

Anon, *A Pictorial and Descriptive Guide to London and its Environs*, London, Ward, Lock & Co., 1923 edn.

Anon, *Chronicle of London from 1089 to 1483*, London, 1827, reprinted Felinfach, Llanerch, 1995.

Archer, Rowena E., 'Brotherton [Marshal], Margaret, *suo jure* duchess of Norfolk (c. 1320–1399)', ODNB.

Arnould, E.J.F., 'Henry of Lancaster and his *Livre des seintes medicine*', *Bulletin of the John Rylands University of Manchester*, 21, 1937.

Barber, Bruno, and Christopher Thomas, *The London Charterhouse*, London, MoLAS Monograph 10, 2002.

Barber, Richard, ed., *Fuller's Worthies*, London, Folio Soc., 1987.

Barber, Richard, ed., *The Chronicle of Geoffrey le Baker of Swinbrook*, Woodbridge, Boydell & Brewer, 2012.

Barber, Richard, *Edward III and the Triumph of England*, London, Allen Lane, 2013.

Barker, Juliet R.V., *The Tournament in England, 1100-1400*, Woodbridge, Boydell, 1986.

Barlow, Frank, 'Freeman, Edward Augustus (1823–1892)', ONDB.

Barnes, Frederic Richard, 'The taxation of wool, 1327-1348', in George Unwin, ed., *Finance and Trade Under Edward III the London Lay Subsidy of 1332*, Manchester, 1918.

Barron, Caroline M., and Matthew Davies, eds, *The Religious Houses of London and Middlesex*, London, University of London, 2007.

Bearcroft, Philip, *An historical account of Thomas Sutton, esq.; and of his foundation in Charter-house*, London, 1737.

Beltz, George Frederick, *Memorials of the Most Noble Order of the Garter, from its foundation to the present time. Including the history of the order in the reigns of Edward III and Richard II*, London, William Pickering, 1841.

Benedictow, Ole J., *The Black Death 1346-1353: The Complete History*, Woodbridge, Boydell, 2004.

Beresford, Philip, and William D. Rubinstein, *The Richest of the Rich: The Wealthiest 250 People in Britain since 1066*, Petersfield, Harriman House with the Social Affairs Unit, 2007.

Bernard, G.W., *The King's Reformation: Henry VIII and the Remaking of the English Church*, New Haven & London, Yale UP, 2005.

Bothwell, James, *Edward III and the English Peerage: Royal Patronage, Social Mobility and Political Control in Fourteenth-Century England*, Woodbridge, Boydell, 2004.

Brereton, Geoffrey ed., Froissart, *Chronicles*, London, Penguin, 1968.

Brie, Friedrich W.D., ed., *The Brut; Or, The chronicles of England*, London, Early English Text Soc., 1906.

Byng, John, Viscount Torrington, *Rides Round Britain*, ed. Donald Adamson, London, Folio Soc., 1996.

Capron, Emma, *The Charterhouse of Bruges*, London, Frick Collection & D. Giles, 2018.

Carlin, Martha, and Joel T. Rosenthal, eds, *Medieval London: Collected Papers of Caroline M. Barron*, Kalamazoo, Medieval Institute Publications, Western Michigan University, 2017.

Chandler, Alice, 'Sir Walter Scott and the Medieval Revival', *Nineteenth-Century Fiction*, 19, 1965.

Clough, Cecil H., 'Rastell, John (c. 1475–1536)', ODNB.

Connors Logan J., ed., Pierre-Laurent De Belloy, *Le Siège de Calais*, London, Modern Humanities Research Association, 2014.

Crouch, David, *Tournament*, Hambledon & London, Hambledon, 2005.

Curtis, G.W.S., ed., *The Passion and Martyrdom of the Holy English Carthusian Fathers: The Short Narration by Dom Maurice Chauncy*, London, Church Historical Soc., 1935.

Cushway, Graham, *Edward III and the War at Sea: The English Navy, 1327-1377*, Woodbridge, Boydell, 2011.

Darmesteter, Mary, *Froissart*, London, T. Fisher Unwin, 1895.

Davies, Gerald, *Charterhouse London: A Historical Sketch*, London, John Murray, 1911.

Davies, Gerald, *Charterhouse in London*, London, John Murray, 1921.

Derheims, Jean, *Histoire ... de la ville de Saint-Omer*, Saint-Omer, 1843.

Desplats, Edouard, 'Des chartreux à Marly et Valenciennes (1297-1791)', *Cercle Archeologique et Historique de Valenciennes et de son Arrondissement*, 88, May 2013.

Dick, Oliver Lawson, ed., *Aubrey's Brief Lives*, London, Penguin, 1972.

Erasmus, Desiderius, *Praise of Folly*, ed. Betty Radice, London, Penguin, 1993.

Evans, H.F. Owen, 'Charterhouse, London', *Trans. of the Monumental Brass Soc.*, IX, 1962.

Ewan, Elizabeth, 'Crab, John, (c. 1280–c. 1352)', ODNB.

Exwood, Maurice, and H.L. Lehmann, eds, *The Journal of William Schellinks' Travels in England 1661-1663*, Camden Soc., fifth series, vol. I, 1993.

Fowler, Kenneth Alan, Henry of Grosmont, First Duke of Lancaster, 1310-1361, PhD thesis, University of Leeds, 1961.

Fowler, Kenneth, *The Age of Plantagenet and Valois*, London, Ferndale, 1980.

Fryde, E.B., 'Financial Resources of Edward III in the Netherlands, 1337-40 (2nd part)', *Revue belge de Philologie et d'Histoire*, 1967.

Fryde, E.B., 'Parliament and the French War, 1336-40', in E.B. Fryde and Edward Miller, eds, *Historical Studies of the English Parliament, Volume I Origins to 1399*, Cambridge, CUP, 1970.

Gasquet, F.A., *Henry VIII and the English Monasteries*, London, Bell, 1893.

Gilbert, Jane, 'Valenciennes', in David Wallace, ed., *Europe: A Literary History, 1348-1418*, I, Oxford, OUP, 2016.

Given-Wilson, Chris, *The Royal Household and the King's Affinity*, New Haven & London, Yale UP, 1986.

Given-Wilson, Chris, *Chronicles: The Writing of History in Medieval England*, Hambledon & London, Hambledon, 2004.

Given-Wilson, Chris, *Henry IV*, New Haven & London, Yale UP, 2016.

Gleig, George, *Lives of the Most Eminent British Commanders*, London, 1835.

Green, David, *Edward the Black Prince: Power in Medieval Europe*, Harlow, Pearson, 2007.

Green, J.R., *A Short History of the English People by John Richard Green*, London & Toronto, Dent, 1915.

Gribit, Nicholas A., *Henry of Lancaster's Expedition to Aquitaine, 1345-1346: Military Service and Professionalism in the Hundred Years War*, London, Boydell & Brewer, 2016.

Gwyn, Peter, *The King's Cardinal: The Rise and Fall of Thomas Wolsey*, London, Barrie & Jenkins, 1990.

Hale, J.R., ed., *The Travel Journal of Antonio de Beatis*, London, Hakluyt Soc., 1979.

Harding, Alan, 'Rastell, John (by 1468-1536), of London', in S.T. Bindoff, ed., *The History of Parliament: The House of Commons 1509-1558*, London, HMSO, 1982.

Hawkins, Duncan, 'The Black Death and the new London cemeteries of 1348', *Antiquity*, 64, 1990.

Hendriks, Lawrence, *The London Charterhouse, its monks and its martyrs, with a short account of the English Carthusians after the dissolution*, London, K. Paul, Trench, 1889.

Hope, W. StJ., 'The London Charterhouse and its old water supply', *Archaeologia*, LVIII, 1902.

Hope, William St.John, *The History of the London Charterhouse*, London, SPCK, 1925.

Horrox, Rosemary, *The Black Death*, Manchester, Manchester UP, 1994.

Howell, James, *Londinopolis: An Historicall Discourse or Perlustration of the City of London ... whereunto is added another of the City of Westminster*, London, 1657.

Jack, R. Ian, 'Grey, Reynold, third Baron Grey of Ruthin (c. 1362–1440)', ODNB.

Jack, R. Ian, 'Hastings, John, thirteenth earl of Pembroke (1347-1375), ODNB.

James, G.P.R., *A History of the Life of Edward the Black Prince*, London, Longman, Orme, Brown, Green & Longmans, 1836.

Jarrassé, Dominique, *Rodin: A Passion for Movement*, Paris, Terrail, 2005.

Johnes, Thomas, ed., *Sir John Froissart's Chronicles*, I, 1803.

Knowles, David, and W.F. Grimes, *Charterhouse: The Medieval Foundation in the light of recent discoveries*, London, Longmans, Green, 1954.

Lambert, Craig L., *Shipping the Medieval Military: English Maritime Logistics in the Fourteenth Century*, Woodbridge, Boydell, 2011.

Langland, William, *The Book Concerning Piers the Plowman*, trans. Donald and Rachel Attwater, ed. Rachel Attwater, London, Everyman, 1957.

Lasocki, David, and Roger Prior, *The Bassanos: Venetian musicians and instrument makers in England, 1531–1665*, Aldershot, Ashgate, 1995.

Lawne, Penny, *Joan of Kent*, Stroud, Amberley, 2015.

le Bel, Jean, *The True Chronicles of Jean le Bel, 1290–1360*, trans. Nigel Bryant, Woodbridge, Boydell & Brewer, 2011.

Livingston, Michael, and Kelly DeVries, eds, *The Battle of Crécy: A Handbook*, Liverpool, Liverpool UP, 2015.

Loades, David, *Mary Tudor*, Stroud, Amberley, 2011.

Lucas, H.S., *The Low Countries and the Hundred Years War, 1326-1347*, Ann Arbor, University of Michigan Press, 1929.

Lucas, Henry S., 'John Crabbe: Flemish Merchant, Pirate, and Adventurer', *Speculum*, 20, 1945, pp. 334-50.

Luxford, Julian, 'Carthusian Monasticism and the London Charterhouse', in Cathy Ross, ed., *Revealing the Charterhouse*, London, The Charterhouse & D. Giles, 2016.

Macaulay, G.C., ed., *The Chronicles of Froissart*, London, Macmillan, 1895.

MacCulloch, Diarmaid, *Thomas Cromwell: A Life*, London, Allen Lane, 2018.

MacGregor, Neil, *Shakespeare's Restless World*, London, Penguin, 2013.

Mackay, Lauren, *Inside the Tudor Court*, Stroud, Amberley, 2014.

Mackintosh-Smith, Tim, ed., *The Travels of Ibn Battutah*, London, Macmillan, 2002.

Major, Ralph H., *Classic Descriptions of Disease*, Springfield and Baltimore, Charles H. Thomas, 1932.

Mason, Anthony, *Mons: European Capital of Culture*, Chalfont St Peter, Bradt, 2015.

McCullum, Robert, and James Davis, 'Robert Gyen of Bristol: A 14th-Century Merchant, Crown Official and Swindler Extraordinaire', *Trans Bristol and Gloucestershire Archaeological Soc.*, 136, 2018.

Melchiori, Giorgio, ed., *King Edward III*, Cambridge, CUP, 1998.

Merchant, W.M., ed., Christopher Marlowe, *Edward the Second*, London, A & C Black, 1967.

Mills, A.D., *Oxford Dictionary of London Place-Names*, Oxford, OUP, 2001.

Montizambert, E., *Unnoticed London*, London & Toronto, Dent, 1923.

Moore, Jerrold Northrop, *Edward Elgar: A Creative Life*, Oxford, OUP, 1984.

Morgan, D.A.L., 'The Charterhouse of Cadzand and the Serendipities of Empire', in Huw Pryce, John Watts and R.R. Davies, eds, *Power and Identity in the Middle Ages: Essays in Memory of Rees Davies*, Oxford, OUP, 2007.

Morrison, Elizabeth, ed., *A Knight for the Ages: Jacques de Lalaing and the Art of Chivalry*, Los Angeles, J. Paul Getty Museum, 2018.

Mortimer, Ian, *The Perfect King: The Life of Edward III*, London, Cape, 2006.

Mottistone, Lord, [John Seely}, 'The Ancient Buildings of the London Charterhouse', *Journal of the London Soc.*, 1951.

Mynors, R.A.B., and D.F.S. Thomson, eds, *The Correspondence of Erasmus*, vol. 4, Toronto, University of Toronto Press, 1977.

Nash, Thomas, *Christ's Tears over Jerusalem*, 1593, reprinted London, 1815.

Nichols, J.G., ed., *Chronicle of the Grey Friars of London*, Camden Soc., Old Series, 53, 1852.

Nichols, J.G., ed., *The Diary of Henry Machyn, citizen and merchant-taylor of London, from A.D. 1550 to A.D. 1563*, Camden Soc., 42, 1848.

Nohl, Johannes, *The Black Death: A chronicle of the plague compiled from contemporary sources*, trans. G.H. Clarke, London, Unwin, 1961.

Ormrod, W.M. 'Montagu, William [William de Montacute], first earl of Salisbury (1301–1344)', ODNB.

Ormrod, W.M., 'Henry of Lancaster [Henry of Grosmont], first duke of Lancaster (c. 1310–1361)', ODNB.

Ormrod, W.M., 'Ufford, Robert, first earl of Suffolk (1298–1369)', ODNB.

Ormrod, W. Mark, *Edward III*, New Haven & London, Yale UP, 2011.

Palmer, J.J.N., ed., *Froissart: Historian*, Woodbridge, Boydell, 1981.

Parrott, J. Edward, *The Pageant of British History*, London, Nelson, 1908.

Pfizenmaier, Sam, *Charterhouse Square: Black Death Cemetery and Carthusian Monastery, Meat Market and Suburb*, London, MOLA, 2016.

Prestwich, Michael, *Armies and Warfare in the Middle Ages*, New Haven and London, Yale UP, 1996.

Prestwich, Michael, *A Short History of The Hundred Years War*, London, I.B. Tauris, 2018.

Rawcliffe, Carole, 'Stafford, Ralph, first earl of Stafford (1301–1372)', ODNB.

Richardson, Douglas, *Plantagenet Ancestry: A Study in Colonial and Medieval Families*, 2nd edn, Salt Lake City, Genealogical Publishing, 2004.

Rickert, Edith, *Chaucer's World*, ed. Clair C. Olson and Martin M. Crow, New York, Columbia UP, 1948.

Riley, H.T., ed., *Chronicles of the Mayors and Sheriffs of London 1188-1274*, London, Trübner, 1863.

Rogers, Clifford J., ed., *The Wars of Edward III: Sources and Interpretations*, Woodbridge, Boydell and Brewer, 1999.

Roper, W.J.D., *Chronicles of Charter-house*, London, Bell, 1847.

Sandeman, G.A.C., *Calais Under English Rule*, Oxford, Blackwell, 1908.

Sargent, Frank, 'The wine trade with Gascony', in George Unwin, ed., *Finance and Trade Under Edward III*, London, Routledge, 1962.

Saul, Nigel, *For Honour and Fame, Chivalry in England 1066-1500*, London, Bodley Head, 2011.

Seebohm, Frederic, *The Oxford Reformers*, London, Longman, Green, 1911.

Sharpe, Reginald R., ed., *Calendar of Wills Proved and Enrolled in the Court of Husting, London, A.D.1258-A.D.1688*, II, 1890.

Sloane, Barney, *The Black Death in London*, Stroud, History Press, 2011.

Smythe, Robert, *Historical Account of the Charter-House; compiled from the works of Herne and Bearcroft*, London, 1813.

Sneyd, Charlotte Augusta, ed., *A Relation, or rather a true account, of the Island of England*, London, Camden Soc., 1847.

Spedding, James, *The Letters and the Life of Francis Bacon*, London, Longman Green, 1861-74.

Stow, John, *The Survey of London*, ed. H.B. Wheatley, Dent, London, 1987.

Strype, John, *A Survey of the Cities of London and Westminster*, London, 1720.

Sumption, Jonathan, *The Hundred Years War Volume I: Trial by Battle*, London, Faber & Faber, 1990.

Sumption, Jonathan, *The Hundred Years War Volume III Divided Houses*, London, Faber & Faber, 2009.

Temple, Philip, *The Charterhouse*, Survey of London monograph 18, 2010.

Thomas, A.H., ed., *Calendar of the Plea and Memoranda Rolls of the City of London: Volume 1, 1323-1364*, London, HMSO, 1926.

Thomson, Elizabeth McClure, *The Chamberlain Letters*, London, John Murray, 1966.

Thornbury, Walter, *Old and New London*, II, London, Cassell, Petter & Galpin, 1887.

Vernier, Richard, *The Flower of Chivalry: Bertrand du Guesclin and the Hundred Years War*, Woodbridge, Boydell, 2003.

Walker, Simon, 'John ['John of Gaunt], duke of Aquitaine and duke of Lancaster, styled king of Castile and León (1340–1399)', ODNB.

Warner, Kathryn, *Philippa of Hainault*, Stroud, Amberley, 2019.

Whibley, Charles, ed., *Henry VIII by Edward Hall*, London, T.C. & E.C. Jack, 1904.

Wickham, Chris, *Medieval Europe*, New Haven & London, Yale UP, 2016.

Wright, Thomas, ed., *Political Songs and Poems relating to English History*, London, Longman, Green, 1861.

Young, Alan, *Tudor and Jacobean Tournaments*, London, George Philip, 1987.

Young, G.M., 'Scott and the Historian' in Sir Herbert Grierson, Edwin Muir, G.M. Young and S.C. Roberts, *Sir Walter Scott Lectures 1940-1948*, Edinburgh, Edinburgh UP, 1950.

INDEX